Arthur Levine

# WHY INNOVATION FAILS

State University
of New York Press

ALBANY

Published by
State University of New York Press, Albany

© 1980 State University of New York

All rights reserved

Printed in the United States of America

No part of this book may be used or reproduced
in any manner whatsoever without written permission
except in the case of brief quotations embodied in
critical articles and reviews.

For information, address State University of New York
Press, State University Plaza, Albany, N.Y., 12246

*Library of Congress Cataloging in Publication Data*

Levine, Arthur.
Why innovation fails.

Bibliography: p.
Includes index.
1. Universities and colleges—United States.
2. Educational innovations—United States. I. Title.
LA227.3.L46     378.73          80-14950

ISBN 0-87395-412-2
ISBN 0-87395-421-1 (pbk.)

# Contents

Preface — vii

### PART ONE  QUESTIONS AND ANSWERS ABOUT INNOVATION
1 Innovation and Failure: Some Questions — 3
2 Organizations and Innovations: Some Answers — 11

### PART TWO  A STUDY OF FOURTEEN INNOVATIONS
3 The Colleges: From Creation to InstitutionalizationI — 29
4 The Colleges: Continuing Institutionalization — 89

### PART THREE  CONCLUSIONS
5 How and Why Innovation Fails — 155
6 Implications: A Literature Review — 167

Appendix A  Methodological Note — 201
Appendix B  A Synthesis of Theories on Planned Change — 210
Bibliography — 212
Index — 218

# *Preface*

*Why Innovation Fails* is a book about innovation and change. Despite its title, its goal is to understand how change can be accomplished successfully. The book concentrates on colleges and universities, but I think much of what is said between these covers is applicable to organizations in general. Parts One and Three of the volume are written with this belief in mind.

Preparation of this book has been a wonderful experience in learning just how nice people can be. Of the hundreds of people I asked for assistance, I cannot remember one who refused to help. In fact, more people offered their time generously and their thoughts conscientiously than I might ever have imagined possible. Without the assistance of these people there would quite literally have been no book.

I wrote this book about innovations on the east coast while living and working on the west coast. This could not have been done without the help of several individuals who offered aid far beyond the call of duty. I owe a special debt of gratitude to three persons — Lionel Lewis, Michael Farrell, and Walter Hobbs of the State University of New York at Buffalo. Lionel Lewis, despite deadline pressures for a book of his own, managed to read chapter drafts and return them with stinging comments in what seemed like hours after I mailed them. His telephone bill for cross-country calls to me would likely have earned him an ambassadorship had he used the money for other purposes. Eagle-eyed Lionel Lewis even picked up typos and spelling errors except for the 312 times I misspelled *compatibility*. Mike Farrell and Wally Hobbs were always available when I needed help. They were gentle in their criticism and always perceptive in their comments.

*Preface*

Several others at the State University of New York at Buffalo, the site of the innovations studied, were also very helpful. Diane Marlinski transformed the 3000-mile distance between Berkeley and Buffalo from an insurmountable problem to a mere headache. She cut through layers of bureaucracy with the speed and grace of Peggy Fleming. Irving Spitzberg was terrific. He dropped the appropriate word for me to gain access to most meetings that I sought to attend, gave much time to this project, and read and commented extensively upon earlier drafts of this book. Claude Welch talked with me for hours and dredged from his files a seemingly endless supply of useful historical documents. President Robert Ketter and the university chartering committee permitted me to sit in on closed meetings germane to this study. I followed them around like a note-taking shadow for three months. All of the members of the chartering committee gave liberally of their time in one or more interviews. Jon Reichert had four interviews totaling over nine hours and, like Claude Welch, gave generously from a well-endowed filing cabinet.

I owe a debt of thanks to JB Hefferlin, my very close friend whom I repaid for inviting me to his home for the first time by asking him to read a draft of this manuscript. His advice made this a better book.

I am also grateful to an ex-Buffalo administrative staffer who shared with me a partial manuscript that had written about the Martin Meyerson presidency at Buffalo. This individual asked that his/her identity be kept secret. I have tried very hard to do this, but I must say that the manuscript was an essential ingredient of Chapter 3 of this book. My promise to protect my source made it impossible to cite this person's contributions without jeopardizing his/her identity. So I say thank you very much to my secret source. I could not have written this book without you. I hope you will finish the manuscript and decide to publish it someday. It is very good.

Sandra Loris deserves a special word of thanks. She typed this manuscript day and night, weekdays and weekends, as the publication deadline drew closer. She was calm, pleasant, and never once complained. I don't understand how she did it all, but I am terribly grateful to her.

Several organizations were generous in their assistance to this project. Financial support came from the National Academy of Education in

*Preface*

Washington, D.C. and the Spencer Foundation through the Spencer Fellowship Program. The Carnegie Council on Policy Studies in Higher Education generously provided office space and equipment.

My parents also spurred me along through our telephone conversations. Each week, one or the other would invariably say, "I thought you finished that book already."

This book goes back several years. It is the first I wrote without benefit of a collaborator, even though others have preceded it to publication. And so it is the book I have saved to thank two people who have been very important in my life, Rae and Henry Kalman. They are responsible for my college education and hence, this volume.

Finally, I dedicate the book to Linda Christine Fentiman, my wife and my best friend, with appreciation, love, and respect.

ARTHUR LEVINE

PART ONE

# QUESTIONS AND ANSWERS ABOUT INNOVATION

CHAPTER 1

# *Innovation and Failure: Some Questions*

In 1969 the faculty of Brown University voted to replace, *in toto*, their traditional program with a progressive, new student-centered curriculum. The change was widely noticed in the educational community and was the subject of much praise. Commenting on the program 5 years later in an article entitled, "Brown University Trend: Back to Old Curriculum," Robert Rheinehold said, "Today the reforms which were hailed as the most flexible and progressive undergraduate curriculum to be found in any major American university are struggling for survival against heavy odds" *(New York Times*, February 24, 1975, p. 47). He went on to chronicle the de facto collapse of the program.

Across the continent, Stanford University, in 1969, introduced a major curriculum change that included two experimental programs. After more than a year of operation, John Weingart and I reviewed those programs and were so impressed with their success that we recommended they be profiled as part of a planned network television documentary on higher education. On January 14, 1975, Stanford announced that it was terminating both programs (*San Francisco Chronicle*, January 15, 1975, p. 3).

One thing the new curriculum at Brown and the experimental programs at Stanford had in common was that they were both innovations. The key words to describe them or any innovation might be *new* and *different*. Innovation combines the elements of reform and change; *reform* implying new and *change* implying different. *Innovation* can operationally be defined as any departure from the traditional practices of an organization. As a result, the element of newness inherent in innovation is a relative phenomenon—what is new in one place is old in the next. The same might be said of time. Much that we call innovation is in fact renovation, trying the ideas of the past once again. For instance, the University of California at Santa Cruz was considered one of the most innovative schools of the 1960s for its use of the cluster college concept, a departure from the traditional pattern of mass education adopted at UCLA and Berkeley. *Clustering* involves dividing the university into smaller, more liveable, residential liberal arts colleges. This is an example both of renovation and the relative character of innovation. As it turned out, the Claremont Colleges near Los Angeles had been using the cluster arrangement since 1925. And the idea itself dates back almost 800 years to the colleges of Cambridge and Oxford in England.

## What's Known About Innovation

We know a lot about innovation. We know about its forms. Different people slice innovation up in different ways and so there are a cornucopia of typologies to choose from. This author divides organizational innovations into five basic types: new organizations, innovative enclaves within existing organizations, holistic changes within existing organizations, piecemeal changes within existing organizations, and peripheral changes outside of existing organizations. Each form has its own advantages and disadvantages as well as its own rationale. For example, in colleges and universities, the form of organization this author is most familiar with, this means:

*The establishment of new colleges.* A new college is the easiest way to establish a nontraditional institutional mission. For example, Bennington College in Vermont was a product of the desire to extend the progressive philosophy of education into the college years where it was absent in the late 1920s. And Metropolitan State University in St. Paul, Minneapolis, was designed to develop a nontraditional program especially for older adults who fit uncomfortably into existing institutions. The creation of a new college avoids the expenditure of enormous amounts of time and effort that would be required to transform

## Innovation and Failure: Some Questions

an established institution and reorient its staff and students. Creating a new college, however, is by no means a guarantee of success for a nontraditional mission. New schools rarely fulfill all of the expectations of their founders. There are external pressures as well as internal ones to revert to the tried and true. There is also a tendency for participants to force their own dreams and hopes on a new institution whether or not these conform with the college's mission. Creating a new college is expensive and when colleges are underenrolled as at present and existing institutions of higher education have unused capacity for lack of students, it is a high-risk, inefficient form of innovation.

*Innovative enclaves within existing colleges.* The development of new enclaves involves setting aside a specific location within the institution for change. It may be an experimental subunit as at Stanford, an experimental period during the calendar year, or any other innovation separate from the mainstream of traditional campus activities. Innovative enclaves are relatively inexpensive and easy to implement. They can serve as institutional laboratories for change and as sources of institutional self-renewal if the practices are adopted elsewhere around the school or involve large numbers of people—faculty and students—who participate in both the enclave and the rest of the institution. The disadvantages of enclaves are that they can become appendages isolated from the rest of the campus, sanctuaries for dissatisfied faculty and students, and a means of preventing an institution from making needed organizational changes.

*Holistic changes within existing colleges.* Holistic change involves the adoption of a major institutional innovation characterized by a unified and coherent purpose. The curriculum change at Brown University is a good example. Of all the forms of change, holistic reform is the most defensible when major change is necessary; the most efficient since it involves substituting new programs for old rather than new additions; the most difficult to get adopted; the least likely to succeed, particularly in large organizations; and the least common. It is risky because it involves already established institutions with built-in resources, habits, and staff—and a staff at that usually lacking in consensus about institutional purposes. But holistic change is especially risky because it replaces the old with the new. If the change does not succeed, nothing is left to fall back on.

*Piecemeal changes within existing colleges.* Piecemeal change involves minor innovations such as the use of a new piece of equipment, the adoption of a new course, or a procedural change in personnel practice. It is the most common form of change, the easiest to implement, and a series of such changes can, in sum, produce holistic change, but this is unlikely since piecemeal changes tend to rely more on political negotiation than on coherent and unifying purposes.

*Peripheral changes outside existing colleges.* Peripheral change involves the establishment of institutions or changes within institutions that are not traditionally associated with higher education, but that have an effect on the activities of existing colleges and universities. A recent example is the establishment of college-degree-granting programs by several commercial corporations such as Xerox and American Telephone and Telegraph. As Sir Nevil Mott said "The infallible recipe for stirring up a university is to set up a rival" (Hefferlin, 1969, p. 3). Peripheral programs can alert existing schools to unmet students needs as well as potentially profitable program additions. They can also compete with colleges and universities by drawing away their clientele.

The strengths, weaknesses, and reasons for these five types of innovation are paralleled in nonuniversity organizations as well.

We are also aware of the times when innovation is most likely to occur. Marvin Bressler (Levine, 1978, pp. 431-432) of Princeton University finds a close connection between environmental conditions and innovation. The likelihood of change is enhanced when there is a crisis in the environment, when people have a shared interest in change, when there is a power imbalance in the environment, when the environment has experienced structural changes, and finally when it is consistent with the zeitgeist or spirit of the times.

We know, too, about the process of innovation. It involves a series of predictable, sequential stages. So say a number of organizational studies (Hage and Aiken, 1970; Mann and Neff, 1961; Rogers, 1962; Rogers and Shoemaker, 1971; Smelser, 1959). Unfortunately, there is little in the way of consensus among the studies about how many steps there might be in the sequence or what the individual steps are.

## Innovation and Failure: Some Questions

Be that as it may, all of the studies and this author's own research are consistent, as shown in Table 1.1, with a process having four fundamental steps: 1) recognizing the need for change—it is realized that some organizational need is not being satisfied; 2) planning and formulating a means of satisfying the need—a concrete plan is developed; 3) initiating and implementing the plan—the plan is put into operation on a trial basis; and 4) institutionalizing or terminating the new operating plan—either the operating plan is routinized and integrated into the organization or it is ended.

The fourth stage is the period described in the accounts of Stanford and Brown. It is less familiar than the earlier three stages and

Table 1.1  Stages in the Innovation Process

| Levine | Hage and Aiken | Rogers | Smelser | Mann and Neff |
|---|---|---|---|---|
| 1. Recognition of need | 1. Evaluation | 1. Awareness | 1. Dissatisfaction with sense of opportunity | 1. State of organization before change |
|  |  | 2. Interest | 2. Symptoms of disturbances | 2. Recognition of need for change |
|  |  | 3. Evaluation | 3. Handling disturbances |  |
| 2. Planning and formulating a solution |  |  | 4. Channeling disturbances |  |
|  |  |  | 5. Attempts to specify | 3. Planning change |
| 3. Initiation and implementation of plan | 2. Initiation | 4. Trial | 6. Implementation by entrepreneurs | 4. Taking steps to make change |
| 4. Institutionalization or termination | 3. Implementation |  |  |  |
|  | 4. Routinization | 5. Adoption | 7. Routinization | 5. Stabilizing change |

*Source:* Hage and Aiken, 1970, p. 113.

*Note:* This table contains examples of a few of the better known theories or models. Zaltman et al. (1973, p. 61-62) engaged in a similar exercise with eleven theories, two of which are included in the above table. Their own model has two stages—initiation and implementation—and five substages. It differs from this author's theory in that the process of recognizing need is omitted. The implementation stage does include a process comparable to institutionalization or termination, however.

that brings us to what we don't know about innovation. There is a tendency to think of the third state of the process (implementation) as its conclusion. The goal of innovation or change is to adopt something new and different. At the end of the third stage, that is done. The innovation is in place, there is apparent closure to the story, and there is a presumption of success. It is not dissimilar from the way fairy tales are told. Most involve something akin to the first three stages of the innovation process. Take Cinderella for instance. In that story we have a prince who recognizes a need, which is the loss of his extraordinary dance partner of the night before. That's stage one. He develops a stage two plan to marry her that involves taking a slipper the young woman left at the dance, transporting it all over the countryside, asking every women to try it on, and marrying the person it fits. Stage three of the plan is put into operation, Cinderella is found, and the story ends happily ever after. The reader never wonders whether the marriage was a good one. We assume it all worked out and are quite shocked when we hear differently from *People* Magazine.

This is approximately what has happened with the research on innovation and change. It concentrates almost exclusively on stages one through three. This literature is far too extensive for casual discussion here, although key works are examined in the concluding chapter of this book. The interested reader might also turn to one of the excellent annotated bibliographies on the topic, such as that prepared by Research for Better Schools, Inc., entitled *Administering for Change* (Maguire, Tompkin, and Cummings, 1971). Stage four, institutionalization or termination of the innovation, 1970, has received only scant attention in published research (Hage and Aiken, 1970, p. 104; Johnson, 1969). Notable are case studies by Selznick (1949) on the Tennessee Valley Authority, Corwin (1974) on the Teacher Corps, Zald (1963) on the Young Men's Christian Association, Gusfield (1963) on the Women's Christian Temperance Union, Grant and Riesman (1980) on experimentation in higher education, and Erikson (1966) on Puritan America. Yet even these studies shed little light on the institutionalization-termination stage. Though the authors focus on events that occurred during this period, it was not their intent to describe the process of institutionalizing or terminating innovation. As a result, very little is known about what happens after an innovation is adopted.

*Innovation and Failure: Some Questions*

This is unfortunate, particularly so because the institutionalization-termination stage is a critical period for any innovation and the organization adopting it. During 1970-71 John Weingart and I conducted a study of the innovative undergraduate programs of the 1960s at 26 colleges across the United States. In the years since, a number of the schools have been revisited to see what fate has brought them. Through it all, we discovered that during the institutionlization-termination stage, innovations are usually transformed or die, and many of the universities and colleges housing innovations, which will be called *host organizations*, change. As at Stanford and Brown, most innovations declined, some have eroded away, as at Brown, and others are terminated, as planned at Stanford.[1] Only one innovation was able to move the host organization substantially in its direction. Subsequent research has confirmed these impressions time and time again.

The 1960s was a decade of widespread change. A great deal of excitement and energy were expended on efforts like those at Brown and Stanford. In the ensuing years we have learned that much of that change has dissipated and we shall hear in the future that much of the change of the 1970s has disappeared as well. In many cases the loss is desirable. There is nothing intrinsically good about innovation for innovation's sake. Yet, in some cases, the loss is unfortunate and unnecessary. It is too often largely a result of what we didn't know about innovation.

That is the subject of this book. This volume focuses on the institutionalization-termination phase of change and attempts to explain why innovation fails—that is, why it declines prior to achieving its intended purposes. In understanding how and why innovations fail, we gain an understanding of what it takes to make them work. This book tries to answer four questions:

1. Why do innovations decline or fail after being adopted?
2. In what manner do innovations decline or fail?
3. Why do innovations persist or prosper after being adopted?
4. In what manner do innovations persist or prosper?

---

[1]Despite its plans, Stanford did not terminate the two units as announced.

## Questions and Answers About Innovation

The text is divided into three parts. Part One, entitled "Questions and Answers About Innovation," sets the stage for the rest of the book. It consists of Chapters 1 and 2. Chapter 2 is concerned with innovations in organizations and provides a detailed description of the fourth stage of the innovation process—the institutionalization-termination phase. A model is presented of the ways in which innovations prosper, persist, decline, and fail after they have been adopted. The reasons for this are explained and examples are provided of how the model works in the case of three similar innovations that met very different ends.

Part Two, "A Study of 14 Innovations," applies the institutionalization-termination model in a study of structurally similar innovations. All were experimental colleges at the State University of New York at Buffalo. The model presented in Chapter 2 is deficient in two respects: It lacks empirical confirmation and it is sketchy, meaning it fails to describe fully the associated events, interactions, and processes. Part Two is intended to respond to these deficiencies. Chapter 3 discusses the character of the State University of New York at Buffalo, the origin and development of the 14 innovations, and their early institutionalization-termination. Chapter 4 concentrates on the subsequent results of the institutionalization or termination stage. A methodological note is contained in Appendix A.

Part Three is entitled "Conclusions." Chapter 5 answers the question that this volume began with—how and why do innovations fail and succeed? The final chapter provides context. It discusses the already existing literature on innovation and change in terms of what has been learned from this study.

CHAPTER 2

# *Organizations and Innovations: Some Answers*

### *The Four-Stage Innovation Process*

All kinds of organizations have been chronicled—service organizations, community organizations, voluntary organizations, complex organizations, formal organizations, social organizations, and work organizations of many stripes, to mention just a few. They are all different, yet they all share three characteristics—norms, values, and goals. *Norms* are the commonly prescribed guides to conduct in the organization—means of communication, patterns of authority and control, rules of membership, and all of the other characteristics that describe the way people should interact. *Values* are the commonly shared beliefs and sentiments held by people in the organization. And *goals*, which are reflective of organizational values and are attained according to organizational norms, are the commonly accepted purpose and direction of the organization.

Every organization has a different set of norms, values, and goals. Even similar types of organizations differ in this respect. No two colleges, for example, are exactly alike. And this is important because the unique set of norms, values, and goals that an organization possesses constitutes its character or personality. That personality is very much the same as an individual's personality. It is an essential aspect of the organization and just as integral to its well-being.

Accordingly, organizations guard their personalities against potentially entropic forces both within the organization and in the external environment. The tools they use are called *boundaries*. Kai Erikson describes boundaries as a "symbolic set of parentheses" which control an orgainization's social space in order to retain "a limited range of activities and a given pattern of constancy and stability within the larger environment" (Erikson, 1966, p. 10). This means simply that boundaries circumscribe or stipulate the personality appropriate to the organization. Their function is to strictly maintain the status quo. Any change in an organization's norms, values, and goals requires a comparable change in its boundaries.

In the bounded organization, innovation is likely to occur when environmental change makes existing boundaries unworkable, when the organization fails to achieve desired goals, or when it is thought that goals can better be satisfied in another manner. Each of these conditions may trigger the first step in the four-stage innovation process. That is, only if the condition is recognized as a failing or need. As a matter of fact, the labeling of need and subsequent innovation does not have to be the response to any of these conditions. Recognition of need can take quite a while. It may not occur until there has been an extensive internal or external examination or it may, in fact, never occur. There are limits to how long inaction is possible, though. Organizations that continually neglect to respond to goal failure or environmental change are likely candidates for extinction. Problems can be ignored only so long without "paying the piper". Nonetheless, once a need is recognized and the organization seeks a vehicle for satisfying it, no matter what the vehicle, it represents an innovation for that organization. It is a departure from its traditional practices.

The actual contact between an innovation and an organization can occur during any of the first three stages of the innovation process. During the first stage (recognition of need) and the second stage (planning and formulating a solution) the innovation is, at its point of greatest development, nothing more tangible than an idea. Participation in these two stages may vary from an organization—wide to an individual phenomenon. The possessor of an innovative idea need be only a single individual, and possibly even an individual external to the organization. For example, at colleges and universities, one person, the entire university community, or even an outside source such as the U.S. Department of Labor may identify the failure of the university to consider the problems of women as a need. The planning and formulation of the solution can vary from an individual designing an independent study; to the faculty, students, and administration of the university forming a joint committee to create a women's studies program; to the U.S. Department of Labor imposing affirmative action guidelines upon the university. In any case, when the innovation or solution is implemented, which is the third stage of the innovation process, there is necessarily contact between the organization and the innovation, whether or not the organization approves of the innovation.

The third stage is a trial period. During this time the innovation is tested as a solution to the unsatisfied need. Every organization has one or more mechanisms for approving innovation or change. In a university, the function might be the purview of the senior faculty or curriculum committee at the departmental level, and at the institutional level the job of a senate, university administrators, or trustees. If the organization has formally approved the innovation and thereby permitted its implementation, it usually grants the innovation some degree of initial autonomy, a grace period of sorts, in order to work out unresolved questions and solve unanticipated problems. Thereafter, the organization begins to send a gradually increasing number of cues to the innovation—initially subtle, subsequently unsubtle—about how it should begin fitting in with the organization. These cues are intended to begin the fourth stage of the innovation process-institutionalization or termination designed to make the innovation just a routine part of the organization, a necessary occurrence if the organization is to achieve a common set of goals.

If the innovation is not approved by the organization, the grace period prior to institutionalization or termination described above is unlikely. Autonomy is a prize that an organization grants only after it has legitimized an innovation, and formal approval is the way in which it confers legitimacy.

Because innovations are by definition departures from traditional organizational practices, the innovation and the host organization have at least a somewhat different set of goals, norms, and values, and, as a result, a differing set of boundaries. This is apparent in the unapproved innovation soon after its adoption and in the approved innovation by the end of the trial period, which is of variable length and dependent entirely on the grace period granted by the host. The presence of two separate and divergent boundary systems combines to provide multiple or blurred definitions of organizational character. An organization cannot function in this manner because each boundary system pulls it in a different direction. This results initially in disagreements and ultimately in conflict between the host and the innovation. The conflict can only be resolved by making the diverging boundaries congruent, which is essential for organizational health. Otherwise the organization expends its resources on internal conflict rather than the attainment of its goals, the raison d'etre for organizational existence.

Conflict resolution and boundary convergence are the functions of the institutionalization or termination stage. There exist two mechanisms for accomplishing these ends. The mechanism selected is largely at the discretion of the host organization since the innovation is typically dependent upon it for resources and the people associated with the innovation have likely developed a survival wish. The first mechanism is called *boundary expansion* and involves the adoption of the innovation's personality traits by the host, or more simply an acceptance by the host of some or all of the innovation's differences. Owing to the dominant position of the organization, there is very rarely a complete acceptance of innovation differences; far more common are mutual changes in both host and innovation personalities, agreed upon through joint negotiation and resulting in a hybridization of the two. In boundary expansion, the convergence of organization and innovation boundaries and conflict resolution occur when the organization legitimizes some or all of the innovation's differences and agrees to live with or absorb those differences. Acceptance or absorption can involve establishing the innovation as an enclave or diffusing it throughout the organization. *Diffusion* is the process whereby innovation characteristics are allowed to spread through the host organization, and *enclaving* is the process whereby the innovation assumes an isolated position within the organization.

The second institutionalization-termination mechanism is called *boundary contraction* and involves a constriction of organizational boundaries in such a manner as to exclude innovation differences.

*Organizations and Innovations: Some Answers*

The innovation, which is then outside organizational boundaries, is viewed as illegitimate and labeled "deviant". The deviant label serves to define and highlight the organization's boundaries by singling out previously not unaccepted norms, values, and goals as now clearly inappropriate for the organization. Having identified the presence of a deviant subpart, the organization has two available sanctions. A sanction must be applied in order to formalize and reinforce the organization's legitimate boundaries and end the internal conflict. This necessitates a showing that deviance of the innovation's variety will not be tolerated. The two sanctions of boundary contraction are resocialization or termination of the innovation. *Resocialization* occurs when the innovative unit is made to renounce its past deviance and institute the acceptable norms, values, and goals it failed to incorporate previously. *Termination* occurs when the innovation is eliminated. Boundary contraction, then, fosters boundary convergence and conflict resolution by excising contested innovation differences. This process is shown in Figure 2.1.

## *Compatibility Versus Profitability*

In order to gain a rudimentary understanding of the factors determining the four outcomes of the institutionalization-termination stage — diffusion, enclaving, resocialization, and termination — a study (unpublished) was conducted of two similar innovations in comparable organizations that resulted in quite opposite institutionalization-termination results. The innovations were experimental colleges, the organizations were large universities, and the opposite results were boundary expansion via diffusion and boundary contraction via termination. An analysis of innovation differences with respect to the university environment yielded a series of characteristics or indicators that broke down primarily along two dimensions — compatibility and profitability. The diffused innovation was found to be profitable for the host and compatible with its personality, while the terminated innovation was incompatible and unprofitable.

Subsequent investigation into the literature of the field revealed that the wheel had been rediscovered, as both compatibility and profitability have long been prominent considerations in the literature on innovation diffusion. That literature is especially poignant because the institutionalization-termination decision is very similar to the acceptance rejection choice involved in the diffusion of innovation; however, the findings of the research are far from crystal clear. Griliches (1957) found profitability to be the cause of farmers adopting a new hybrid sorghum breed. Bradner and Straus (1959), in a reexamination of the Griliches data, found congruence (synonymous with compatibility) a more influential factor. Fliegel and Kivlin (1962) found relative advantage (close kin of profitability) and compatibility the attributes most significantly related to innovation adoption; however, most followup research has failed to confirm one or the other (Rogers and

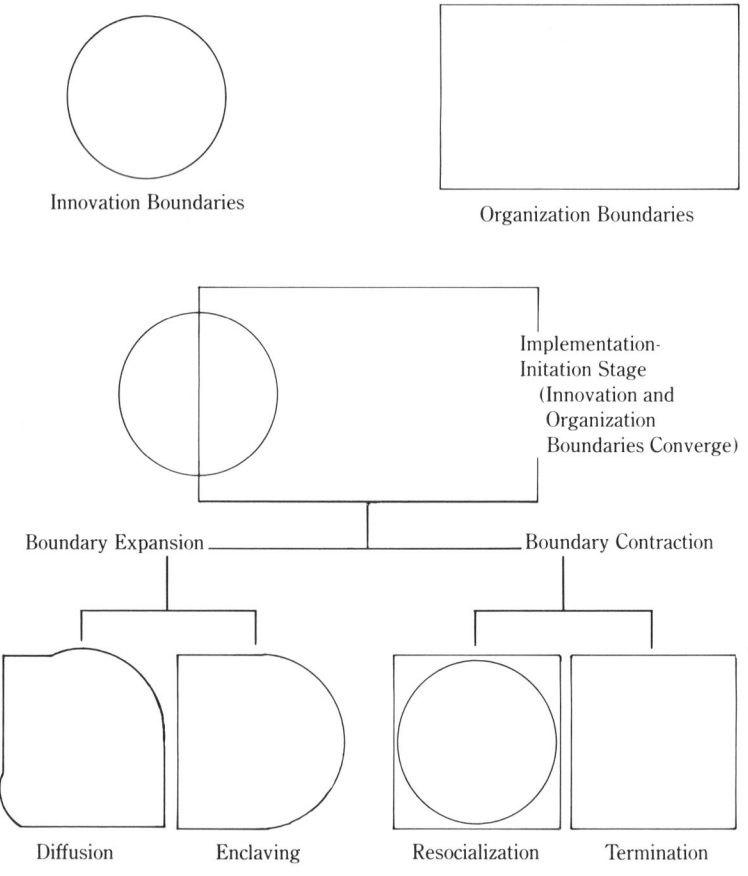

Figure 2.1. The Institutionalization or Termination of Innovation in Organizations.

Shoemaker, 1971, pp. 140-141). Compatibility tends to be supported less often than profitability.

A major difficulty with this literature is that three forms of research bias confound the issues—researcher's world view, research setting, and research methodology. With regard to researcher's world view, anthropologists and sociologists—scientists of culture—are prone to emphasize compatibility, while economists and psychologists—scientists of the individual—tend to stress profitability.

Concerning the research setting, research conducted in industrialized Western countries has emphasized profitability, while that conducted in nonindustrial, non-Western countries has emphasized compatibility. This results in large measure because most innovations studied have been Western and industrial in origin, making them more likely to be incompatible with non-Western, nonindustrial countries than their own. For instance, a new breed of beef cattle is more likely to be rejected in the United States because of profitability than compatibility considerations. On the other hand, in India, where the consumption of beef is taboo, the rationale for rejection would undoubtedly be compatibility. Unfortunately, a good deal of diffusion research has been based on an American rural agricultural setting, and therefore minimizes the importance of compatibility.

With regard to research method bias, studies utilizing in-depth, long-term, participant-observation case studies have stressed compatibility more often than survey research methods, especially when conducted in a post facto fashion and when designed only to gauge the acceptance-rejection choice. This is because all innovations lacking cultural compatibility are not rejected, but are often manipulated in a manner designed to make them more congruent with culturally shared orientations. Profitability, however, is not as easily adapted. Survey research studies have almost uniformly missed such compatibility manipulations. Given all of this, one would have to conclude that both compatibility and profitability play an important part in the institutionalization or termination of an innovation.

Compatibility may be thought of as the degree to which the norms, values, and goals of an innovation are congruent with those of the host. Profitability cannot be so easily defined. In the rural agricultural studies mentioned, profitability was treated as an objective and solely economic variable. Under no circumstances can it be construed as an objective phenomenon; profitability is subjective. To illustrate, because a new crop was shown to have a very high economic return in 1958 does not mean that the farmers who adopted it in 1959 did so for financial reasons. Others have taken exception to this inference as well. Rogers and Havens (1961), for instance, note that "profitability as any other item of information about an innovation must be diffused. . . . It is our contention that what really counts is an adopter's perception of profitability, and not objective profitability" (p. 414).

The solely economic concept of profitability encourages the objectification of it. There are a multitude of noneconomic profits available to the innovation adopter, such as security, prestige, peer approval, growth, efficiency, and improvement in the quality of life, to name only a few. Different organizations have different needs, so that an unpopular or unaccepted organization might overlook an innovation promising financial profit in favor of another offering peer approval. An innovation may then be defined as profitable so long as it satisfies the adopter's needs or satisfied them better than the existing mechanism. This definition incorporates both the subjective and noneconomic elements of profitability in emphasizing simply adopter needs. A state of profitability exists when needs are effectively satisfied. The greater the satisfaction, the higher the profitability.

There are two forms of profitability—self-interest profitability and general profitability. *Self-interest profitability* is that which motivates the individual subunits and the individual staff within an organization to adopt an innovation. *General profitability* is that which motivates an organization to choose or maintain an innovation, but is such that neither subunits nor individuals would adopt it themselves. For instance, an innovation adopted at a university by one department in response to declining revenues that results in increased enrollments, more faculty lines, and a large foundation grant might motivate other individuals and departments with similar needs to adopt the innovation. This is self-interest profitability. On the other hand, an example of general profitability might be a learning skills center which was established because students lacked basic reading, writing, and arithmetic skills. The success of such a center would obviate the need for subunits or individuals to adopt similar programs. Such an innovation would be profitable because it satisfied a recognized need and allowed the college to pursue its goals without the prior encumbrance of students lacking basic skills.

With this background in mind, compatibility and profitability can be placed in their roles as the determinants of the institutionalization-termination outcome. Compatibility is a measure of the appropriateness of an innovation within existing organizational boundaries. It is a measure of dissatisfaction. Compatibility does not determine whether an innovation will work; it indicates the degree to which an innovation is inconsistent with the norms, values, and goals of the organization. In seeking compatibility, an organization attempts to maintain its personality, to protect the status quo, and to avoid changes in established boundaries. Organizations continually monitor and seek to preserve cherished boundaries. The word *maintenance* is a key to compatibility. The greater the compatibility of an innovation with the organization, the lesser the degree of dissatisfaction within the organization that will be aimed at the innovation.

In contrast to compatibility, profitability is a measure of satisfaction. It is a measure of the effectiveness of an innovation in satisfying adopter needs. In measuring profitability an organization evaluates whether the innovation: 1) satisfies the specific need for which it was created, and 2) positively (+) or negatively (−) affects the rest of the organization. Unlike compatibility considerations, which aim at preserving a particular array of organizational boundaries, profitability concerns deal strictly with a pragmatic assessment of gain irrespective of the boundary system.

This brings us back to the outcomes of the institutionalization or termination stage. Boundary expansion via *diffusion* occurs when an innovation is compatible with the norms, values, and goals of an organization and the innovation is, in itself, profitable—self interest profitability. Boundary expansion via *enclaving* occurs when an innovation is compatible with the norms, values, and goals of the organization and the innovation exhibits general profitability. Boundary contraction via *resocialization* is associated with incompatible but profitable innovations. And boundary contraction via *termination* occurs when an innovation is either compatible or incompatible with the norms, values, and goals of the organization, but is unprofitable. This plus or minus evaluation scheme is shown in Figure 2.2.

A few illustrations may be helpful. For simplicity's sake each is based upon a similar innovation in a similar organization—an experimental college in a major university—but in each of the illustrations, the outcome of the institutionalization-termination stage is different.

*Boundary expansion via diffusion.* In 1970, after two years of preliminary study, a student-faculty-administration committee at the University of Alabama recommended the creation of an experimental

*Figure 2.2 The Institutionalization or Termination of Innovation in Organization.*

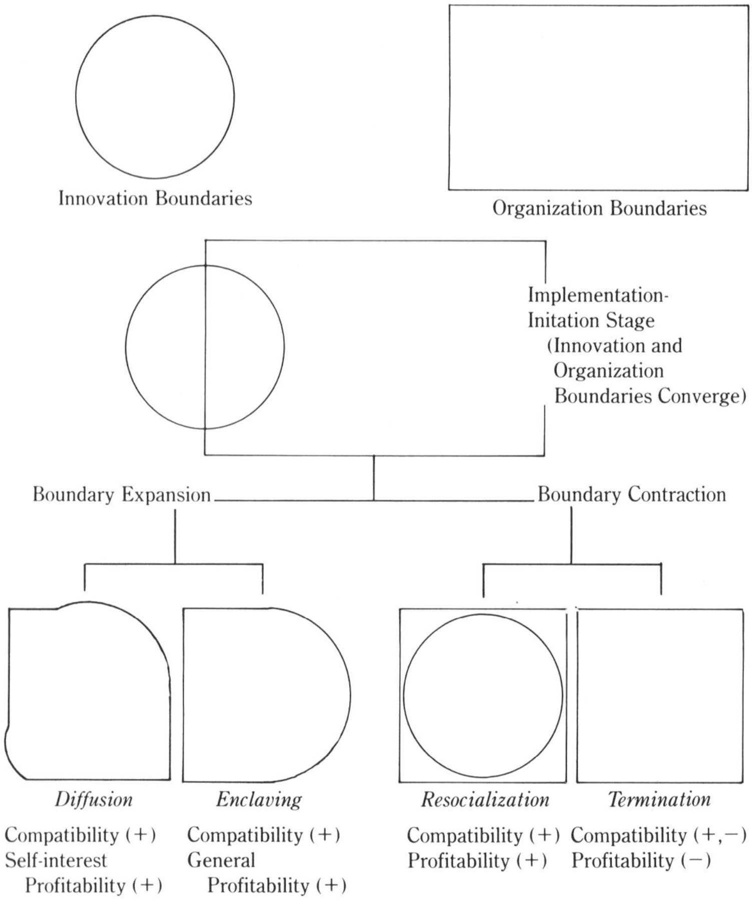

Innovation Boundaries

Organization Boundaries

Implementation-Initation Stage
(Innovation and Organization Boundaries Converge)

Boundary Expansion — Boundary Contraction

| *Diffusion* | *Enclaving* | *Resocialization* | *Termination* |
|---|---|---|---|
| Compatibility (+) | Compatibility (+) | Compatibility (+) | Compatibility (+,−) |
| Self-interest | General | Profitability (+) | Profitability (−) |
| Profitability (+) | Profitability (+) | | |

## Organizations and Innovations: Some Answers

subunit, New College. The faculty senate of the College of Arts and Sciences voted to table the recommendation, feeling the college would usurp arts and sciences prerogatives and thinking the cost of the venture excessive. Despite the opposition, David Matthews, president of the University of Alabama, established the college one month later. He appointed Neal Berte as its dean.

Berte and his staff began by trying to create a positive image for the experimental college. They spoke at civic clubs, on television, and at high schools across the state. Berte also reached out to the University of Alabama faculty. He explained the purpose of the college to opponents and invited them to participate in it. They did so as advisors, guest lecturers, and members of a review committee.

Berte and his staff also structured the college in a manner that was designed to reduce discord. Students admitted to the college were representative of a cross-section of the university rather than being either all honor students or all way-out types. The number of students admitted to New College was limited to a few hundred despite the fact that a large number of applications were received. In addition, all New College students were encouraged to take two-thirds to three-quarters of their courses in the existing departments of the university. Faculty appointments at New College were of two types— joint appointments with existing university departments and a small number of full-time appointments within New College. Full-time New College instructors had credentials comparable to those of other university faculty. Furthermore, New College was planned to be a temporary. Berte promised that the college would phase itself out when the university adopted the programs that made it unique. With the aid of David Matthews, Berte also built an endowment for New College and obtained large foundation grants, including a $250,000 Ford Venture Fund Grant targeted for the whole university, not just New College.

For the faculty and administration of the University of Alabama, New College came to be perceived as compatible with the norms, values, and goals of the university. The faculty of New College was like the faculty of the university; the New College student was like the university student; the faculty of the university helped to shape the New College curriculum; and, most of the courses New College students took were in the existing departments of the university.

New College also proved to be of self-interest profitability for University of Alabama faculty. New College managed to obtain grant money and an endowment at a time when funds were tight. It also attracted large numbers of applicants at a time when enrollments were declining in several departments. And the innovations at New College were the basis of lay and professional kudos.

Compatibility and self-interest profitability are the conditions associated with boundary expansion via diffusion, which is what occurred at the University of Alabama. A large number of New College programs, practices, and even administrative procedures diffused throughout the university. For instance, departments such as physics, and colleges such as Business and Commerce, adopted more individualized programs that they attributed to New College. In addition, the arts and sciences college adopted the student-designed major's program which originated at New College. The College of Business and Commerce adopted internships from New College and the School of Education hired a New College student to act as a consultant in the development of a program based upon her independently designed major.

*Boundary expansion via enclaving.* In 1932 a dean's committee with enthusiastic support from University of Minnesota President Lotus Coffman recommended the establishment of the General College. It was a two-year, lower-division, open-admissions liberal arts program intended for students who had interests that could not be satisfied elsewhere in the university, students without time for a four-year degree, students wanting a broad general education, and students lacking the qualifications to be admitted to other units of the university.

The best instructors at the University of Minnesota were recruited to teach in the General College when it began operation in the fall of 1932. Emphasis was placed upon creating interdisciplinary general education courses.

The college proved compatible with the university. Its mission of interdisciplinary general education and quality teaching was compatible with and, in fact, improved upon the university's own lower-division program. The initial faculty of the General College, all of whom already had appointments with other university departments, were certainly compatible with the University of Minnesota faculty.

The only way in which the General College seemed at all incompatible with the university was in respect to students. The General College never became a place for the excellent student who was unhappy with the university program. Instead, it attracted primarily the student who would not otherwise have been admitted to the university, and this is what made the college profitable in the manner that was earlier described as general profitability. The General College kept the selective university open to all students, which was a social necessity. In taking primary responsibility for educating the nontraditional student, the General College permitted the university to continue its own programs with few changes, which would not have been the case if other units of the university were made to adopt the General College mission.

Because the General College was compatible with the norms, values, and goals of the university and exhibited general profitability, it was institutionalized by boundary expansion via enclaving. Even from its earliest days the college was somewhat peripheral to the University of Minnesota and was never fully integrated into its social structure. Obtaining resources from the university, for example, often involved a struggle. The General College developed a faculty separate from that of the rest of the university. The joint faculty appointments of the first year ran into opposition from university departments and began decreasing as early as the late 1930s. Today, the General College has a separate faculty, very few of whom have joint appointments with any other university department, even though the majority with positions of assistant professor or higher have Ph.D. degrees. General College students were not fully integrated into the university either. Although they are permitted to take courses in the university, they are not automatically granted upper-division admission to the university for satisfactory performance. Instead General College graduates must apply for upper-division admission just as students from any other institution outside the university. In short, General College is an enclave or isolated island within the University of Minnesota.

## Questions and Answers About Innovation

*Boundary contraction via termination.* In 1926 a senior faculty and administration committee identified weaknesses in the University of Wisconsin's educational programs in the areas of instruction, advising, and the relationship between the university and secondary schools. To combat the weaknesses, Alexander Meiklejohn, a member of the committee, proposed an experimental college that was approved by the university faculty and the state regents. Meiklejohn was made director of the college.

The college began operation in 1927. Its staff consisted of parttime faculty loaned by the university departments. The college offered an unusual two-year course of study that focused on fifth-century B.C. Athens during the first year and contemporary America during the second year. There were no course or subject matter divisions in the curriculum.

The college proved incompatible with the norms, values, and goals of the university. The curriculum was quite unlike anything else on the campus. In addition, the college violated accepted university policy by withholding student grades until the end of the second year. The Experimental College students differed sharply from the rest of the students at the university as well. Very early the college and its students acquired a reputation for being radical, causing local high schools to discourage their students from applying to the Experimental College. As a result, most of the Experimental College students were from out of state and a majority were Jews. In an age of overt antisemitism this was incompatible with the social make up of the university. Indeed, the composition of the Meiklejohn student body also raised the ire of both the state legislature and campus fraternities.

Another consequence of the college's reputation was a decline in enrollments at the height of the depression, which made the underenrolled college very costly to the university. Moreover, the college failed to satisfy one of the needs for which it was created—it worsened the relationship between the high schools and the university, and brought the university bad local press as well. In addition, the college utilized financial resources and new university facilities that other academic departments or more traditional students would like to have used. The short of it is that the Experimental College was unprofitable to the university.

*Organizations and Innovations: Some Answers*

Meiklejohn's college then was both incompatible with the university and unprofitable for it. Accordingly, it was terminated in 1932, only five years after it began.

Boundary contraction via resocialization is conspicuously omitted from these illustrations. It's not for lack of examples; merely as a courtesy for the reader. Boundary contraction via resocialization is the principal focus of Part Two of this book.

# PART TWO
# A STUDY OF FOURTEEN INNOVATIONS

CHAPTER 3

# *The Colleges: From Creation to Institutionalization*

*Stage 1 of the Innovation Process: Recognition of Need*

The State University of New York at Buffalo was founded in 1846 as a private university. Unlike most schools that began as liberal arts colleges and grew into universities by adding graduate and professional divisions, the University of Buffalo as it was named began as a professional school—a medical school, to be precise. For the next 67 years, it grew by adding new professional schools—a school of pharmacy, a school of law, and a school dentistry. It was not until 1913 that the College of Arts and Sciences was created. Some attribute its establishment to the prominent Flexner report of 1910 on medical education which panned in no uncertain terms the preparation of Buffalo's entering medical students. As a matter of fact, the report did not have a whole lot of nice things to say about the university in general, except for its medical library. It went so far as to call the University of Buffalo a "fiction," simply a collection of independent professional schools, "each living on its own fees" and masquerading under a common charter (Flexner, 1960, p. 26). The university did not change a great deal as a consequence. Development continued as it had in the past. In subsequent years, an evening division and summer school were organized; schools of business, education, social welfare, nursing, and engineering made their appearances; and, a graduate school was introduced just before World War II.

It was not that Flexner was wrong either. Until well after the First

World War, the University of Buffalo really was no more than a collection of independent professional schools held together in name by a common administration. The school of arts and sciences was treated as an unwanted stepchild. Robert Hutchins once described the university "as a series of separate schools and departments held together by a central heating system" (Kerr, 1963). Buffalo lacked even that, but there was a unifying concern—the training of local practitioners as lawyers, doctors, and pharmacists to serve western New York state. University admissions were largely regional; enrollments were, in part, limited by the community's capacity to absorb graduates; and, most instructors were community professionals.

By 1950, though, Buffalo had changed a bit, but the changes were more in degree than in kind. The university began to grow, but admissions requirements remained low. Each of Buffalo's colleges had its own admissions standards, curricula, graduation requirements, faculty and the like, so there was little change in this regard. However, the act of growing caused some changes. The first dormitories were opened in 1952. Class size increased. In fact, students were given identification numbers, and admissions became increasingly geared toward grades and standardized test scores as the 1950s progressed.

The most damaging outcome of growth, however, was the entrapment of Buffalo in an escalating growth cycle. Increased enrollments necessitated more faculty and more buildings, which required more money, which meant either increased tuition or increased enrollments. Since Buffalo established itself as a local service university, only limited increases in tuition were possible or it would have priced itself out of the market. The same constraint militated against large enrollment increases. It became obvious that only state aid would save this private university. The next several years found Buffalo trying to check the expansion of New York public higher education in favor of state support for private schools. But this was not in the cards, and the University of Buffalo merged with the State University of New York in 1962.

At the time of the merger, Clifford Furnas (a former Assistant Secretary of Defense) was Chancellor or Chief Executive Officer, of the University of Buffalo (U.B.). He was a Buffalonian, though some-

*The Colleges: From Creation to Institutionalization*

what less of a local than many of his predecessors. In negotiating the merger with New York State, he aggressively sought to preserve a high degree of autonomy for his campus. He feared U.B. would become "a numbered restaurant in a Howard Johnson chain.'" This sort of colorful language, and a lack of reticence in making his opinions publicly known, alienated the State University of New York (S.U.N.Y) central administration from Furnas and prevented him from staying on as chancellor past retirement age (Bennis, 1973 p. 113-114). In all fairness, there were very real differences in the interests of U.B. and S.U.N.Y. which would likely have prevented any University of Buffalo representative negotiating the merger from becoming popular with the State University of New York.

Furnas was succeeded by Martin Meyerson, who had just completed a fairly successful term as Acting Chancellor of the University of California, Berkeley. After the riots of 1964, he was the individual selected by the California Regents to restore quiet on campus. He might well have been appointed permanent chancellor had he not demanded as a precondition the Regents' assurances of nonintervention in his campus affairs (Heirich, 1970, p. 276). Prior to the acting chancellorship, Meyerson served as Dean of Berkeley's College of Environmental Design. He came to Berkeley via the University of Chicago, and Harvard University, where he had been Director of the Harvard-M.I.T. Joint Center on Urban Studies.

The transition from the Furnas to Meyerson administration and merger of Buffalo into the S.U.N.Y. system transformed the University of Buffalo from a local to a cosmopolitan institution.[1] For U.B. the change meant a break with local western New York ties. There was an influx of students from the New York City area, who competed for admission with local residents. In the four years between the merger and Meyerson's presidency, western New York enrollments declined from 73 percent to 55 percent of the total. By 1968, 80 percent of the entering freshmen were in the top tenth of their high school graduating classes as compared with 10 percent 10 years earlier. Almost 75

---

[1]The terms *cosmopolitan* and *local* were popularized in separate works by Merton and Gouldner in 1957. They were earlier used by Zimmern, who equated "local" and "cosmopolitan" with Tönnes' "gemeinschaft" and "gesellschaft."

percent of the Buffalo faculty in 1973 were recruited under Meyerson (Bennis, 1973, p. 126). They were largely Ph.D.'s from highly rated universities, not professionals from the Buffalo area with Buffalo degrees dedicated to training Buffalo practitioners.

Not only did the people constituting the U.B. population change, but its mission changed as well. In fact, the new mission resulted in the new people. A comparison of University of Buffalo goals just prior to the merger with those of the State University of New York for a university center makes clear the nature of the change.

A few years prior to their merger, both U.B. and S.U.N.Y. carried out studies of their goals and purposes. Buffalo's research was part of a self-study prepared in 1955 for the Middle States Association of Colleges and Schools. Though 1955 was early in the Furnas administration, the statements capture well the ethos already described.

> The Furnas statement noted that the first goal of the university was "deliberately and officially to foster the advancement of knowledge." This was to be done through instructional offerings in the academic disciplines and professional studies "represented in the constituent schools of the university." Further the university was to encourage and provide resources for carrying out research.
>
> "A second goal was to serve the local community and region. This was to be done by providing "a local opportunity for study and learning . . . and for teaching and research." The university was to work "with industry, commerce, government and institutions for educative and social welfare in finding answers to current problems." The university was to furnish social services "which are appropriate to a university" and which other agencies might not be able to provide. It was to keep the professions informed of scientific advances affecting the work of practitioners. It was to offer opportunities for understanding other cultures. It was to inform all types of citizens "of great moral, political, and aesthetic values which have been distilled out of recorded civilization."
>
> The third goal of the university as defined in the Furnas document was to insure the accomplishment of the others by providing "a setting in which intellectual freedom may be exercised and the search for truth may be prosecuted unhampered" [S.U.N.Y., 1972, p. 3].

The S.U.N.Y. statement was part of a 1960 report to the Governor and Board of Regents entitled, "Meeting the Increasing Demand for Higher Education in New York State," by a blue-ribbon panel chaired by a former head of the state university system, Henry Heald. The recommendations of that report resulted in the State University of New York's decision to merge with Buffalo. The panel urged that a graduate university center be established in upstate New York, "either through the conversion of an existing private university or through the development of one of the present campuses of the State University and should be reasonably large in size and scope" (Heald, 1960 p. 31). The university center was to "be designed to stand with the finest in the country and to attract and hold able young men and women from all over the world." [It] "would bring to the state and help to advise the technical and scientific industries that are playing an increasingly important part in our national economy. The faculty and research staffs would provide additional sources of advice and expert service for all the public and private interests of the people of the state. With their twin missions of advanced education and basic research, graduate schools are the keystones of modern universities. A great graduate school cannot exist in isolation, however, it must be a part of a great university with all this implies in undergraduate and professional education as well as graduate instruction (p. 31)."

The differences in the S.U.N.Y. and U.B. statements were several. First, the mission of the University of Buffalo was regional and that of the State University of New York was at least statewide with suggestions of national and international involvement. To adequately serve this new clientele, U.B. was required to expand in size. Enrollments increased 55 percent from 9,582 the year before the merger to 14,831 in 1966 when Meyerson assumed office.

A second difference was the emphasis of the S.U.N.Y. document upon graduate study and research. Though research was mentioned in the Furnas statement, it was not nearly as central to the mission of the university. Advanced education and basic research were viewed as "keystones" and "twin missions" of the S.U.N.Y. university center. As a result, new academic units were introduced at U.B.: Schools of Health Related Professions, Information and Library Science, and Architecture and Environmental Design. The number of Ph.D. degrees awarded by U.B. increased almost 475 percent from 19 in 1961 to 90 in 1966.

A third difference was in institutional character. At the risk of a slight hyperbole, the University of Buffalo was a passive university, one that responded primarily to community needs: It *furnished* services, *worked with* industry, *kept* professions and practitioners informed, *offered* opportunities for understanding other cultures, *provided* opportunities for study, *informed* all types of citizens. The S.U.N.Y. university center, on the other hand, was vibrant. The community responded to it. The university center was to *attract* and *hold* able young men and women, *bring* industry into the state, and *stand* among the finest universities of the country.

The S.U.N.Y. dream was a Berkeley of the East. For the first few years of the Meyerson administration, the State University of New York at Buffalo (S.U.N.Y.A.B.) was promoted, in faculty recruitment, as exactly that. Unfortunately for S.U.N.Y., it was easier to recreate the negative aspects of Berkeley than the positive. A truly excellent university requires both money and time to create, but large size, impersonality, and attendant unhappiness come rather quickly. Soon after the meger with S.U.N.Y., Buffalo began to develop the traits students reacted against at Berkeley in 1964. An increasingly elite student body was being admitted. Such students are historically most prone to campus dissent (Flacks, 1971). The university was staffed by a growing number of departmentally oriented faculty with strong research and disciplinary training who were dedicated to basic research and graduate training. This situation is notorious for isolating faculty and ignoring and alienating the undergraduate (Scott and El-Assal, 1971). Enrollments were growing. And because the new state university was founded with an almost arrogant self-directedness, all the subsequent repercussions were just a little worse.

Martin Meyerson was well aware of the similarities when he accepted the S.U.N.Y. at Buffalo presidency. Some maxim like, "once burned, twice warned" would seem to apply. In any case, Meyerson sought to avoid a repeat of his Berkeley experience at Buffalo. The first opportunity to do that occurred in the summer of 1966, just a few months before he took office.

In 1965, S.U.N.Y. asked Clifford Furnas to prepare a 10-year plan for the growth and development of his campus. A year later a student newspaper characterized his plan as: lacking a coherent educational philosophy, expressing unmerited satisfaction with the quality of student services and campus education, being preoccupied with the quantitative aspects of mass education, and disregarding individual identity (*Spectrum*, 1966 editorial). In short, Furnas failed to recognize the conditions that lead to Berkeley's unrest and the need for change in these respects at Buffalo. Meyerson, though professing no dissatisfaction with the plan, established his own committee consisting of key Buffalo faculty and administrators. Their charge, preparing "an academic plan for the university," was essentially to redraft the Furnas document.

Meyerson's immediate rationale for the committee was that a new campus was soon to be constructed for S.U.N.Y.A.B. It was a $650 million "dowry" that came with the merger. Like the 10-year plan for development, the new campus had been rather conventionally designed by the Furnas administration. Meyerson felt that the new campus should reflect the objectives of the new university. This was, of course, necessary and desirable, but on a larger scale it permitted Meyerson the opportunity to begin the transformation of S.U.N.Y.A.B. into the academic jewel coveted by the State University of New York, but tempered by his experience at the gem of the California system.

By the time Meyerson assumed office, a need for change had been recognized at the State University of New York at Buffalo. The need resulted from a fundamental change in the nature of the University of Buffalo. The norms, values, and goals of this local university were radically altered via merger with the cosmopolitan S.U.N.Y. system. The need was recognized through a change in personnel—a former Berkeley chancellor was matched with a Berkeley aspiring university.

## *Stage 2 of the Innovation Process: Planning and Formulating a Solution*

Martin Meyerson's committee was the very first step in planning and formulating a programmatic solution. The committee consisted of the most important U.B. people who would continue into the Meyerson administration. It was chaired by the dean of the graduate school, Robert Ketter, who would succeed Meyerson. The Ketter committee, or MAC 1 (Meyerson Advisory Committee 1) as it was called, met from mid June through early September of 1966, one or more times a week for at least 2½ hours a session. The mood was rancorous, so much so that the deliberations of the committee were still sealed in the S.U.N.Y.A.B. archives 10 years later. Ketter said it was not clear that the committee would reach any agreement until its last session, at which time he showed up with a bushel of apples and suggested that no one leave until there was a consensus about something. Even so, it was pointed out, in presenting the final report, that it in no way reflected the opinions, *in toto*, of all members.

The acrimony was not surprising in view of the membership of the committee and its charge. The committee was, in essence, deciding what the university was to be, what it would be like to live and work there, and how life at S.U.N.Y.A.B. would be structured. The membership was a polyglot indicative of the transition from U.B. to S.U.N.Y.A.B. There were people with Furnas-like and S.U.N.Y.-like views of the university. There were individuals representing the once dominant professional schools, the once dominated arts and sciences colleges, and the newly prominent graduate school. There were persons interested in preserving and extending the power of departments as well as those interested in minimizing their importance. There was much to disagree about and the subjects were hardly trivial.

What was surprising about the committee was that it proposed a potentially innovative program for the university. Committees, especially those like MAC 1, that are ideologically divided do not typically seek out the best solutions to problems. Rather, they try to form a consensus among members. This is a political process which involves simply finding something everyone can live with. For the Ketter committee, the political process levied a heavy toll, not in terms of producing an innovative outcome since Meyerson influenced that, but in terms of the committee's inability to spell out the specifics of the new program. In fact, different members of the committee had very different perceptions of what they had approved.

MAC 1 chose a collegiate concept for S.U.N.Y.A.B. It was designed to capitalize on the large size of the university, which was to stabilize at an enrollment of 40,000, but to minimize the impersonal and alienative aspects of mass education. This was a redefinition of the

## The Colleges: From Creation to Institutionalization

university aimed at satisfying the recently recognized need. The committee described the college concept as follows:

> The "college concept" derives from the idea of the wholeness of the educational process: the horizontal and vertical involvement of the student, the faculty member, the administrator and the community at large in the educational program of the college. The curricular/cocurricular aspects of college life should combine to reach the "whole" individual. For this type of experience to be meaningful, each participant must be committed to, and have a substantial involvement in, college life.
>
> Ideally, the collegiate system embraces the following four features: residence, faculty, program and organizational coherence. The first three of these are directly related to the enhancement of the "total educational experience." The fourth is necessary for vitality. . . .
>
> A "college" will be a self-contained educational entity, with its own living accommodations for resident students and some faculty members, classrooms, faculty offices, laboratories, dining halls, student centers for the commuting students as well as residents, library, reading lounges, etc. This is not to say that teaching cannot and should not be done more effectively in special facilities outside the college, or possibly even outside the university. . . .
>
> The "college" has as one of its fundamental concepts and keystones the "living learning unit." Therefore, the coordination of the cocurricular aspects of the educational experience with those normally thought to be academic must be given special attention. Management of living, dining, social, cultural, and athletic activities must be considered within the whole educational experience, and not separate and distinct from it. This dictates the development of comparatively small living units, of probably less than 500 resident students. It should be recognized, however, that the nature and mission of the various colleges may differ markedly. Therefore, there should not be specified any uniform fixed size of "college" or living unit for the "campus" as a whole. . . .
>
> A unique and distinctive feature of the collegiate university being proposed is the degree to which the various components may differ. There should be created a framework of operation which allows the natural formation, and correspondingly the natural dissolution, of parallel colleges serving completely different needs and functions. For example, we are presented with the opportunity to create such colleges as a College of Social Science, a Center for Conservation Studies, a "Reed College," and an Institute of Technology, as well as a School (or College) of Education, Business, Engineering, etc. More than this, there should be encouraged the development of special experimental programs, and "Experimental Colleges" should be established with this special goal in mind. . . .

> In certain areas of the university, traditional academic departments and departmental groupings afford the most natural and logical college units. These should not be discouraged from continuing their present affiliations. At the same time it must not be presumed that current disciplinary boundaries are necessarily sacrosanct... [Ketter, R., 1966].

Changes in university governance were also proposed and five plans for implementing the collegiate concept were offered.

The Ketter committee report was interesting in several respects. First, it provided both a rationale for the university, consistent with the notion of a S.U.N.Y. university center, and mechanisms for translating that rationale into a plan for the new campus. Second, it emphasized the concerns that the Furnas report was criticized for omitting. This is not at all surprising, as Meyerson created the committee for that purpose. But the MAC 1 report went even further in recommending that the entire campus be academically reorganized in light of its new needs. All organizations have need hierarchies, but the satisfaction of an advanced need is inadequate if it results in dissatisfaction at a more basic level. Buffalo's faculty had not been recruited for a collegiate university, and so might badly have adapted to one. As a matter of fact, the faculty had been recruited for more than one university: some for a cosmopolitan first-rate graduate school, others for a local service university. The Ketter report might have been a potential threat to the very basic security needs of the faculty because it challenged their multiple beliefs about appropriate values and norms.

Third, the major reorganization recommended was organizationally vague and possibly unworkable. This was probably the result of the composition of the committee. A more definitive and explicit statement would likely have failed to win approval. The Ketter report explained neither the scope nor the magnitude of the colleges.

Edward Spicer has said that people resist change under three conditions: 1) if the change is a threat to basic securities; 2) if the change is not understood; and 3) if the change is imposed upon them (Spicer, 1967, p. 18). Conditions 1 and 2 were likely consequences of the MAC 1 report for the reasons just noted, and many at S.U.N.Y.A.B. suspected that condition 3 was a factor as well.

*The Colleges: From Creation to Institutionalization*

Meyerson, however, did not seek to impose the Ketter report on S.U.N.Y.A.B. He disseminated it widely throughout the university, stating that he hoped it would inaugurate "a colloquy which will lead us to a plan which is reflective of both our practical needs and our visions of greatness," Meyerson asked recipients to "study the prospectus and communicate to me any of your views on the matter" (*Monthly Reports*, 1966).

On September 20, 1966, the Ketter report was the subject of the university's annual fall planning conference. It was an off-campus, day-long retreat attended by President Meyerson; the MAC 1 members; the faculty senate; special invited faculty, students, and staff; and outside experts including A. H. Halsey, an expert on British higher education, and David Riesman, an eminent social scientist and commentator on American higher education who had been a U.B. law professor years before. In the course of the session all of the seemingly possible objections to innovation were raised without ever really getting to the specifics of the proposal before the group. Perhaps the potential scope of the change frightened the participants. In any case, the student body president objected to the absence of students on the Ketter committee; a department chairman said the proposed change flew in the face of departmental excellence; a nationally famous English professor thought the report just tinkering and felt it better to fail with a truly new and utopian vision of the university than one that trifled with the plumbing; and a graduate student representative said that undergraduates and graduates had dissimilar interests and needs, so that a single curriculum would be inadequate for both. At the start of the meeting, Riesman and Halsey offered long discourses on collegiate education, and from time to time Meyerson or Riesman told the retreatists that they were on the wrong track, but to no avail.

Meyerson pushed his colloquy for approximately two more months, and on November 28, after discussions with the principal faculty, student, and administrative bodies, offered his own proposals. Meyerson's statement—delivered during his first 100 days in office at the first faculty senate meeting of fall 1966—set the tone for his administration and the future policy directions for the State University of New York at Buffalo. It posed a set of goals for the university and, based upon these goals, recommended the academic reorganization of S.U.N.Y.A.B.

The goals were a mix of the 1955 Furnas statement, the 1960 S.U.N.Y. Heald report, and Meyerson's own feelings about what a university should be. Their point of origin appeared to be the Furnas statement, but their emphasis was clearly reflective of the Heald report as carried out in a Meyerson-organized university.

Goal five of the seven goals set dealt with the college concept. It stated: "As a community of scholars we must take advantage of the diversity which large size can provide and at the same time establish centers of identification for students and faculty in which both intellectual and social values can be realized." In so formulating the collegiate notion, Meyerson made both the need and the solution a permanent part of the university, at least for his administration. The fact that it was one of the lower ranking goals meant that it was not a top priority for Buffalo.

This was certainly true in Meyerson's placement of the colleges among his recommendations. At the tail end of the report, in a section entitled "'Other Features," the collegiate concept was the last item mentioned. To give a better idea of its importance, it was immediately preceded by a proposal to create a Board of Visitors to occasionally review the programs of each of seven reorganized and broadly based faculties that Meyerson planned to establish. His description of the colleges was as follows:

> No organizational plan can be developed without consideration of the role of the student in educational policy or of the noncurricular provisions which enrich the lives of resident and nonresident students. As for the role of the student, we must all resolve in the period ahead how he may best take part in the deliberations of the University. In respect to living and study arrangements, I propose that all students, graduate of undergraduate, men or women, married or single, have the opportunity to associate with or live in a college which will include residential and dining facilities, study and recreation space, overnight accommodations for commuters, reading and seminar rooms, as well as cultural facilities. Some faculty as well as the Masters of these colleges will live in them, and other faculty may be associated with them.
>
> Each of the colleges may be expected to develop a character of its own and educational programs to supplement formal instruction. Exper-

## The Colleges: From Creation to Institutionalization

imental seminars may be offered through the colleges. For example, such seminars, after appropriate educational review, may provide pass-fail credit for undergraduates. The colleges would also be suitable centers for advisement. Each college would have no more than a thousand students selected from a variety of fields, although the sizes of colleges would vary. Similarly the mix of graduate and undergraduate, men and women, single and married students would vary. The Masters will have important leadership roles not only for their colleges, but for the university as a whole.

In developing these colleges, we must be aware of the great diversity of life-styles and life ideals we must satisfy. Too often students are considered deviant because they do not fit the models created by institutions. More often the institution does not provide a sufficient diversity of models to meet the variety of human types which it serves. A university must, of all places, be free of this accusation [Insert Source?].

Meyerson's goal statement was exactly that of MAC 1, but the recommendations, growing out of it departed widely from the Ketter statement. The seemingly most obvious distinction between the two was the approach each took to change. The Ketter report suggested holistic change at Buffalo while Meyerson recommended an array of piecemeal changes. However, the vagueness and indecision of the Ketter document minimized the virtues of coherence associated with holistic change, while the interlocking and extensive nature of the Meyerson proposals made his recommendations something more than the sum of their parts—so both reports appeared to be very similar.

They were alike in another way, too. Both proposals stressed structural changes, and that was all they really could do. In 1966, S.U.N.Y.A.B. was still in the midst of the transition from the old U.B. to the new state university. As a result, a whole mix of norms, values, and goals permeated the institution.

There were significant differences in the two approaches as well, particularly in regard to the colleges. Meyerson's colleges were a supplement to the university program rather than the substitute of the Ketter Committee. Accordingly, the Meyerson colleges were less central and more peripheral to S.U.N.Y.A.B. than those of the Ketter report. Meyerson also altered the target population of the colleges. The faculty, who were one of four basic elements of the MAC 1 colleges, were only marginal in Meyerson's. His emphasis was almost exclusively upon students. Meyerson also streamlined the functions of the collegiate units and doubled their maximum enrollments. The academic program was de-accented, planned research centers were moved out of the colleges into the seven faculties, and the mission of the colleges was shifted to filling in the affective gaps in the S.U.N.Y.A.B. curriculum. The courses that were offered by the colleges were to be experimental and graded on a pass-fail basis. This did potentially provide an experimental enclave for the university, but at the same time, the mandatory pass-fail grading system demeaned the academic currency of the college courses and served to further reinforce the affective image, which is of dubious merit in a cognitively oriented university.

The faculty senate unanimously approved "in principle" Meyerson's proposals on the day they were recommended. This was quite a contrast with the negative reception of the MAC 1 proposals at the annual planning conference. When the senate approved Meyerson's proposals, it tentatively sanctioned the planning and formulation of the colleges and so permitted the new program to be initiated and implemented. Planning and formulation, however, was to continue through much of the initiation-implementation stage as the very broad outlines of the proposal were translated into an operational design. In a similar manner, the need stage continued well into the planning and formulation of its solution. It ended only with the approval of Meyerson's report. At that time, the faculty senate transformed Meyerson's personal recognition of new university needs into an organizationally official and permanent recognition.

In retrospect, the proposals of the Ketter committee can be viewed as a trial solution for Meyerson's personal recognition. They served both to inform S.U.N.Y.A.B. of a need and to present a possible solution. MAC 1 emphasized the ideal more than the practical and aimed more at the effectiveness of the solution than its adoption or acceptance. Unfortunately, reports advocating fundamental change as a rule do not become policy (Ladd, 1970, p. 205). They are modified by community reaction, the realities of the adoption process, and a realization of the difficulties of implementing such change. At Buffalo, the result was the Meyerson report calling for an assortment of changes. He emphasized the practical more than the ideal, and easy acceptance and adoption over effectiveness and impact. The differences in the two approaches points to the centrality of organizational facts of life in shaping change.

Meyerson came to Buffalo with a record as a reformer. After the Berkeley rebellion, he called for the creation of a committee to examine education there and recommend change. Like the Ketter report, it was visionary in proposing reform. Despite 11 months of deliberations, the academic senate, counterpart of the Buffalo faculty senate, enacted few of the recommendations. The obvious moral of the story for a reformer like Meyerson was that future change efforts should be geared to the realities of the organization being changed. Changes should occur step by step, each step building on the previous one. This speaks to an emphasis initially on piecemeal change and multiple solutions that would become more holistic as extended over time. In terms of the three Spicer conditions for resisting change, Meyerson's report was not very threatening, it was not imposed upon the university, and it was clearer than the MAC 1 report.

Meyerson's choice of a more practical, less far-reaching solution permitted him to be more explicit in his formulation. Because his proposals were not particularly threatening, the greater detail offered enhanced clarity not internal chaos and university criticism, as would have been the case with the Ketter committee. Nonetheless, Meyerson left several major questions about the colleges unanswered. Though he had the advantage over MAC 1 of operating from a single value and norm perspective, Meyerson was far more reform-minded than the Buffalo faculty as a whole, and as a result still had to play his cards very close to the chest in order to insure the adoption of his recommendations. Undoubtedly some of his ideas were kept vague for this reason. In addition, there were the circumstances common to all new programs. Some retrospectively important things were just not considered in the planning and formulation of a new program, and others simply could not or did not develop until the initiation-implementation phase. As previously noted, this is one of the reasons for an initial autonomy period during the initiation and implementation of an innovation.

## Stage 3 of the Innovation Process: Initiating and Implementing a Program

For more than a year after Meyerson's speech the colleges remained only a proposal. There were a number of reasons for this. The physical plant required for them had not been constructed—nor would it be for eight years, but that was not known or even thought possible at the time. The faculty senate had not specifically approved the colleges. It acted on Meyerson's "early implementation" proposals within a few months, but not on the colleges for almost 3½ years. The senate's tacit approval in principle might have been sufficient for the new president to press ahead with the colleges, but because several of the other proposals were of higher priority, they occupied his attention during 1967.

In December 1967 Meyerson asked the 28-year-old dean of University College (lower division of S.U.N.Y.A.B.), Claude Welch, a product of the Harvard and Oxford Colleges, to take charge of the implementation and initiation of the Buffalo colleges. Welch saw two possible approaches to his task and, in turn, each prevailed. The colleges could be built around great people or upon great ideas. That is, the colleges could be launched by finding vibrant, visionary, and accomplished people who would, according to plan, bring both imagination and university wide support; or, they could begin with ideas solicited from the university at large. The best of the ideas would be rewarded by becoming colleges.

The great-person approach was based upon the assumption that innovation is a difficult and human process. Approval and success grow out of the interaction of people, so a very special person would be necessary to cope with the resistance and to accept the frustration attendant in translating an idea into reality. The great-ideas approach acknowledged the difficulty of innovation, but glossed over the role of the superbeing. Instead, change was viewed as an institution-wide phenomenon that the university community was far more likely to support if it was involved in the planning. Participation encourages recognition of a new program and fosters a sense of ownership.

The great-person approach was tried first. In early 1968 a committee was appointed to screen potential college master director candidates. Over 100 different people inside and outside S.U.N.Y.A.B., including a mideast potentate, were considered. By fall 1968, six masters had been selected.

All came from within S.U.N.Y.A.B. and, with few exceptions, their stature was local and not quite of great-person quality. Moreover, two were made masters because they were having difficulties in their present positions.

The six included Allan Sapp, a composer with a Harvard background, who was dean of the U.B. College of Arts and Letters and a member of the Ketter committee; John Huddleston, a professor of engineering who had been active in the Yale colleges; Mac Hammond, an associate professor with a Harvard education and an interest in linguistics; Lyle Borst, a nuclear physicist inclined in recent years more toward undergraduate teaching than research; Charles "Chip" Planck, a young political scientist who had written two books before receiving his Ph.D. from Johns Hopkins; and, Fred Snell, a Harvard M.D. with a Ph.D. from M.I.T. Shell had been appointed dean of the graduate school in 1967, where he enjoyed an innovative, yet short and conflict-ridden tenure of slightly more than a year. Meyerson believed he and, Snell shared similar views on education; Snell had the academic stature to be respected by the university faculty — in fact, in 1970 he was elected president of the International Biophysical Association; and as graduate dean he had developed an excellent rapport with students. Snell and the colleges seemed the perfect match.

In concert with Meyerson's preference for decentralized academic administration, each of the college masters ran off in his own direction and began planning the substance of his college. All developed faculty advisory groups. The masters also met together with Meyerson administration officials and planned the future of the collegiate system. Their conversations were heady and freewheeling. There was talk of 30 full-time faculty per college in three years, and elaborate innovative programs. Early on, Meyerson suggested that one-quarter of all student programs be the prerogative of the colleges, a return to the MAC 1 conception of the colleges. There was talk of admissions requirements, of whether the colleges would strike out on their own or build on existing departmental programs, of how commuting students might be integrated into the residential facilities.

The six colleges were given letter designations until such time as an appropriate name was selected. When the masters were named, it was assumed that the new campus facilities for the colleges would be available by the time their initial planning was completed. Not surprisingly, the planning took significantly less than eight years.

The colleges quickly developed their own missions. Snell's College A was to study and improve the greater community; Sapp's College B was to be concerned with the arts; Huddleston's College C was to study the relationship between technology and society; Borst's College D was to study the natural sciences with an emphasis on scholarship; Hammond's College E was to examine literature and film as symbolic forms; and Planck's College F was to study new forms of education, politics, and living.

As the planning for the first six colleges proceeded, steps were taken to expand their number via the great-ideas approach. In December 1968 Warren Bennis, vice president for academic affairs, wrote a letter to the *Gazette*, an in-house organ, inviting all members of the university to propose new ideas for colleges. It was a chance to see one's dream curriculum come true; all that was required was a description, a statement of advantage, and advocacy before the committees considering the proposals. A total of 70 proposals were submitted. There were proposals for five international colleges, seven health or ecology colleges, five black studies or interracial colleges, and a slew of history colleges. On the more extreme side, there were suggestions of a college for 14-year olds, an expertise college, a life-styles college, a child day-care college, a commuter hotel conference college, a synthesis college, an esthetics and modern tribalism college, and a peripatetic college. A goodly number of more traditional ideas for interdisciplinary programs or undertakings lacking in the undergraduate curriculum were offered as well. These included sociotechnical systems college, law and society college, education college, ancient history college, Western civilization college, and women's college.

By June 1969, 10 more colleges were created: Law and Society College, International College, Afro-American Studies College, Sociotechnical Systems College, Comparative Historical Studies College,

Ecology College, Modern College (to study modernization), Health and Society College, Communications College, and Mathematical Science College. These college had the blessings of the president, the faculty senate educational policy and planning committee, and a specially created student, faculty, and administration committee called the colleges committee. The new colleges were called workshops and were given the authority only to plan a program. The use of the term *workshop* was intended to convey a lesser status than *college*, and marked a differentiation in the collegiate system by developmental stage. This was the first step in beginning to structure the new innovation.

The selection process was conservative, as none of the less traditional colleges were selected. Also, quantity seemed as important as quality since all of the multiply proposed colleges were included among the 10. It was hoped that the conservative approach would serve to make the colleges more compatible with the university, and the choice of popular colleges would get more people involved. Again, all of the masters were S.U.N.Y.A.B. faculty members.

Meanwhile, back at the original six colleges, only five remained. The rosy picture of the collegiate future quickly turned gray. The new campus with its collegiate facilities had progressed little further than Governor Nelson Rockefeller's 1968 shovelfull of groundbreaking dirt, not only because of unavoidable strikes and disputes over racism in construction, but because of increased costs that the New York State legislature was unwilling to assume. Expected increases in the university budget that were to be shared by the colleges did not materialize. Talk of huge masters' expense accounts and rapidly increasing numbers of staff lines remained only talk, and it was feared by the masters that the colleges would become only a shoestring operation. John Huddleston, perhaps because of his experience with Yale's well-supported college system, resigned in 1969. He resigned soon enough so that Sociotechnical Systems College could be selected to replace College C, which folded with his departure. Sociotechnical Systems College was based on the same ideas as "C" and staffed by many of the same people. Within a year, Mac Hammond resigned for the same reasons, but more so because financial conditions had deteriorated even further—there were then 15 colleges to share the available resources. College E continued, however, because Hammond had already gotten a small program off the ground.

When it became apparent that there would be additional delays in constructing the new campus, the colleges were asked or permitted to offer trial or pilot programs. It was felt that this arrangement would be only short-term, as the physical plant would soon be available to house them.

In any case, each college was assigned temporary facilities. S.U.N.Y.A.B. at that time was a very crowded campus—faculty, students, staff, and academic units had expanded rapidly during Meyerson's first few years. An interim campus was rented in 1967 and 11 departments found homes there, but the main campus grew more and more to approximate a sardine can. The situation was temporarily liveable because, to use what is beginning to sound like a punch line, a new campus would soon be available. There was no room on the campus for the new colleges, so they were located at its periphery. Colleges A and F found adjoining storefronts on the main street of Buffalo across the street from the campus, and College E found a frame house on Winspear Avenue, contiguous with the campus. Several departments were also located on Winspear Avenue in one-and two-family residential units owned by the university. Colleges B and D got off to a late start and missed the initial real estate rush. Allen Sapp went on sabbatical during 1969-70 and Lyle Borst operated out of his own office.

Allen Sapp's philosophy of educational change was that it must be slow and initiated with the support of the existing social structure, so College B did not offer a program until fall 1970. Lyle Borst had a similar outlook. He did not wait as long to get his college going, but did so by cross-listing courses already offered by established departments. His college, which was to be based on the Oxford and Cambridge educational model, attracted a large conservative faculty group. It was, in fact, the only one of the original six to do that.

College A, which was the first college to offer courses, became the most visible of the five, and as a result appeared the prototype of the new innovation to most in the university and local community. The fortunes of College F were closely tied to those of College A because of the bordering storefronts. "F" cross-listed courses with several departments and offered three of its own. Early on Charlie Haynie, a Cornell University A.B.D. (all but dissertation) in mathematics with a recent background in social activism and community organizing, was hired as a full-time fellow of College F. More about Haynie and "F" later.

Fred Snell based College A on a radically progressive philosophy of education. Its focus was the liberation of people in the local community and at the university.

With regard to the university, Snell pointed out the essential meaninglessness of a college education:

> "Right now, I would have to say that by-and-large, students are lazy, irresponsive, irresponsible, apathetic, and superbly lacking in intellectual curiosity to the extent that it borders on the anti-intellectual. The dominant motives, furthermore, are those that seem to channel them toward the B.A. degree, which has become so institutionalized in our society as a symbol of success. Of course in the drive toward this end, which as a matter of fact is an end in itself, they would like an impressive record, for even the QPA [Quality Point Average] has its societal and monetary rewards"—[Communication with Claude Welch, May 8, 1969].

Today, much of his critique strikes a sympathetic chord; this was not nearly as true in 1968. His remedies were even less appealing. Education at College A would free people to learn, not to exalt the outmoded oppressive patterns of education. The formal university was a vehicle of bondage—College A would depend heavily upon informal or experiential education. At College A the capricious domination of the teacher would be replaced by the freedom of the learner. The learner was best able to judge how much and how well he or she had learned.

All of this and one additional ingredient were contained in a course CAx02, entitled, "Conflict and Change in the Local Community." The additional ingredient was activism in and around Buffalo. In January 1969 the course was approved by the university college curriculum committee for the spring and summer of that year. Five hundred students enrolled during the very first term. The format was group and individual independent study. Students were to choose what they wanted to learn and grade themselves on how well they did it.

Snell hit a nerve. The activities at College A attacked the authority system, the power structure, the day-to-day operations, and the basic rationale for S.U.N.Y.A.B. and other universities. The function of the university has traditionally been the creation, transmission, and application of expert knowledge. With regard to power, this meant that the faculty senate or a body like it determined educational policy because it best represented the collective wisdom of the faculty. Similarly, a physics department determined the physics curriculum because of its collective expertise in that area. With regard to authority, expertise in theory was the means by which faculty were ranked. With regard to the day-to-day operation of the university, faculty experts were necessary to guide and evaluate students in their learning. Expertise is the glue that holds academia together. It is the reason that every American professor presumably carries in his wallet a picture of Mark Hopkins, his log, and his tutee. College A said everyone was an expert.

Needless to say, the criticism of College A was widespread, loud, and pragmatic. It was challenged for its size, for student self-evaluation, and for lack of faculty supervision. Ironically, Snell's basic critique of current university practice was not joined, it was probably not even heard, and if it was, it was ignored. Rather, Snell was forced to defend his college on traditional grounds. It was felt that with a group as large as 500 (1 out of every 20 students at S.U.N.Y.A.B.), students could not possibly receive adequate attention or guidance. Many of Snell's critics rallied around his analysis of college education—at least his acknowledgment that students were "irresponsive", "irresponsible", and "apathetic". Students given the freedom Snell proposed would simply goof off. Snell said fewer than 10 percent were doing so, and opponents at the university cited examples to the contrary. In September 1969 Dean Welch tried to limit enrollments to 250 in CAx02. The university forced College A to evaluate the course twice in its first three months of operation. For the second evaluation College A students brought into his office what Claude Welch described as a loud and noisome chicken with a cassette bearing Fred Snell's evaluation of CAx02 tied to its leg.

## The Colleges: From Creation to Institutionalization

Ninety percent of the students in College A gave themselves course grades of A. Around the university people angrily joked, "Why do you think its named College A?" The banner of standards and excellence was raised high and often by S.U.N.Y.A.B. faculty and administrators. On May 14, 1969, the university college curriculum committee approved self-regulation and self-evaluation. After the results of self-grading became known, a long, hard fight ensued. Dean Welch, Vice President Bennis, and their successors attempted to institute pass-fail grading and to require a product: an exam, a paper—something.

College A began with a faculty advisory committee, but the number of faculty involved dwindled quickly perhaps because faculty were not used to being dominated by students, who by sheer numbers had more power in the governance of "A" than they; or because Fred Snell's views on education differed radically from their own; or because of the shabby condition of the storefront; or because of the very negative impact involvement with "A" would have on their futures at S.U.N.Y.A.B. Each was advanced as the reason by several people active in the colleges or university during this time. Who knows? In any case, College A, in a very short time, became the only college lacking significant and formal faculty participation. Fred Snell often said that many faculty were involved, but they feared career retribution if they made themselves known. The existence of a covert faculty contingent did not receive much credence, and College A was criticized for its lack of faculty guidance and evaluation. The lack of faculty, in fact, was the real issue underlying both the enrollment and grade questions. There were no experts.

The storefront home was not particularly esteemed either. The storefront was, at best, dilapidated. One observer noted that its principal decorations were "a burglar alarm and a slogan on the wall, 'We love you Fred,' followed by 20 signatures." The storefront was also an advertisement to the local community of the S.U.N.Y.A.B. schism. Some felt that if College A were closer to the campus, Fred Snell would come to his senses and the students would reassume their proper places. An attempt was made in August 1969 to move "A" back to a campus building, but the college declined the offer.

As 1969 came to a close, a wide discrepancy existed between

Meyerson's concept of the colleges and the reality that had been initiated and implemented in the form of College A. College A was, in practice, an antagonistic alternative to S.U.N.Y.A.B. Meyerson had specifically planned the colleges as a supplement. In fact, he used that very word in his senate speech. The difference between alternatives and supplements is important. Alternatives aim to confront and supplant existing organizations, while supplements are designed to broaden, complement, and perhaps reform. Colleges B and D were supplements.

The alternative nature of College A and the manner in which it had been approved deprived it of the initial autonomy often characteristic of the initiation-implementation trial period. Almost from the moment CAx02 began, College A was the subject of close scrutiny and criticism, not to mention the two evaluations in three months. The decentralized governance structure, which permitted Snell to plan "A's" program essentially alone, and the lack of specific approval by the faculty senate did not make the college illegitimate. On the other hand, these conditions in no way served to establish "A's" legitimacy. College A was an unknown quantity which, combined with Snell's rhetoric and the lack of faculty involvement, tended to make the university faculty and administration suspicious and distrusting. The first evaluation was an attempt to clarify the situation. It was the first cue to College A about how it should begin to fit in with the rest of the university. In this instance it was a very obvious comment that College A was not fitting in.

If "A" had responded by self-censorship or by showing that everything was indeed fine, perhaps more autonomy would have been granted in the form of peace and quiet. For those who requested the evaluation, College A's response was insufficient or inadequate. A second evaluation was demanded; the response was no better than the first. An enrollment ceiling followed; it was scotched. An attempt to impose pass-fail grading and a project requirement came next; College A successfully opposed it.

The process of sending cues moved from the level of requests for self-evaluation (censorship) to impositions of sanctions by the university. The initial query was designed to test the waters. As the waters proved chilly, the level of cue or sanction escalated fairly dramatically.

## The Colleges: From Creation to Institutionalization

The response of the host changed from questioning uncertainty to certainty and an attempt to control. College A reacted at first with annoyance and subsequently with growing solidarity, anger, and defensiveness. In the end the situation could only be resolved via institutionalization or termination of the colleges.

Three factors caused the divergence of the colleges from the original plan. One was the lack of resources. The lack of physical plant meant that the colleges could not possibly become the physical entities envisioned. The lack of funding caused the demise or decline of two of the more innovative colleges, which were certainly more compatible with the university than College A.

The second factor was publicity. Reports of deviance are more newsworthy and spread more quickly than accounts of success at conformity. Colleges B and D got off to plodding uncontroversial starts. College F was linked to College A by proximity, similar facilities, and ultimately by joint activity. College A was the college people at S.U.N.Y.A.B. heard about, and it was the way many came to picture the colleges. As a result, the perceived divergence of the colleges from plan was much greater for a lot of people than the reality.

The third factor was people. The choice of Fred Snell as master determined the way College A would develop, but that was only possible because of Martin Meyerson, who believed in decentralized governance. This kind of governance structure permitted Fred Snell the freedom to operate relatively independently. Other principals such as Claude Welch and Warren Bennis were in a rather unenviable position. They acted as a buffer between the colleges and the rest of the university. Both were committed to the colleges as envisioned by Meyerson, not Snell. In 1969 and 1970 the colleges were fragile, still subject to veto by the faculty senate, but strong in student enthusiasm. In fall 1969, 900 students were involved in the credit and noncredit activities of College A. Bennis and Welch acted to avoid a confrontation between the faculty of S.U.N.Y.A.B. and the colleges, perhaps out of feelings of proprietorship of the collegiate concept.

The faculty was in the midst of reorganizing the senate during the early Meyerson years and became only peripherally involved in the first college sorties. Though there was a good deal of anti-Meyerson feeling among the faculty, the college idea evoked more questions than opposition. In 1967 Peter Regan, S.U.N.Y.A.B. executive vice president, conducted a faculty senate poll of academic units and student organizations. This survey of Meyerson's proposals showed that all groups, with the possible exception of the graduate student association, accepted the collegiate notion. This might have encouraged an initial suspension of action against the colleges, despite the fact that conservatives remained in key positions throughout Meyerson's administration.

This assortment of people at Buffalo added up to a political situation in which Fred Snell and a student contingent had more clout than the Meyerson administration and a disorganized faculty. Moreover, the well-organized but relatively small College A interest group was able to use the administration's advocacy of decentralized and participative decision-making to defeat the imposed control measures.

Before digressing for a bit, an important point about College A needs to be highlighted. For all the turmoil "A" caused and would cause, it performed admirably in meeting the need for which it was created. In a large university, College A did an excellent job of providing a sizeable number of students with a personal center of identification. The rhubarb was over the way College A did that. The institutionalization-termination stage would focus not on the need, but on the way the formulated plan was implemented and initiated — compatibility, not profitability.

## When the Horn of Plenty Turned Steady State: An Informative Digression

In January 1970 Martin Meyerson resigned the presidency of the State University of New York at Buffalo to become president of the University of Pennsylvania. The S.U.N.Y.A.B. he left after 3-1/3 years was very different than the S.U.N.Y.A.B. he imagined in 1966. At the fall 1966 planning conference, David Riesman told participants not to plan their university too pragmatically because the State University of New York is a rich university in a rich state. Five years later, Earl Cheit, dean of Berkeley's business school, looked at the conditions of colleges and universities around the country and described them as "the new depression in higher education."

## The Colleges: From Creation to Institutionalization

Wealth came to higher education with World War II. After the 1957 Sputnik launching, college and university enrollments increased at the rate of almost 8 percent a year until 1970. At that rate, enrollments more than doubled in 10 years. "The total number of students in degree-credit courses reached 3.6 million in 1960 and 7.9 million by 1970" (Carnegie Council on Policy Studies in Higher Education, 1975, p. 25). At Buffalo, between the time of the merger in 1962 and a 1972 accreditation study, undergraduate enrollments doubled and graduate enrollments tripled.

Finances increased even faster than enrollments. From 1957 to 1968, more money was spent on higher education than the total for all previous years since the founding of the American college in 1636. "In 1959-1960 the annual operating expenditures were $7.6 billion" (Carnegie Council, 1975, p. 25). At S.U.N.Y.A.B., operating budgets grew fourfold between 1962 and 1972. Large departments grew where there had been none. From the time of the merger through Meyerson's resignation, Buffalo attracted a large number of distinguished scholars; many were internationally known. During 1967-68, nine new department chairpersons and two deans were hired. S.U.N.Y.A.B. raided faculty from Harvard, Yale, and Princeton; eight Ph.D.'s were recruited en masse from M.I.T. Warren Bennis observed further that:

> Each new appointment meant an increase in enthusiasm, new ideas, the Meyerson optimism. The tiny crowded campus seemed barely able to contain all the excitement within it. Intellectual neighborhoods sprang up across the campus each dominated by the personality of a "new look" appointee. Lawrence Chisolm inaugurated a radical American studies program that emphasized the study of non-American cultures as a way of overcoming chauvinistic biases. David Hays inherited a good, but narrowly defined, linguistics program and made it magnetic by insisting that linguistics was no less than a focus for intellectual integration. John Eberhard, the dean of architecture and environmental design, attracted a nucleus of nonestablishment designers interested in creating living systems, rather than monuments. To head a new library school a dean with an applied math background was hired. He shocked an assembly of catalogers by asking who exactly Melville (Dewey Decimal System) Dewey was and then proceeded to attract to the school a flock of media freaks, sensitivity trainers, and, less unusual for a library school,

systems specialists. The new social welfare dean, Franklin Zweig, young enough to be called "boy dean" by his detractors, turned the social work school upside down. Social work at Buffalo was no longer to be the handmaiden of psychiatry. Under Zweig, the emphasis would be on community organization, legal and social policy. Richard Brandenburg, new dean of the school of management, also broadened the scope of the management school to include public institutions. Changes were seen in the least likely places. For example, Leroy Pesch, who came from Stanford to head the medical school, took steps toward streamlining the medical curriculum. Talk at the medical school was somewhat less of the narrow professional concerns of private practice and more of the health care needs of the public [Bennis, 1973, p. 125-126].

Camelot died even before Meyerson resigned; in fact, its death hastened his departure. By 1970 the trends of the 1960s were reversed; where money once flowed like water, the streams reached drought level. The U.S. Departments of Commerce and Labor found that the rates of college attendance among 18- and 19-year-old men increased from 37.7 percent in 1962 to 44 percent in 1969, but by 1972 returned to the 1962 level (Glenny, 1974-1975, p. 24). The causes were at least fourfold and included: 1) the abolition of the draft, 2) the poor quality of the job market for college graduates, 3) the rising costs of college attendance associated with inflation, and 4) the growth in popularity of the concept of life-long learning with its associated acceptance of deferred entrance and periodically dropping out of college. S.U.N.Y.A.B., however, did not lose enrollments. It was the top school in an area with a number of private colleges, several community colleges, a state college, and a state university. S.U.N.Y.A.B. was able to attract students who would ordinarily attend the state college. More than that, it was cheaper than a private college. The cost to S.U.N.Y.A.B. was a very slight decline in the quality of student admitted, but even that was a jolt to a school aiming at such a high level of excellence.

The students who did enroll changed their majors to those fields offering the best occupational opportunities. Nationally, the Bureau of the Census found that between 1962 and 1972 enrollments in the biological and health sciences increased by 68.1 percent, the social sciences increased by 48.6 percent, business and commerce increased by 30.3 percent, and the humanities and mathematics increased by somewhat smaller amounts. In contrast, engineering enrollments decreased by 33.1 percent, the physical and earth sciences decreased by 30.5 percent, and education decreased by 9.9 percent (Carnegie Council, 1975, p. 25). Buffalo's major enrollments were indicative of the national trend. The impact of the change was a shift in the full-time equivalent enrollments in academic departments. Highly tenured departments with shrinking enrollments suffered, as did the university since it was unable to add faculty to oversubscribed departments or to build in new or desired areas that might bring additional students. As a result, there was fear that total full-time enrollments would be lost which would be a disastrous occurrence because the university's budget was determined by enrollments.

Changes in state and federal funding affected Buffalo more than enrollments. Public attitudes toward higher education turned sour in the late 1960s and early 1970s owing in large measure to student unrest. Higher education fell in public priority as well. Unemployment, health, and environment are among the concerns that replaced it. The late Berkeley Center for Research and Development in Higher Education found that the proportion of revenue going to higher education has dropped steadily since 1968 in the Midwest and since 1971 in the rest of the country. The graduate university was particularly hard hit, declining from 62.3 percent of the total state funds for higher education to 49.6 percent (Glenny, L.; 1975, p. 25). For Buffalo, the discrepancy between the budget granted by the New York State legislature and that requested by the university grew larger each year. In 1970 and 1971, a freeze was put on hiring, even for replacements. And beginning in fall 1970, the academic complement of the university decreased each year.

Federal funding declined in the same manner as state funding, with one exception— there was a change in who got the money. Money went to student aid instead of institutional aid. The greatest victim was the research university. For Buffalo, research money nearly quadrupled between 1962 and 1970. Beginning in 1969, it increased only slightly: 12 percent in 1969-70 and 1970-71 combined, and 1.5 percent between 1972-1973 and 1973-1974. Graduate student fellowships and traineeships plummeted.

Even though there were small increases in state and federal funding,

## A Study of Fourteen Innovations

they were eaten up by an inflation rate reaching what was then the scandalous level of 6 percent per year. In real dollars, S.U.N.Y.B. was losing money. The impact on the campus was devastating. Meyerson came with a promise of growth—not only growth, but growth with excellence. He and the people he recruited came with an expectation of bigger and better each year, but after only one year the increases began to decrease. The dream of a Berkeley of the East died with the budget.

Meyerson became quickly disillusioned. There were rumors that he would leave after his first year. David Bazelon commented, "In every other university I've been to, the faculty hated the administration. Here they worry about desertion" (Bennis, 1973, p. 144). In fall 1969, Meyerson went on two-thirds leave of absence to chair the American Academy of Arts and Sciences' Assembly on University Goals.

Buffalo's faculty also became disillusioned. They were recruited to S.U.N.Y.A.B. with Meyerson's vision of the future. When they arrived, they were stuffed into an overcrowded campus and shortly found out things were not going to get any better. Warren Bennis described the situation as follows:

> Inadvertently we had cooked up the classic recipe for revolution as suggested by Aaron Wildavsky, "Promise a lot; deliver a little. Teach people to believe they will be much better off, but let there be no dramatic improvement. Try a variety of small programs, but marginal in impact and severely underfunded. Avoid any attempted solution remotely comparable in size to the problem you are trying to solve."
> The intensity of the disaffection felt by some of those I had brought to the university came to me as a shock. . . . The disparity between vision and reality became intolerable [Bennis, 1973, p. 37]

There was a mass exodus of faculty. Many of the superstars left, including John Barth, James Dannieli, Edgar Friedenberg, Gabriel Kolko, and C. H. Waddington. Most major Meyerson appointments turned ultimately into a resignation or termination. Perhaps the mood was best captured by an interchange between Theodore Mills, who left Yale to head Buffalo's sociology department, and Warren Bennis, just before he left S.U.N.Y.A.B. to assume the presidency of the

*The Colleges: From Creation to Institutionalization*

University of Cincinnati (Bennis, p. 129):

> Mills: "You know, I never asked you about this, Warren, but do you feel guilty about bringing me to Buffalo?"
> Bennis: "Yes."
> Mills: "Well you should."

Meyerson was succeeded by Robert L. Ketter, after an interim acting presidency by Peter Regan. Ketter's academic career had been characterized by steady advancement through the Buffalo hierarchy. He rose from chairman of the civil engineering department, to secretary of the faculty senate, to dean of the graduate school, to vice president for facilities planning, to president of the university. His ascent was only halted once when, in 1969, he resigned as vice president for facilities planning. The Meyerson people felt he did it abruptly and in so doing intimated that President Meyerson was responsible for the building delays on the new campus. That resignation, combined with a tough stand on the student disruption that racked S.U.N.Y.A.B. in 1970, won Ketter the support of the middle-of-the-road to conservative faculty caucus, and the local residents on the body charged with nominating the new president.

Different times call for different leaders. Martin Meyerson was an innovator, and Robert Ketter was a consolidator. Good times, like those from the end of World War II to the late 1960s, demand the visionary leader or the innovator. When resources are plentiful, growth and change are the order of the day. This situation is possible only because the central functions of the university are secure. Anything else that happens is gravy. The pattern of innovation or change during good times is by addition to that which already exists.

Bad times, like those since the late 1960s, require the services of a consolidating leader or integrator. When resources are meager, retrenchment is the appropriate response. Because the university grew by addition in good times, there is a need to integrate the mass of new activities and programs with the existing core, but more importantly, a cut in resources means that some things have to be eliminated. Bad times are characterized by an acceptance of innovation largely for survival and only when accomplished via substitution.

## A Study of Fourteen Innovations

It was precisely because of conditions at the time that both Meyerson and Ketter became president. In Catholic Buffalo, Meyerson was "that Jew from Berkeley"; yet the times demanded Meyerson or someone like him. Ketter was one of two candidates for president. The other was Warren Bennis, who was right out of the Meyerson mold and had comparable strengths and weaknesses. Bennis had been chairman of the organization department at M.I.T.'s Sloan School of Management prior to coming to Buffalo, where he served first as provost of the social sciences division and subsequently as vice president for academic affairs. He was the author of numerous books and articles on interpersonal relations, group dynamics, and change. Bennis taught at Harvard, the University of California, and Boston University. Those were impressive qualifications, but they were not what was needed at S.U.N.Y.A.B. in 1970. Robert Ketter had the appropriate qualities. He was an insider or, more unkindly, a local who had shown the ability to make fast, tough decisions in a time when fast, tough decisions had to be made.

Different presidents and different times meant different goals for S.U.N.Y.A.B. Meyerson's goals for the university dated back to the fall of 1966 and were part of his faculty senate speech. Ketter's goals were formulated in 1972 as part of the university self-study for accreditation. Meyersons' goals for the university were:

1. We must become a preeminent graduate center for the advancement of knowledge through research and teaching in academic and professional fields.
2. We must evolve ways in which we can do this so as to reinforce the traditional disciplines and transcend them by new approaches to research and teaching.
3. Despite a large increase in organized research activity since we became a State University, the weight continues heavily in favor of the health sciences, and for all fields, the level of resources available to research is much below that of other major institutions and must be supplemented substantially.
4. It is also our conviction and our State mandate that we be a great undergraduate center. All estimates of our future enrollment point to a majority of our students being undergraduates. We must provide a breadth and quality of education so that when the student receives

## The Colleges: From Creation to Institutionalization

his first degree he may rightly be regarded as liberally educated and at the same time prepared for advanced study.

5. As a community of scholars we must take advantage of the diversity which large size can provide and at the same time establish centers of identification for students and faculty in which both intellectual and social values can be realized.
6. Located as we are in a large metropolitan area, we must have a close and dynamic relationship with the community while recognizing our national and international ties.
7. The administration of the University must be conducted with a style which encourages the greatest degree of freedom for students and faculty to study and do other creative work not only in conventional, but also in new fields and through new ways of learning [Meyerson, 1966, unpublished].

These were goals for a golden decade. No limit on resources was envisioned, expectations of growth and development were based on common knowledge, and innovation was the order of the day. Innovations were specifically proposed in goals two, five, and seven; five calling for the creation of the colleges. The themes of growth, expansion, and increasing resources were prominent in goals two through six. The first depended upon it and the seventh grew out of it. Goal seven offered the rationale for Meyerson's decentralization of university governance. A plan allowing students and faculty "the greatest degree of freedom" was very expensive. Decentralization is said to decrease organizational efficiency because of duplication, oversight, subgroup politics, and the like; and to decrease the volume of task work accomplished, due to the increased involvement of people in governance at the cost of the goal-defined work of the organization (Weber, 1947, p. 334-40).

In contrast, the new realities of what has come to be called "the steady state," or bad times, shaped the Ketter goals.

1. The University will continue its evolution towards becoming one of the nation's preeminent graduate and professional centers with a firm commitment to the advancement of knowledge through teaching and research in selected academic and professional disciplines.
2. The University will continue to accept the obligation inherent in its graduate center aspirations of creating both an outstanding under-

graduate division, with a rigorous academic orientation which challenges the individual to test the limits of his intellectual and personal development, and an outstanding continuing education division dedicated to the concept of education as a life-long pursuit.

3. In each of its major divisions—undergraduate, graduate, professional, and continuing education—the University will act to maintain existing academic strengths, to strengthen areas of promise, and to develop new areas which possess indications of future importance to the University and to society.

4. The University will remain unequivocally committed to academic freedom; it will simultaneously insist upon a commitment to academic responsibility.

5. In its academic programs, policies, and organization, the University will be open to innovation and sensitive to the needs of faculty and students, both present and prospective; yet it will never lose sight of its academic purposes and of the need to determine and discriminate in favor of the most effective methods of advancing and transmitting knowledge, understanding, and abilities significant and valuable to mankind.

6. The University will recognize the importance of an environment conducive to learning, teaching, and research; it will seek to provide the facilities, services, and personal examples which create such an environment.

7. The University will continue to recognize a special relationship with the community and region, and it will serve in this relationship according to its academic interests and abilities.

8. The University will never be bound to the traditional forms of higher education; it will be willing to create new forms which will further the realization of its aspirations, purposes, and goals.

9. The University will strive to organize and govern itself in such a manner as to make the most productive use of those resources entrusted to it by society for the achievement of these goals [State University of New York at Buffalo, 1972].

No longer were the sights of S.U.N.Y.A.B. set at such lofty heights; a stable plateau might be a more apt description. Limited resources required selective development. S.U.N.Y.A.B. was open to innovation, but innovation would not be as integral to its operation as it was to Meyerson's university. The Ketter goals were far more concerned with preserving the core functions of the university than were Meyerson's. This was not because Meyerson did not believe in them, but rather because they were never in doubt. The twin sentiments underlying Ketter's goals were evaluation and accountability. Organizations that lose the faith of their supporters pay the price in autonomy. Such organizations are scrupulously monitored (Faris, 1964, p. 522). Disruptions at Buffalo during 1969-70, combined with the lowered public priority of higher education, put S.U.N.Y.A.B. in exactly that position with the New York state legislature and the local community. The word that explained the university's reaction to the phenomenon was *accountability*, and it was accompanied by more centralized internal governance. Indicative of the change in times is the contrast in Meyerson's governance statement, which sought the greatest freedom for creative work, with Ketter's, which aimed to make the most productive use of resourses.

There was also a shift in the scope of S.U.N.Y.A.B.'s mission. Though the first goal proclaimed Buffalo desires to be a preeminent graduate and professional center, the seventh realized it would become a regional or local university. Accordingly, continuing education was included among the goals.

U.B. boarded the gravy train a little too late. Had the merger with the State University of New York occurred in the 1950s, S.U.N.Y.A.B. would probably have come much closer to fulfilling its dreams.

## Stage 4 of the Innovation Process: Institutionalization or Termination

The formal process of institutionalization or terminating the colleges began for the first time in early 1969 during Martin Meyerson's last full semester as president of S.U.N.Y. at Buffalo. It continued through the acting presidency of Peter Regan and was completed early in the presidency of Robert Ketter. In all, the process took approximately two years.

When Martin Meyerson became president of U.B., one of his aims was to bring the faculty together. His administration in reality did a little to encourage that outcome and a little to discourage it. On the positive side, he gave the faculty significantly more decision—making power via decentralized governance, and sought to mitigate the isolation of the staff with the creation of the seven interdisciplinary faculties. On the negative side, he increased the rate of growth and spurred the development of conflicting value systems that encouraged greater division. Some measures worked faster than others. Unfortunately, the unifiers were the slower. Faculty members resisted the seven faculties. The seven provosts, who were conceived as minipresidents for each faculty and whose function it was to begin the integration, turned into lobbyists for the various faculties. Each provost was forced to act as an advocate with the central administration in demanding a larger piece of the stabilizing university pie, and then to return to his faculty to mediate the sharing of the meager slice. It was not a time for solidarity.

Furthermore, the campus quickly reached 134 percent of its occupant capacity and faculty were divided among several campuses: a law school downtown, an interim campus, a main campus, and assorted departments in the neighborhoods surrounding the campus. The divergence of norms, values, and goals added to the geographical and departmental divisions by splitting people ideologically as well. Very quickly, faculty developed a liberal-conservative schism. The groups were formalized as caucuses in 1970.

The one countervailing force was the enhanced decision-making role Meyerson ceded the faculty. As we all know, nature abhors a vacuum (even significant scientific laws can be turned into trite maxims). Gradually, the faculty dribbled into the more powerful position he offered it, being pushed and shoved by leaders straining at the bit. The fact of the matter is that it took a lot to overcome the divisions. A widespread disillusionment with Meyerson and his promises of greatness helped decrease divisiveness, as did happenings such as College A, about which there was widespread agreement that something had to be done.

The concerns of the faculty senate, the legislative body advisory to the president, centered specifically on those areas that Meyerson left vague in his 1966 recommendations. The colleges had been established programs by 1969, so they necessarily filled in the gaps in the proposed idea. The way College A did it was at least questionable to

## The Colleges: From Creation to Institutionalization

many faculty. Organizations respond to clashes of interest by creating or modifying the laws by which norms in the disputed area are governed (Coser, 1956, p. 126). Laws are statements about an organization's acceptable norms and are premised upon the values of the organization. The creation and modification of laws are, as a result, means of adjusting organizational boundaries. That was the course S.U.N.Y.A.B. followed with its colleges.

Perhaps fearing the inevitable faculty reaction or perhaps being personally offended by the direction the colleges were taking, Warren Bennis initiated the law-making process. He assembled a faculty-student-administration group to write the law that would govern the colleges in early 1969. The resulting legislative proposal, called a prospectus, was redrafted several times after comments by four faculty senate committees, the college masters, the provosts, university administrators, and the college committee. Widespread approval was crucial because if people do not believe in a law, it does not work. And given the situation, Bennis needed something that would work.

The Bennis prospectus filled in the gaps and answered the faculty senate's questions. Its emphasis was on collegiate review, not academic innovation. The document was based upon three hopes:

1. Relationships between the colleges and the departments and other academic programs must be such that the nature of their interaction is collaborative, not competitive.
2. There must be assurances (and insurance) that whatever standards of academic excellence exist elsewhere in the University also pertain to the academic portions of the colleges as well.
3. Mechanisms for change and redefinition must be built into the development program for the colleges as problems, needs, and capabilities are revealed, discovered, or developed [Bennis, 1969].

The document was firmly committed to Meyerson's notion of the colleges as residential entities. It wavered, however, on his original position on faculty involvement and academic courses, but so had Meyerson. Admissions requirements were discussed. Colleges would have a good deal of freedom in this regard, but specific criteria, which had to be defined and published, would be reviewed by the appropriate university bodies. Faculty associated with the colleges had to be university staff. Appointments were to be negotiated with the individual's employing unit. Participation in the colleges was to be considered in tenure and promotion decisions. Tenure could not be granted through the colleges. The job title "fellow" was created so that colleges could appoint a limited number of nonuniversity people to their staff. Their appointments were to be of limited duration and required a complicated approval process involving all of the faculty in the college making the appointment, the collegiate committee, and the vice president for academic development. Each group was required to act affirmatively before an appointment was permitted. The collegiate committee, nominated by the faculty senate executive committee, was to be faculty and administration dominated.

Governance and supervision were to be democratic, but the specific design was at the discretion of the individual college with review by the appropriate faculty senate subcommittee. Every college was to be under the guidance of a scholar, a master, who would have a limited term and "overall coordinating responsibility for the internal and external affairs of his college."

A three-stage plan for collegiate development was also included in the Bennis prospectus. Passage from stage to stage would be regulated by the collegiate committee, the faculty senate committee on educational policy and planning, the council of college masters, and the vice president for academic development. The nature of the stages—collegiate workshop, collegiate development, and college authorization—was somewhat vague. "Workshop" appeared to be a planning stage, "development" seemed to be a trial period, and "authorization" involved full participation in collegiate governance.

The living-learning character of the colleges was reaffirmed, as was the importance of physical facilities. Up to 25 percent of a student's undergraduate education was to be offered through the colleges, but students would continue to take their majors through academic departments. Three kinds of college courses were envisioned: 1) courses offered by departments and cross-listed with their permission by colleges, 2) courses initiated by the colleges, but cross-listed by departments, 3) courses offered solely through the colleges. Any course initiated by a college for credit would have to be approved by the college committee and the appropriate faculty or university-wide

## The Colleges: From Creation to Institutionalization

curricular body before it could be credited toward a university degree.

Before becoming law, the prospectus required ratification by the faculty senate and approval by S.U.N.Y.A.B.'s president. In June and November 1969, the executive committee of the senate discussed the document and amended it at several points. Most notable of the amendments was a restriction during the workshop and development stages limiting enrollments to 150 in courses not cross-registered with one of the faculties. It was the perfect restriction. It succeeded both in slapping the wrists of the university administration for its sloppy management of the colleges and in limiting the perceived excesses of College A.

The executive committee of the faculty senate was described in the senate by laws as "the medium through which the senate functions and which shall represent and act on behalf of the senate in all matters within the jurisdiction of the senate." In practice, the executive committee was the leadership of the senate and served as the liaison between the senate and all other groups inside and outside the university. All university committees reported to the executive committee and the executive committee reported its opinions and recommendations to the senate when it felt appropriate or necessary, which was most of the time.

With Meyerson on two-thirds leave and the presidency in the hands of a caretaker, the executive committee flexed its muscles and expressed its disapproval of academic policies. It did so by appointing at least one ad hoc committee to examine College A, and it did so by trying to tighten the prospectus. But it did not consider how students would react.

At its June meeting, the executive committee gave the prospectus tentative approval and, at its November meeting, final approval. Warren Bennis distributed the proposal widely and asked for comments. In October, the prospectus was printed in the *Gazette*, an in-house organ. Despite all of the consultation, few university students were involved and even fewer college students.

On December 4, 1969, the prospectus went to the faculty senate with a recommendation that it become effective on January 15, 1970. One hundred and sixty-nine faculty members attended the meeting and they voted to admit observers. While all of the jockeying with the prospectus went on, College A did a little of its own politicking. The "Up the Colleges Committee" was formed and its motto was self-determination for the colleges. College A turned out a large student group for the senate meeting. The gathering took on the appearance of a parliamentary Little Big Horn. Students filled all the remaining seats in the meeting room, far outnumbering the senators. Senators who spoke for approval of the prospectus were made aware of the hostile audience that had quite a different point of view. Those who spoke against it were cheered. One senator felt that the room crackled with tension. The prospectus was amended by an 88 to 81 vote requesting modifications, recommendations, and advisement by "existing students and their successors." On March 15, the faculty senate would reconvene to consider the responses, but in the interim the colleges would continue as they were.

The next task for College A and the "Up the Colleges Committee' was the creation of an alternative to the Bennis prospectus. What must have been especially galling to the executive committee and the university administration was that some students got academic credit for drawing up the new prospectus and participating in the "Up the Colleges Committee" through CAx02, "Conflict and Change in the Local Community."

Spring term, 1970, began noisily. In the name of self-determination, College A demanded that the registration limit for "Conflict and Change in the Local Community" be lifted from 500 to 2000. Dean Welch refused on the grounds that development of the colleges was in a delicate state. Students would have to be responsible, it was argued, or they would wash the whole thing down the drain. In response, the "Up the Colleges Committee" held mass meetings to stop oppressive, arbitrary administrative rulings and press for self-determination.

In February, the issue spread to the local community; in March, it spread throughout the state; and in the summer of 1970, the U.S. Senate considered the problem of weapons allegedly confiscated outside of the College A storefront. The two Buffalo daily newspapers, *The Buffalo Courier Express* and *The Buffalo Evening News*, had run stories on the colleges since their beginning, but in January 1970, coverage became almost daily. The provoking incident was the distribution of leaflets at six local high schools by the Youth Collective

## The Colleges: From Creation to Institutionalization

Conspiracy and the Organization of Afro-American Awareness. The leaflets included phraseology like, "Let's get out of the fucking system," "Come to the storefront and let's talk it over." Free "brew" was promised. The storefront was, of course, College A and many of the students were getting credit for their leafletting through CAx02, "Conflict and Change in the Local Community."

A bit of perspective is needed to understand the events that followed. The local community harbored a good deal of resentment against S.U.N.Y.A.B. After all, in becoming a state university it had attenuated its ties with Buffalo. Clean-cut local youngsters were being rejected in favor of "long-haired, occasionally foul-mouthed, frequently ill-dressed, political activists" whose New York City origins were plainly obvious in their accents. S.U.N.Y.A.B. was derisively called "Jew B" and Meyerson was thought the cause or at least a good reflection of the problem. Not too much provocation was necessary to get Buffalo angry. Nor was much needed to set off S.U.N.Y.A.B. students. Like the faculty, they too had been promised the moon and, like the faculty, had been terribly disappointed. Many students came back to Buffalo angry in the fall of 1969 for this reason and because of the national mood associated with the war in Vietnam.

Throughout the fall, there were sporadic protests related to ROTC, institutional racism, student participation in governance, and government-sponsored research. School leafletting was the very tame beginning to a tumultuous spring, but it was sufficient to draw the ire of the Buffalo City Council. Council people bipartisanly denounced Meyerson, sex and drugs, permissiveness, obscene language, offering high school students free "brew," and the harboring of runaway boys and girls on campus. College A was described as a "new and revolutionary departure from university concepts" in the strictly worst sense of the words *new* and *revolutionary (Buffalo Evening News, 2/11/69)*. A city councilwoman called for an investigation of the incident and declared that, "the time has come in this city to clean out that university and weed out the revolutionary students ... who are polluting the minds of the young who venture onto that campus" *(Buffalo Evening News, 2/11/69)*.

In late February the whole S.U.N.Y.A.B. campus erupted. On February 24, several hundred students occupied the court during a basketball game between Buffalo and S.U.N.Y. at Stony Brook, charging racism in the S.U.N.Y.A.B. athletic department. The next day things snowballed as rumors and misunderstandings spread. That evening ended with the appearance of the Buffalo police on campus and the medical treatment of 27 individuals, including five policemen injured in the resulting fracas. March brought student vandalism, around-the-clock police patrols of the S.U.N.Y.A.B. campus, a student strike, a faculty senate vote of "no confidence" in Acting President Regan, and the sit-in and arrest of 45 faculty members protesting the police occupation. S.U.N.Y.A.B. took on the appearance of an armed camp. Warren Bennis described his experience walking across campus one Sunday:

> The parking spaces had been cleared for police vans, prowl cars, and K-9 wagons. . . . I stopped twice to let squads of police go by. There were sixteen men and two dogs to a squad. They passed in double columns, the sun flashing off the visors of their plastic riot helmets [Bennis, 1973, p. 91-92].

In April, an uneasy quiet reigned; but in May, after the Cambodian invasion and the killings at Kent State and Jackson State Universities, violence shook the campus once again. Fighting between students and the police spilled out into the streets of Buffalo. Students marked the battlelines with barricades on Main Street. Blocks away, tear gas drove people from their homes. Police allegedly fired birdshot at students on the campus. Somehow, all of this became tied to the colleges, notably A and F. It was an unreasonable association.

At the end of February, two state assemblymen asked the Republican caucus, an influential group in a Republican-dominated legislature, to initiate a probe of College A. Soon after, concerned mothers began to picket outside college A demanding that it be shut down. Stories were told of elementary school children who had been seduced into the storefront by means of coloring books and toys. Even the obviously beneficial activities of College A, such as the tutoring of local students and the creation of alternative schools, were denounced. For instance, after Fred Snell talked of a tutoring relationship with St. Joseph's Collegiate Institute, the Catholic diocesan educators issued a statement denying any connection with College A. Similarly,

## The Colleges: From Creation to Institutionalization

a faculty person who was listed as a member of the curriculum committee that approved College F's 302 course, "Social Change in America," wrote a letter to the *Buffalo Evening News* indicating in no uncertain terms that he had not participated in the committee.

In March, another assemblyman asked Acting President Regan to close College A as "the source of much of this disorder on campus and in the community." He went on: "Without immediate and strong action we can only assume that your administration supports such disorder" *(Buffalo Evening News,* 3/1/70). Elementary school parents charged that College A encouraged their children not to attend church or school. Professor Robert J. Good, in a letter to *The Reporter,* a university newspaper, asked the question "high in the minds of most faculty members." "How many of the students in College A have taken part in the disruption, arson, and assault of the past week? How many of the militants whom we have seen joyfully trooping around campus, tripping fire alarms, barricading doors, screaming obscenities were students in College A?" *(The Reporter,* V1, n. 7, 3/5/70).

The pressure on the colleges increased. The Bishop's Lay Council of Buffalo denounced College A, claiming that Buffalo officials should "remove this temptation from our youth before it becomes a larger festering sore which will further spread contamination" *(Buffalo Evening News,* 3/3/70). Though the city government found it was unable to prosecute for the leaflets, a viable alternative was discovered that involved the inspection of the storefront by the city fire department and the county health department. Twenty-seven violations of building codes were uncovered. City and county officials concluded that the building did not "comply with Buffalo building code and cannot be used for school purposes because of height and area limitations" *(Buffalo Courier Express,* 3/6/70). The city declared that College A would have to close and put the university on notice that other off-campus properties might be examined, including 19 buildings on Winspear Avenue.

By April of 1970, the state government determined its response. Excerpts from the *Courier Express* had been read into the New York State Senate record in March. State Senate Majority Leader Earl Bridges from Western New York met with representatives of the Governor's office and the chancellor of the S.U.N.Y. system. Samuel

## A Study of Fourteen Innovations

Gould, the chancellor, said the university had circumvented the S.U.N.Y. approval process. He chided the Buffalo faculty for inaction and appointed a faculty advisory committee to make recommendations to him by April 15 on the future of the colleges and U.B. rioting. Gould also defended College F's "Social Change in America." (That will be discussed shortly.) Legislators pointed out that College A would not be shut down immediately, but it would be phased out over time. "An immediate shut down it was feared would be a potential (source) of further campus-wide disturbances involving not only the radical elements on campus but more moderate students as well" *(Courier Express*, 3/4/70).

Toward the end of March, College F's 302 course, "Social Change in America," began making headlines. The course, sponsored in cooperation with the American Studies Department, was divided into 45 topically different sections, including: "Monopoly Capital Imperialism," "The School as an Institution," "Radical Research," "Radical Organizing in Professional and Community Groups," "The U.S. as a Militaristic Authoritarian State," " Personal Awareness and Political Consciousness," "Studies in the Dynamics of Culture," "Youth Collective Conspiracy," "Science and Ideology," "The American Family," "Revolutionary Anarchism," and "Professional and Intercollegiate Sports: A History of Institutional Racism." The course was intended

> to remedy a deficiency at this university: the lack of a systematic critique of present day industrial society in America and the potential for radical change. Students will find that while most university course offerings presume the ideology of bourgeois capitalist society, this will decidedly not be the case in this course. This will be a radical course and we shall attempt to review the time-honored dialectic fusing thought and action ["Social Change in America" Catalogue, *Introduction,* 1970].

Instructors were primarily graduate students, though a number of faculty participated. The course began in spring 1970, and by March 20, 500—900 students had enrolled. The rioting made an absolute accounting impossible.

The *Courier Express* ran a four-part, page-one series on the course. Articles were titled: "Violence Stressed in Courses" (3/20/70), "Rebel Class Approved by U.B. Officials" (3/21/70), "25% of Staff Face

## The Colleges: From Creation to Institutionalization

Campus, Court Action" (3/22/70), "Sweeping Changes Bring U.B. Anguish" (3/23/70). The articles were slanted and inflammatory, harping on the greatest weaknesses of the course. Much of the activism of course 302, in fact, involved simply learning to do research on social issues. In any case, the *Courier Express* linked the moral collapse of U.B. to the ideas of Martin Meyerson.

There were covert threats by legislators to cut off funding in April, when the U.B. portion of the state budget was being considered. Acting President Regan explained that the colleges were not funded with state money, but through a foundation established at the time of U.B.-S.U.N.Y. merger. The foundation head denied it and charges of fiscal mismanagement were lobbed about until Regan could prove his story. At about the same time, Fred Snell received a letter threatening his life, written on Buffalo police stationery.

Sometime in the midst of all the havoc, the faculty senate deliberations on the colleges were postponed from March 15 to April 10. There were those on the faculty senate executive committee who suggested in lieu of a delay that the December 4 prospectus simply be declared law in the absence of a student government alternative. For them, the prospectus offered by the college students and approved by a mass of from 900 to 4000, depending upon whom one talked to, lacked legitimacy. The executive committee had long been conservative in orientation, but in 1970 the committee began exerting stronger leadership in the university. Even before the riots, the executive committee started taking a hard line with the colleges. In early February the executive committee seized upon the debate between Claude Welch and College A over whether the enrollment ceiling should be raised from 500 to 2000 and strongly urged administrative adherence to the 150 students-per-class limitation of the December prospectus. On February 25, the day after the basketball game sit-in, the executive committee discussed the possibility of noting self-evaluated courses on student transcripts. Such notation was intended as a stigma to students.

Then came the riots. In their aftermath, the executive committee developed a tougher new prospectus. The key feature was that all existing colleges and workshops would face a complete review, entailing possible program revision, by a special advisory committee appointed by the vice president for academic development and composed of individuals inside and outside the university. The aim of this measure was resocialization, at least for Colleges A and F. After the review, an assembly or division of colleges would be formed consisting of one representative from each collegiate unit, the dean of undergraduate studies, dean of graduate studies, and student representatives as determined by the assembly. The assembly, under the direct supervision of the vice president for academic development, was to rule on trial courses (new nondepartmentally approved courses) and the final establishment of collegiate units. The notion of a collegiate division or assembly was part of the college's plan for self-determination, but the powerful role of the vice president of academic development in the executive committee plan was to insure not too much self-determination in view of CAx02 and CF302. Students would be permitted to enroll for up to four credits of trial courses per semester, provided that the instructor was a regular faculty member and the courses were approved by the assembly. The faculty member and assembly requirement grew out of criticism of graduate student instructors in "Social Change in America." College courses could satisfy major, distribution, or elective requirements upon approval of the appropriate university body. Fellows could be appointed without the possibility of tenure.

The executive committee document was quite a contrast to the college's proposal. In February, college students proposed a prospectus calling for acceptance and preservation of the practices that many in the university abhorred. It emphasized self-determination of the individual college units, self-determination of student programming within colleges, and autonomy for the colleges within the university. Nearly all of the review procedures of the Bennis prospectus were scrapped. The college's prospectus called for the establishment of a division of collegiate studies comparable to the existing divisions of undergraduate education, graduate education, and continuing education. The division was to be coordinated by an 11-member committee elected by the colleges. The committee was to lend strong support in defending the autonomy of the individual collegiate units, obtain academic approval of their programs, and control the collegiate budget. The division would be headed by a dean appointed by the university administration. The dean would facilitate the needs of the individual colleges and serve as their agent in negotiation with other segments of the university. A very simple procedure was specified for creating colleges. Any group of students, faculty, and/or staff could define themselves as a college. After a clear statement of intent, the college could offer trial programs for credit on a one-semester experimental basis without review by the university or the collegiate division. After the trial period, approval would be requested from the appropriate university bodies. Upon approval, the colleges would automatically gain self-determination over the life and death of their programs. There was also a call for college representation on the curriculum committees with which they would deal.

Students begged, cajoled, and attempted to moralize faculty into supporting their prospectus. On February 19, an open letter to the faculty from the "Up the Colleges Committee" urged them to "edge over, join up, and grow with us." By April, the suggestion bore a certain similarity to inviting the faculty to vacation in a leper colony. Whatever small chance there was that the student prospectus would be approved when it was written dropped to naught by the end of March, but neither the Bennis nor the executive committee prospectus was very popular either. Prospectus-writing became a common institutional pastime. Robert Stern, chairman of the faculty senate college's subcommittee in 1970, joked that everytime any two people got together a new prospectus was born.

Warren Bennis, a strong believer in consensus governance, quickly realized that his prospectus did not represent a consensus, particularly with regard to students and the people in the colleges, so he threw in his lot with the faculty senate committee on educational policy and planning. Robert Rossberg, chairman of the committee, could not endorse the college student prospectus because there was little likelihood that the senate executive committee would approve it and pass it on to the senators for a vote. His goal was a similar liberal alternative with a chance for success.

The Rossberg prospectus established a committee to create a collegiate division. The committee was dominated by the colleges, being composed of two representatives from each existing collegiate unit, three university-wide deans, the vice president for academic devel-

## A Study of Fourteen Innovations

opment, and would likely have produced the governance structure recommended in the student prospectus. According to the Rossberg prospectus, the governing body would have the same function prescribed in the student prospectus, as would its director. The only significant differences were that students were limited to eight credits of trial courses per term and only a limited number of fellows, without tenure possibilities, could be appointed. Self-determination was not specified, though there was no disavowal of the principle and no means of prohibiting it other than the generous limit on trial courses and an unspecified limit on fellows.

Robert Stern and members of his faculty senate college committee balked at the Rossberg prospectus and filed a minority report somewhere in tone between the executive committee and educational policy and planning committee prospectuses. It was a compromise proposal more severe than the Rossberg document, but still advocating expansion via enclaving—a position unlike the executive committee's.

The Stern prospectus created a governing body slightly different in composition from that recommended in the other documents, but it was still college-dominated. It consisted of five faculty appointed by the executive committee, one representative from each college, three student representatives, the dean of undergraduate studies, and the dean of the colleges. The assembly's powers were the same as those specified by the executive committee—ruling on trial courses and the establishment of collegiate units. Striking a compromise between Rossberg and the executive committee, the Stern proposal headed the collegiate assembly with a dean who only reported to the vice president for academic development. The Stern prospectus provided that colleges would be funded in proportion to their contribution to university educational goals, as did the Rossberg document. Like the executive committee prospectus, trial courses were limited to four credits per term and assembly approval was required, but like the Rossberg proposal the courses did not have to be taught by university faculty. Departing from both prospectuses, appointment of an unlimited number of fellows required consultation with the dean or director of the colleges. All three senate prospectuses permitted courses to satisfy concentration, elective, or general education requirements with approval of the appropriate university bodies;

## The Colleges: From Creation to Institutionalization

allowed colleges to offer credit and noncredit courses, authorized colleges to choose their own form of internal governance; and encouraged any group of students, faculty, and/or staff to form colleges. They also established procedures for dissolving individual units, permitted nonresidential collegiate units, and urged colleges to appoint university faculty.

The three senate prospectuses, the first Bennis prospectus, and the college's prospectus were the principle prospectuses, but there were a slew of others as Robert Stern suggested. By the time the faculty senate meeting convened, the first Bennis prospectus was dead—Warren Bennis withdrew it. The students that the senate promised to listen to did not want it. The prospectus represented a concept that differed too widely from the reality of the situation to be of use. As there already existed colleges and still no campus, acceptance of the prospectus with its emphasis on residence would have meant a temporary suspension in college operations, which seemed sure to reignite the dormant student riots. The prospectus of the college students was little more than a dream. Indications, which shall be discussed shortly, were that most faculty opposed it on ideological grounds and, as another faculty member said, "to approve it would have meant giving them their cake and eating it too. They gave the university a hard time and had to be punished." The college student prospectus was absorbed into the more conservative Rossberg prospectus. At the April 10 meeting, three prospectuses were presented: the executive committee prospectus, the Rossberg prospectus, and the Stern prospectus.

The executive committee proposal had the support of the conservative faculty caucus and Acting President Regan, who needed something to show the chancellor, state legislature, and governor, who were pressing him for results. At this point, Regan lacked support both inside and outside the university, and everyone knew that. The Rossberg prospectus was supported by Fred Snell; the "Up the Colleges Committee"; Warren Bennis, who had resigned as acting executive vice president after police were called on campus; and the liberal faculty. The Stern prospectus had moderate support and was most people's second choice.

The Rossberg, colleges, and Stern plans called for institutionalization of the college by boundary expansion via enclaving. The prospectuses varied in the extent to which college differences would be accepted by the university and host differences would be accepted by the innovation. The prospectuses were also distinct in the degree to which they imposed controls upon the colleges to avoid future departures from university norms. The college prospectus required the greatest degree of accommodation by the university, the least by the colleges, and the most minimal controls. The Stern prospectus called for the opposite. The Rossberg prospectus occupied an intermediary position, far closer to the student than the Stern proposal.

The executive committee prospectus was predicated upon a control measure, a review of each college, and possible academic program revisions. This review, according to faculty members interviewed, was intended as a means of boundary contraction. "Troublesome colleges" would be made to conform, which is resocialization, or they would be terminated. Troublesome colleges would be defined as units whose norms, values, and goals differed from those of the university. After review, control over the colleges would be more direct and extensive than that recommended by the Rossberg, college, or Stern prospectuses. Similarly, the executive committee plan demanded a greater degree of conformity with university norms than any of the other prospectuses.

The first Bennis prospectus sought a high degree of conformity with the Meyerson concept of the college. Given the existing set of university boundaries, that conformity would have required some form of boundary contraction. Perhaps it could only have been accomplished by terminating all existing units and starting anew. Control and review procedures were direct and extensive.

Of the 1492-member Buffalo faculty, a contingent of 322 attended the senate meeting to decide the fate of the colleges. All nonfaculty were barred. Several previous senate sessions had been disrupted by students, so guards were posted at the doors of the meeting room. The proceedings were broadcast over the campus FM radio station and about 150 students watched the meeting on closed-circuit television. The rival prospectuses were considered two at a time in elimination contest fashion. In the first heat, the Rossberg prospectus beat the executive committee proposal by a vote of 147 to 126 to 12 (abstaining). In the second heat, the Rossberg prospectus was

## The Colleges: From Creation to Institutionalization

defeated by the Stern prospectus by a vote of 151 to 124. Four amendments were added to the Stern prospectus which made it considerably more like the Rossberg document: Advice and consent of the assembly would be necessary to appoint the director; faculty membership in the assembly was increased from five to seven, but appointment was to be made by each of the seven faculties instead of the executive committee; trial courses could be initiated without assembly approval; and, the collegiate assembly was to publish an annual review of its deliberations and decisions. The Stern prospectus was then approved by voice vote. It was to be reviewed in two years.

The faculty senate chose a boundary expansion via enclaving mode of institutionalization for the colleges in preference to a boundary contraction via resocialization mechanism. The important question now is whether that is consistent with the institutionalization-termination model presented in Chapter 2. The two conditions required by the model for institutionalization by boundary expansion via enclaving were compatibility of the innovation with the norms, values, and goals of the host organization, and profitability, which encourages the host to preserve rather than diffuse an innovation owing to its ability to satisfy generalized organizational needs.

With regard to compatibility, there were many sets of norms, values, and goals to guide the university in spring 1970. Goals were offered by Martin Meyerson, the city of Buffalo, Acting President Regan, Robert Ketter, Warren Bennis, the executive committee, the state legislature, the liberal faculty caucus, the conservative faculty caucus, the college students, Fred Snell, the rioters, the student strikers. Which set of norms, values, and goals represented the university? Certainly not Meyerson's or Ketter's. Ketter was not yet president and Meyerson was gone and, for many, hopefully forgotten. In the city of Buffalo, Meyerson's name was an anathema associated with rioting and academic chicanery. Both conservative and liberal faculty at S.U.N.Y.A.B. fought valiantly to turn him into a nonperson in the finest Soviet tradition of de-Stalinization. For conservatives, who were glad to see Meyerson go, he had to be dissociated from the university to prevent intervention by the outside groups that opposed him; and for liberals, who were unhappy to see Meyerson leave, his name was an albatross around the neck of future educational reform. Warren Bennis was too closely linked with Meyerson to be the source of university goals. Peter Regan was a caretaker president who was too busy taking care to have time to formulate goals. Moreover, students struck over his policies, and the faculty senate voted no confidence in him. There was no one else within the university with the authority and power to set S.U.N.Y.A.B. goals. The most powerful group was the rioters who had the ability to disrupt the campus and stop people from making decisions, but did not themselves have the power to establish university goals. In terms of authority, what remained was an assortment of pressure groups with conflicting norms, values, and goals.

The terms *anomie* and *normlessness* are too strong to describe the situation. It would be more accurate to say that the boundaries of the university were extremely blurred. As discussed in Chapter 2, organizations cannot function under such conditions. They need to clarify and stabilize their boundaries. Each of the interest groups mentioned was trying to reconstruct the university boundaries around its values, norms, and goals. It was agreed by all inside and outside the university that the faculty senate would make the decision. The groups were battling over what the norms, values, and goals of the university would be, not over how they would be defined.

At the time the Stern prospectus was voted on by the faculty senate, the boundaries had not yet been stabilized. As a result, the collegiate system was compatible with some groups and incompatible with others. Relative to events like arson and rioting with police, the colleges had grown more compatible with the university as a whole. Relative to the editorials of the *Buffalo Courier Express,* the colleges had grown less compatible with the university as a whole. The fact of the matter was the colleges were never a monolithic whole. Although the college system may not have been compatible with most of the interest groups, each segment was compatible with some interest group. At the extremes, College D had the support of the conservative faculty caucus, and College A's rallying cry of self-determination was a demand of the well-supported student strike in March. The importance of this can be better understood after examining profitability.

As the senate met, S.U.N.Y.A.B. was just getting back on its feet after more than a month of unrest. The prognosis for the patient was

## The Colleges: From Creation to Institutionalization

still guarded, as the resumption of rioting was a real possibility. Universities are work organizations, and the work they do is teaching, research, and service. Rioting disrupts those activities, calls into question the survival of the university, and threatens the security of those working there. Abraham Maslow, in his hierarchy of human needs, classified *survival* and *security* as the two most basic needs (Maslow, 1954). Anything that causes those needs to become unsatisfied would be classified as unprofitable. Interviewees expressed fear that a hard stand on the colleges would have caused further rioting. In addition to a statement to that effect by state legislators cited previously in this chapter, the comment was made by the *Courier Express*. To that extent, preserving the colleges had become a profitable activity for even the most conservative interest groups. The form of profitability was general profitability. There was certainly little incentive for most faculty or departments to adopt the innovation themselves. To establish it as an isolated enclave was more appealing.

This finding represents a refinement of the institutionalization-termination model. According to the model, profitability is a measure of satisfaction. The form of satisfaction associated with the colleges might be described as *negative profitability*. That is, the innovation is profitable because eliminating it would make the organization less satisfied. The negatively profitable innovation creates a need if its status is diminished. In contrast, a positively profitable innovation satisfies an already existing organizational need. Satisfaction is derived by the organization for its presence as opposed to dissatisfaction resulting from its absence.

The lack of legitimate university wide authority at U.B. provided the perfect environment for political interest groups to confront one another. To some extent, all of the internal groups had to be appeased to insure that no group would stalk off and renew hostilities. Approval of a prospectus, then was, a negotiated settlement in which each group sought to win as much as possible without reigniting the conflict. Faculty and student polls showed that there had been a good deal of compromise or, less positively, a realization of the limits to which change in the colleges could be realized.

In late April, all full-time Buffalo faculty were sent a questionnaire.

Seven hundred and ninety-two people, or 53 percent of the faculty, replied. One item dealt with the colleges and asked, "Should Colleges A and F continue to operate pretty much free of control by the university, or should they be brought under firm control, or should they be abolished?" In reply, 50.9 percent (403) of the group voted for firm controls; 26.6 percent (211) were in favor of free operation; 11.5 percent (91) were in favor of abolition; and, 11 percent (87) abstained. The vote seemed decisively to favor the faculty senate executive committee prospectus. Interviewees told of faculty colleagues who failed to attend the senate meeting for fear of harassment, or because they felt the necessary controls would be impossible to obtain or undesirable in the long run.

A few days after the faculty senate meeting, the three prospectuses were sent to the S.U.N.Y.A.B. student body in a referendum. Although less than one-seventh of the students voted, feelings were strong. An earlier referendum on the same subject had been invalidated because of harassment at the polls, which may explain the low turnout and certainly indicates the strength of feeling held. In the final voting, 1722 students voted for the Stern and Rossberg prospectuses, 455 chose the executive committee prospectus, and 745 students abstained. A campaign for abstentions was promoted by segments of the colleges committed to self-determination, feeling that all of the prospectuses were repressive. Fewer than one-sixth of the votes favored the firm control advocated in the faculty poll. With such meager support and such strong emotions associated with the poll, one can only imagine what would have happened if the executive committee prospectus had been adopted by the senate.

All of this adds up to a supercharged political environment in which there was no one predominant set of norms, values, and goals. Instead, there was a mosaic of unshared, very frequently conflicting orientations. In this atmosphere, the colleges were both compatible and generally profitable. They were compatible because one group, or several, with the power to upset the balance found most college practices acceptable. The fact of the matter was that there were no criteria in that environment to judge the colleges incompatible because there were no agreed-upon norms, values, and goals. As hypothesized, the outcome was institutionalization by boundary ex-

## The Colleges: From Creation to Institutionalization

pansion via enclaving.

Among individual groups, the responses to the colleges were quite diverse, and that resulted in the range of prospectuses proposed. By way of example, the faculty senate executive committee, which offered the most stringent prospectus, can be contrasted with the "Up the Colleges Committee," which proposed the least restrictive prospectus. Of all the internal interest groups, the degree of demonstrated incompatibility with the colleges—at least with College A— seemed greatest for the executive committee. Indicative of that was the committee's willingness to intervene in college administration debates and to react more harshly to perceived college abuses, with recommendations such as grossly limiting enrollments in college classes or noting self-evaluated courses on student transcripts. Despite executive committee admiration for College D, compatibility with the existing collegiate system would have been rated as low, and general profitabilty would have been rated affirmatively for the reasons previously discussed. According to the model, this added up to boundary contraction via resocialization, and that was exactly what the executive committee proposed.

For the "Up the Colleges Committee," on the other hand, compatibility was high, certainly the highest in the university because the committee was composed of members of the colleges. Compatibility could only have been higher if the colleges were less restricted in their activities. With regard to profitability, the rationale for enclaving was not that the rioters would tear down the university if they did not get their way, but that the colleges presented a mode of education lacking elsewhere in the university. Right or wrong, students wanted it and felt the colleges eminently profitable. The brand of profitability was necessarily general profitability because the committee had no means of diffusing the innovation, and because they feared diffusion would dilute the experiment. It was not surprising that, as hypothesized, the outcome was a prospectus calling for boundary expansion via enclaving with the fewest controls.

There are often major differences between plans and programs, as we saw in the implementation of the college concept. The same is true of institutionalization plans. The fact of the matter was that different groups had different perceptions of what the Stern prospectus was designed to do. For some, the creation of a separate collegiate unit was intended to secure autonomy for the colleges; for others, it was a means to control them and guard against further developments like College A.

The colleges enjoyed a good deal of autonomy for the first few months after the passage of the Stern prospectus, as campus rioting resumed owing to the invasion of Cambodia and the killings at Kent State and Jackson State Universities. Meanwhile, mothers continued to march outside the College A and College F storefronts demanding that they be moved back to campus; a report sympathetic to the colleges was sent to Chancellor Sam Gould by the 11-member committee he created; a Buffalo grand jury subpoenaed all university records dealing with 64 students and faculty associated with Colleges A, E, and F; and, Peter Regan resigned. While turmoil gripped the campus, the new collegiate assembly began writing bylaws. It defined its quorum only in terms of collegiate-unit presence. Faculty representation in the quorum was rejected. There was talk of appointing Fred Snell director of the collegiate assembly. In late June the assembly, with one dissenting vote, sent a telegram to Governor Nelson Rockefeller, Chancellor Gould, the S.U.N.Y.A.B. trustees, and the S.U.N.Y. trustees stating that the procedures used to select Robert Ketter as president were "distant, unpublic, and insensitive to the wishes of the major constituencies of the university."

The new arrangement seemed to increase the freedom of the colleges, but that was only temporary. On July 1, 1970, Robert Ketter assumed the university presidency. In terms of the political conditions that led to the passage of the Stern prospectus, the Ketter presidency meant a restoration of campus wide leadership, and the summer vacation brought a return of stability to the campus as unrest ceased. Many of the prominent interest groups folded or weakened over the summer. Warren Bennis resigned and a member of the senate executive committee, Albert Somit, filled his long-vacant executive vice presidency, and the dean of the graduate school, Dan Murray, became acting vice president for academic development, retitled vice president for academic affairs. In the fall, Claude Welch resigned as dean of university studies because of differences with the educational philosophy of the new administration. Charles Ebert, an academically moderate department chairman, was named to the position vacated by Welch.

Consolidation and reassessment were the words the Ketter administration used to describe its mission. Ketter's political ideology seemed conservative in contrast to Meyerson's, but was actually moderate for the academic world. The goals of the university were not made explicit for almost two years, but the values that would guide the new administraiton were obvious. One of its first jobs was establishing campus wide norms that corresponded with these values. With the summer lull, the collegiate assembly, which was meeting through July, became a prime location to begin fixing norms.

On July 15, after reaching an agreement with Albany, Ketter made three demands on the collegiate assembly as part of a plan to philosophically, geographically, and financially integrate the colleges into the university. They were: 1) the assembly would soon have to nominate a director personally acceptable to Ketter, 2) Colleges A and F would have to move back to campus, 3) experimental or trial courses would have to be reviewed, despite language to the contrary in the Stern prospectus.

Ketter told the assembly that the Stern prospectus would remain in effect for the next two years, but the impact of the demands was a tightening of the controls on the colleges and, more importantly, an increase in the restrictions of the Stern prospectus. (Furthermore, Fred Snell was certainly not going to be director of the collegiate assembly.)

With regard to the activities of the assembly, the days of autonomy had come to an end. This administration was less compatible with the colleges than had been conditions in April. The problem of student unrest was still a possibility if a hard line was taken on the colleges. The colleges were less compatible with the university, but still generally profitable. This administration was more inclined to boundary contraction and resocialization.

The colleges balked at the Ketter demands, but the executive vice president said too much further delay would logistically jeopardize the collegiate fall budget. The colleges had to give in. An internal course review process was created; Konrad Von Moltke, a Bennis staffer and assistant professor in the history department, was named director; and, Colleges A and F came back to campus.

In early fall the collegiate assembly, with a good deal of internal dissent, approved a new collegiate unit named after the German communist Rosa Luxemburg. Luxemburg combined "Social Change in America's" orientation toward the application of radical theory in the community, with "Conflict and Change in the Local Community's" self-grading system. The acting vice president for academic affairs, Dan Murray, stated that the college was unacceptable and the university would neither pay instructors nor grant credit to students enrolled in Rosa Luxemburg courses. The assembly pointed out the conflict between the vice president for academic affairs and the Stern prospectus which said that experimental courses could be given for one semester without assembly approval, but was later modified by Ketter to read "with" assembly approval. Murray responded by saying that, "I reserve the right to review all courses . . . and [to make] a possible recommendation to the President or the faculty senate that specific offerings not to be given academic credit" *(Spectrum* 9/17/70, p. 3). President Ketter supported him, arguing that the approval of the collegiate assembly was only a recommendation to the vice president of academic affairs. Furthermore, he agreed with the decision on the ground that the overtly political orientation of the college was blatantly at odds with the notion of academic freedom.

In the end, the collegiate assembly again had to give in. Space was found on campus for Rosa Luxemburg courses by unofficially using empty classrooms, and some students got credit for the courses through indirect mechanisms like College A and independent study, but Rosa Luxemburg College never truly established itself. This episode further abridged the Stern prospectus in favor of university control. With this incident a precedent was set. University wide values and norms like academic freedom were sufficiently important to supercede legitimate but incompatible activities of the collegiate assembly. This was a major step in integrating the colleges into the university. Universal norms and values preempted particularistic sub-unit norms and values.

The spring of 1971 brought another attack on collegiate practices. This time, Acting Vice President Murray directed that College A abandon self-grading before he would grant the college any summer funding or permit it to enroll summer students. All students in College A were required to be given grades beginning with the current term. Failure to respond affirmatively would have jeopardized senior graduations and draft deferments for students who were required by Selective Service to be enrolled full-time. Full-time enrollment was determined by credit load. Furthermore, lack of funds and inability to enroll students would have put College A into the same class as Rosa Luxemburg, that being defunct. College A railed at the restriction and the collegiate assembly initiated a grievance against Murray in the faculty senate. A senate grievance committee found it was "not only the right, but the duty of the academic vice president to interfere in the internal affairs of the academic units if policy is being violated." In the interest of equity, and due to previous administration vacillation on the subject, self-grading was permitted for the current semester, but would thereafter have to be ended. The collegiate assembly appealed the decision as far as possible, but eventually had to give in. The close of the term brought an end to self-grading and the resignation of Fred Snell.

Again university wide norms and values, this expert evaluation, took precedence over the collegiate assembly's norms and values, as well as the Stern prospectus. The procedure in this instance was slightly different than it had been for Rosa Luxemburg. After an edict was handed down by Dan Murray, the assembly asked for disconfirmation by a university wide body, the faculty senate. In essence, each edict served as a boundary marker pointing out unacceptable norms and values. Resorting to the senate was the collegiate assembly's way of calling it a borderline case and asking for the judgment of a more representative body. The senate had the ability to ratify or overturn the ruling. The assembly turned to the faculty senate in this instance while it did not for Rosa Luxemburg for two reasons: 1) it was united in this case while it was greatly divided in the other, and 2) less significantly, the assembly felt the university via the senate to have a view similar to its own in this instance. These are the two conditions that made self-grading a borderline case.

Each time one of these incidents—be it college grading, Rosa Luxemburg, or the Ketter demands—was resolved, with or without senate intervention, it served as a boundary marker to the colleges and a record for the university of the limits of acceptable norms and values. For the Ketter administration, each resolution moved the colleges a step closer to having norms and values corresponding to those of the university.

CHAPTER 4

# The Colleges: Continuing Institutionalization

The second round of institutionalizing the colleges at Buffalo began in 1973 after efforts to impose controls upon them proved insufficient from the university's point of view. Like the earlier institutionalization-termination stage, the second took approximately two years to complete. Unlike the earlier institutionalization-termination stage, campus political turmoil was absent during the second. Reinstitutionalization began three years into the presidency of Robert Ketter, and during its course Ketter was named to a second term. The stability of the university was an essential element in the decision to institutionalize the colleges primarily by boundary contraction via resocialization. Institutionalization also occurred in part by boundary expansion via diffusion and boundary contraction via termination. This chapter will describe the conditions, processes, and outcomes of the institutionalization of the colleges and will analyze the consistency of those events within the framework of the hypothesized institutionalization-termination model.

### Adopting a New Prospectus

April 1972 marked the two-year reconsideration point for the Stern prospectus. By any standards, but certainly in comparison with the 1970 proceedings, the reconsideration was routine—routine to the point of being dull. The prospectus was amended at several points to reflect the Ketter administration's victories in its confrontations with the colleges. Growing out of the 1970 Ketter demands, appointment of the collegiate assembly director no longer required advice and consent of the assembly—just advice, and trial courses required the approval of the assembly rather than being an individual college initiative. Growing out of the experience with "wayward" innovations like College A and self-grading, the previously autonomous collegiate units were required to have an authority report to the assembly director. Growing out of the university's precarious financial health, it was specified that the department or academic unit funding each instructor would be credited with enrollment in collegiate courses rather than the colleges since public university budgets are largely enrollment driven, this minimized college competition with departments for funding and encouraged departments to participate in the colleges. For departments with low enrollments relative to staff size, the colleges represented a potentially attractive way to increase enrollments by farming out staff. Finally, growing out of the political atmosphere surrounding the 1970 prospectus, an extramural review of the colleges under the auspices of the faculty senate (with collegiate assembly approval of the nationally prominent members of the review team) was mandated. It was felt that only impartial observers were capable of giving the colleges the assessment they had never received and badly needed to clear the partisan air.

The amended prospectus was a product of the faculty senate colleges subcommittee. Robert Stern resigned as chairman after one full term and was replaced by John Halstead. A change in campus mood was apparent in the different conditions under which the two committees operated. During the Stern tenure, members, in some cases, quit after only a meeting or two because of the intense emotions focused upon them. There were tales of members receiving poisonous telephone calls or rocks through their windows in the middle of the night. At one meeting at a committee member's home, "legend" has it that a student was sent in place of one of the masters. He put his boots on the living-room coffee table and sprayed the group with four-letter words. The result—another faculty resignation. This superheated political atmosphere had cooled by 1972. The overt hostility directed at the Stern committee was not shown the Halstead committee, but there was a consensus among members interviewed

## The Colleges: Continuing Institutionalization

that the current political climate still prohibited a significant revision of the Stern prospectus. The student body was perceived as disillusioned, discouraged, and sullen in temper. Too much of a jolt could set them off again. The committee felt that it would be able to do no more than tinker with the old prospectus. There was hope, however, that in tinkering the colleges might be shown that they needed to put their houses in order.

The colleges certainly were not enamored of the amended prospectus, but that prospectus did no more than reflect the reality of their current existence. By April 1972, the record of lost battles with the university administration showed the colleges that they could not realistically expect to do any better than the amended document, so they cooperated in getting it accepted unanimously by the senate.

The most farsighted provision of the revised prospectus was the external review. For the colleges it was a way to legitimize their existence in a hostile environment, and for the hostile environment it was a way to justify its negative feelings. The evaluation was viewed by almost all of the people interviewed who had been associated with it as the way to resolve the college-university tug-of-war once and for all. The remainder of the prospectus was more or less a holding action continuing the policy of boundary expansion via enclaving, with greater emphasis on control than the original Stern prospectus.

The autonomy versus control tug-of-war was certainly not ended by the 1972 amended prospectus. It was doubtful that it could be for two reasons. First, there were limitations in the nature of a consolidating document like the 1972 prospectus. It did not resolve problems; rather, it stated as hard-and-fast rules the losses and gains of competing groups at a moment in time. Second, the autonomy versus control issue was secondary—the primary concern was incompatible or deviant practices. With each new practice that was so recognized by the host, the issue of control was raised, only to be countered by demands for autonomy by the innovation. In sum, the Halstead prospectus cleaned the slate of already settled grievances and established a procedure for resolving the remainder for once and for all via the external evaluation.

## Airing New Grievances

Four compatibility issues came clearly to the surface in the period following the passage of the new prospectus. They concerned the organization and administration of the colleges, the character of the collegiate assembly, academic freedom, and the academic quality of college courses.

### Compatibility Issue 1: Organization and Administration of the Colleges

Compatibility issue 1 centered on the role of the director of the assembly. College governance emphasized the decentralization and freedom of the Meyerson goals, rather than the centralization and accountability of the Ketter goals. By 1972 the Ketter goals had been approved by the major S.U.N.Y.A.B. faculty and student groups. As a result, the organization and administration of the colleges was incompatible with that of the university.

Konrad Von Moltke resigned as director of the collegiate assembly after two years. His successor, Pat Smith, lasted only one year. On resigning, Smith called the directorship an impossible position because the university administration and the colleges had conflicting expectations of the director's role. The administration wanted a leader who would control the colleges — the collegiate director was expected to relay and enforce university policies among the colleges. The colleges, on the other hand, wanted a spokesperson who would be responsible to the assembly and defend its opinions to the rest of the university.

The basic difficulty lay in the divergent organization and governance patterns of the colleges and the university. The university was hierarchically organized. Departments were subunits of the faculties, and the seven faculties constituted the university. In reporting procedures, a department chairman reported to a provost who reported to the vice president for academic affairs who reported to the president of the university. Technically, the colleges constituted a faculty and the director was expected to act as a provost. Although the other provosts had many of the same competing demands as the director of the colleges, the demands were not as intensely polar. Because the

## The Colleges: Continuing Institutionalization

administration disapproved of several college practices, it shortened the tether of the collegiate director, feeling his loyalty should be to the greater university. Because the colleges felt their autonomy was in serious jeopardy, they did the same. For the other provosts there was not the grave distrust of their faculties by the university, and consequently less of a defensive posture by their faculties. The problem was further exacerbated by the administrative structure of the colleges. Decision making was participatory, not the responsibility of the collegiate director. Budget allocation, course approval, acceptance of new collegiate units, dissolution of old units, and the like were decided collectively by the assembly members. In that scheme of things, the director was not a leader or authority figure; his role was that of communicator to the outside world. If he did not like a decision, he could resign, but he could not reverse it. In contrast, the position of provost carried with it both authority and leadership potential.

After Pat Smith resigned there was a fracas over who would act as interim director. The vice president for academic affairs, Bernard Gelbaum, had a candidate and the colleges had a candidate—each unacceptable to the other. In the end, Gelbaum named himself acting director and appointed his candidate assistant to the interim director, granting him all the authority and powers of the director. The vice president's response to the vacancy was an attempt to control the colleges and the colleges' response was rebellion. Though the colleges really had little power to disobey, they did have the ability to punish the vice president and the assistant through grievance procedures, personal attack, and parliamentary abuse. Those methods were employed fully. Sometimes even an army of ants can be lethal.

At the same time the interim director debate was going on, a faculty dominated committee was formed to select a new permanent director. There was hope that the new dean or director would be a person with sufficient prestige to be able to control the colleges or, alternatively, to be strong enough to chase the administration away when it knocked on the colleges doors. In the end, the colleges would have to compromise more than the administration because 1) the colleges had only two representatives on the faculty-dominated committee, and 2) because President Robert Ketter made the final decision.

As compatibility was being forced upon the colleges by Vice-President Gelbaum's seizure of the directorship and by the appointment of a faculty-dominated committee to choose the next collegiate director, the collegiate assembly protested. The protest was publicized both in the local and campus media. The media spread the news of the basic incompatibility and the protests made the colleges appear all the more deviant.

*Compatibility Issue 2: The Character of the Collegiate Assembly*

Compatibility issue 2 focused upon the collegiate assembly's thwarting of the norms, values, and goals of both the colleges most compatible with the university and the faculty representatives of the collegiate assembly. In so doing, it was felt that the collegiate assembly underlined its own incompatibility with the university.

By 1972 there were 17 collegiate units. Five of the 17 were new colleges; three of the original units were defunct; and one, black studies, became a separate department. For the 1972-1973 academic year, the colleges shared a budget of $257,148, which was an average of slightly more than $15,000 per college—not enough to hire one tenured professor in each unit. In subsequent years, the budget increased by more than 50 percent, but that was still inadequate because the colleges were receiving about one-fifth of the funding of the average department relative to their enrollments (*Spectrum,* 5/30/73). College E supplemented its budget with voluntary contributions from its students, and that caused quite a stir in the university. As might be expected, the division of the college budget caused a good deal of tension in the assembly, given an assortment of collegiate units with divergent goals.

In the course of growth, three varieties of colleges had developed: residential, thematic, and activist units. Activist colleges were those whose central focus was on community involvement at either the personal or group level. The thematic units were more academic in nature and oriented to the concerns that cut across several faculties and departments. Residential colleges were living-learning units based in university dormitory facilities. The residential units were the smallest group, being comprised of two colleges:[1] College D, named Clifford Furnas College and College B. A residential program was more expensive than a nonresidential program, but given the tightness of the collegiate budget and the small number of units in that category, there was little support for adequately funding them.

In addition to this division by function, there was also an ideological division among the colleges; however, there was a fair degree of similarity in the two divisions. The activist and a number of the thematic colleges were the more radical groups in the assembly. Some of these units were dominantly student-administered and student-staffed. Furnas College was all faculty-administered and the most educationally and politically conservative of the collegiate units, being modeled as it was after the Oxbridge schools. Most of its program was a cross-listing of other departmental courses. It resembled S.U.N.Y.A.B. (the host) closely or, more accurately, what S.U.N.Y.A.B. would like to have been academically.

The participatory nature of the assembly resulted in the formation of coalition groups. The residential college were outnumbered by the nonresidential colleges, and the conservative colleges were outnumbered by the liberal-to-radical units. Pat Smith (1972) commented that the collegiate units "are strongly egocentric and in certain areas like residential versus nonresidential, there are irreconcilable differences. It is increasingly difficult to get collaborative cooperation and resource sharing".

With time, the nature of participatory governance became increasingly strident and rhetorical. The only certain thing about it was that minority groups like Clifford Furnas College continually lost. The representatives of the seven faculties, being a minority, did not have much success either. Faculty attendance dropped off sharply. Some claimed they left because they could not take the interminable discussions; others said they left because the assembly never did anything; and still others attributed leaving to the profanity common at assembly meetings. In defense of the assembly, there were those who left because of departmental and career pursuits, as well as those

---

[1]In fall 1974, the number of residential colleges increased to six. At that time the new campus facilities finally became available.

who could not tolerate their powerless situation relative to students, recent graduates, and the young nonstudents in the assembly. A candidate for director described the situation as follows:

> The operating style of participatory democracy became relatively pompous and byzantine and ideologically radical in a manner which alienated faculty, administration, the community at large, and the mass of students [Letter to Collegiate Assembly Director Search Committee, 1973].

The collegiate assembly voted to make faculty representatives nonvoting members of the assembly in 1972-1973, but that was rejected by the faculty senate college committee. The move was intended both as a statement of autonomy and a sign of indignation against faculty who did not attend meetings.

In summer 1973 Clifford Furnas College was permitted by Vice President of Academic Affairs Gelbaum to withdraw from the collegiate assembly and report to the Division of Undergraduate Education. The faculty senate sanctioned the arrangement, showing their own disapproval of assembly operations. There was talk of permitting other residential units to do the same. The collegiate assembly again felt its autonomy violated, appealed the decision, and lost.

The secession of Furnas and the possibility of similar action by other units had the effect of removing the more orthodox colleges from the assembly and thereby shifting the balance of the collegiate assembly more in the direction of the deviant stereotype. This increased the level of incompatibility between the remaining colleges and the university and, according to the hypothesized model, made boundary contraction more feasible. The philosophy behind such a move might have been that that if the university could not get the colleges to conform, it could take the "good" colleges out and terminate the rest. Complaints by the collegiate assembly again magnified and spread the basic incompatibility.

*Compatibility Issue 3: Academic Freedom*

Compatibility issue 3 focused on political tests imposed upon college instructor candidates, which are violations of the tenets of aca-

## The Colleges: Continuing Institutionalization

demic freedom. Academic *freedom* is a "buzz word" often defended more in theory than in practice; however, it is the bedrock foundation underlying the American university and is key in the Ketter goals for Buffalo.

In 1972, there were two cases of possible political tests in choosing staff by the colleges. One case involved the alleged rejection of a course on rock music (based upon the instructor's political ideology) by the Social Science College, whose mission was to "bring people together to study radical social theory" (*College Catalogue,* 1973-74). The other incident involved the refusal by the colleges to grant credit for a course taught by a *Courier Express* journalist who had actively muckraked the colleges during the riots of 1970. The program evaluation committee approved an investigative reporting skills course to be taught on an interim noncredit basis until its members had time to assess the instructor's political attitudes. Ideological tests are a no-no in universities. Measuring competence is not. And given the poor quality of the *Courier Express* articles, one certainly could question the competence of its writers. In any case, university faculty review sided with the colleges in both incidents.

Though the colleges were acquitted of the charges, there remained a lingering doubt. These two incidents proved to many that if the colleges were not flagrant abusers of academic freedom, which some doubted, they certainly were uncommitted and soft on the principle. In fact, doubts about the colleges with respect to academic freedom were voiced by over half of the faculty senators interviewed (50 percent random sample of 1973—1974 faculty senators) as a rationale for the second institutionalization-termination. This was not the chief criticism of the colleges, but it certainly was a common one.

*Compatibility Issue 4: Academic Quality of College Courses*

Compatibility issue 4 concerned a series of curricular practices employed by the colleges that were absent within the rest of S.U.N.Y.A.B. Under the rubric of experimental courses, the practices included employment of instructors without B.A.'s (not to mention Ph.D.'s), inflated grading, and the offering of courses of questionable academic substance. Each of these practices was grossly incompatible with the

Ketter goals in a manner that will be discussed shortly.

By 1973-1974, regular university faculty constituted only 16.6 percent of the total teaching staff of the colleges. The remainder consisted of people from the local community, a goodly number of whom were ex-S.U.N.Y.A.B. students (48 percent), graduate students (23 percent), and undergraduates (12.1 percent). The proportion varied from college to college. For instance, 36 percent of the College F (renamed Tolstoy College) staff consisted of undergraduates, while 54 percent of the colleges used no undergraduate staffers. Vico and Furnas Colleges were 100 percent faculty, while 21 percent of the colleges had no S.U.N.Y.A.B. faculty teaching. The lack of faculty was as much a problem of money as of philosophy. Pat Smith (1972) viewed the situation in the following way:

> There has been a steady withdrawal of faculty from active collegiate participation. In part faculty have moved back within their departments to support and defend them during a tight money period. Departments, too, feel themselves under heavy scrutiny and individuals feel the need to concentrate on discipline oriented publications and successful grant proposals that support their department's position. In part young faculty perceive the collegiate system, as currently constituted, as not tied very well to the university rewards structure. With regard to tenure decisions it is more often a negative connection than a positive one. In part older faculty are tired of the rhetoric of the collegiate assembly that goes on and on seemingly getting nowhere any more except to alienate well-meaning faculty and administrators who are made to feel unwanted.

With regard to grading, the colleges gave more than twice the percentage of A grades as all other undergraduate courses combined. The university average was 23.2 percent in 1973-1974 and the college average was 56.3 percent. Forty-three percent of the colleges gave more than half of their students A's and only 14 percent gave fewer than the university average that year.

Concerning course content, 14 percent of the classes were trial courses that lacked approval from university bodies outside the colleges. Thirty of the 44 experimental college courses were offered by College E and constituted 55 percent of its program in spring 1973. Undergraduate Dean Charles Ebert felt that the courses varied in quality from "very acceptable to unadulterated bilge." He was "not convinced that the standards of College E (offering 68 percent of all experimental courses) are acceptable to a degree-granting university" [Memo from C. V. Ebert, February 12, 1973]. The chairman-elect of the faculty senate, however, was even more adamant in his opposition. The fact of the matter was that the lack of university review of college courses was entirely legal and a matter of standing university policy as it was stated in the 1972 amended prospectus. Moreover, the academic departments did far worse in obtaining approval of their own courses, but then again they were not perceived to be as incompatible with the university. The row with the colleges centered on courses like "Bhakti Yoga," "Light Aircraft," "Mao Tse Tung Thought," "ESP and Hypnosis," "Occult Philosophy," and "Horror Film." There was a fear that was not entirely unjustified that the colleges, particularly "E," were abusing the experimental course option by retitling trial courses that required approval after one term and repeating them semester after semester without approval.

The practices in the three disputed areas—grades, content, and instructional staff—though incompatible with existing university policies had clearly articulated philosophical rationales underlying them. Within certain colleges, such as "E," Progressive Education, and "F," grades were viewed as an obstacle in the development of independent learners, substituting external rewards for internal motivation. Giving all or most students A's left only internal motivation. With regard to instructors, learning was conceived as a process of mutual exploration by student and teacher, not one of an expert teaching the ignorant. For the former activity, a Ph.D. was by no means a requirement. With regard to content, all subjects could be thought of as appropriate to the university. Unfortunately, the university concentrated upon empirically based cognitive learning to the detriment of intuitive, psychomotor, and affective learning.

Such views flew in the face of the Ketter goals for S.U.N.Y.A.B. The inflated grading of the colleges violated the commitment of those goals to "a rigorous academic orientation," as did courses that Dean Ebert described as "unadulterated bilge." Other higher quality courses were off the beaten path of university concerns and challenged the goal to advance "knowledge through teaching and research in selected academic and professional areas"—palm reading, however,

## A Study of Fourteen Innovations

was not one of those areas. Historically, universities are communities of the mind with a very limited range of accepted ways of knowing. Little more than 200 years ago, the natural sciences were barred from Yale and Harvard. What place was there in such a scheme for a course on "Horror Film?" The notion of undergraduates teaching, which caused such a bruhaha, was certainly at odds with the aspiration to become a "preeminent graduate and professional" school with an "outstanding undergraduate division." There is no such excellent university that arrived at its lofty position through the quality of its undergraduate staffers. In fact, President Ketter informed the collegiate assembly that at least one college or university—the University of Illinois, Chicago Circle—would not accept transfer credit for S.U.N.Y.A.B. college courses.

At least one of the four incompatible practices subsumed under the topic of experimental courses was mentioned by every faculty senate member interviewed, and that practice was most often the chief criticism of the colleges. Wildly exaggerated claims about college abuses were quite common. For instance, one individual said that most of the college courses were encounter groups and required no reading. Compatibility issue 4 resulted in S.U.N.Y.A.B. faculty anger, widespread misunderstanding, and a sense of urgency that something had to be done.

The sense of urgency attached to experimental course incompatibility resulted in very serious proposals directed at controlling the colleges. In 1973 Dean Ebert recommended that the experimental courses not be granted credit toward the B.A. degree; that proposal never received serious consideration. The same year, Vice President of Academic Affairs Gelbaum summarily fired the associate master of College B, an older, eccentric graduate student with impressive educational credentials behind him and a penchant for speaking his mind. A year later, Gelbaum cancelled 16 experimental college courses. They were subsequently reinstated by President Ketter because the colleges were, at the time, in the midst of a major transformation. In 1973, George Hochfield, chairman elect of the faculty senate, cited the record of College E and sounded a call for faculty action. A whisper might have been sufficient.

In this atmosphere, many plans were developed by many people to

## The Colleges: Continuing Institutionalization

transform the colleges. The plans went far beyond dealing with the incompatibility of experimental courses.

In fall 1972, Pat Smith proposed a separation of the residential and nonresidential colleges (compatibility issue 2). The assembly made him withdraw the plan.

In spring 1973, John Halstead's college committee proposed significant changes in the 1972 prospectus: Procedures were created to insure the dominance of the director and the vice president of academic affairs over the collegiate assembly (compatibility issue 1); faculty review and evaluation of experimental courses through a half-and-half faculty—college committee (compatibility issues 3 and 4); minimal instructor qualifications in collegiate courses of an M.A. or the equivalent (compatibility issue 4); and the independence of residential units from the assembly should they so desire (compatibility issue 2). In making this proposal, all four of the compatibility issues would be remedied by placing additional controls upon the colleges. The faculty senate executive committee passed the proposal and strengthened it by shifting the balance of the faculty-college review committee in favor of the faculty. The senate, however, returned the report to the Halstead committee pending further evaluation and proof of the need for change.

In fall 1973, Vice President Gelbaum suggested that the colleges be rank-ordered by the external evaluation, and all except the top three to five colleges would be eliminated. This plan was not adopted either.

The period between the passage of the 1972 prospectus and the external evaluation constituted a moratorium. No major changes were tolerated from either side until after the evaluation. Plans by administration or faculty to radically alter the colleges constituted no more than saber-rattling, marking the limits of incompatibility pending the external evaluation. The people proposing the changes were extremists or principals, whose function it became not to curb the incompatibility, but rather to inform the community of it.

## A Study of Fourteen Innovations

### Evaluating the Colleges

During the moratorium, evaluation became a way of life for the colleges. In little more than a year, the colleges were evaluated four times: one self-evaluation, one evaluation by S.U.N.Y.A.B. faculty, and two external evaluations. In Fall 1972, the colleges were scrutinized as part of a Middle States accrediting commission visit. The study team reported that the "colleges were on the minds of most people we met on campus" *(Middle State Association of Colleges and Schools, 1972, p. 11)*. The substance of their observations was that there were serious and major areas of contention between opponents and proponents of the colleges.

In spring 1973, the Halstead committee, in preparation for the external evaluation, required that each college write a self-study to be followed by a S.U.N.Y.A.B. faculty evaluation of the college. Three-person teams were formed to evaluate each college. The teams were composed of two people "lacking bias and previous association with the colleges" and nominated by the faculty senate, and one person nominated by the college to be evaluated. Every team evaluated one college. All of the colleges were evaluated, with the exception of Clifford Furnas College, whose committee refused to release a report. The committees focused on curriculum, instructional capability, and budget. They were additionally requested to determine whether the goals of the colleges were consistent with the Ketter goals for the university, and what directions the colleges should take in the future.

John Halstead summarized the evaluations by saying that, "the consensus was positive and favorable." Though noting that some of the reports were superficial and incomplete, he also said that:

> Repeatedly professors on the teams were pleasantly surprised explicitly or implicitly with the high quality of course material and instructional capability they discovered. The reports *in toto* made clear that whatever the defects, the collegiate system is making a significant and valuable contribution to the university [Memo to the Faculty Senate Executive Committee and the Incoming College Committee, June 25, 1973].

## The Colleges: Continuing Institutionalization

Halstead's analysis was a very fair and accurate assessment of the combined evaluations. Few other people were found who offered such reasoned commentary. The student newspaper, *The Spectrum,* billed the evaluation as "Colleges Succesful" (November 28, 1973). Many in the colleges rallied behind the internal evaluations. There was fear that the faculty senate would minimize the importance of the favorable evaluations *(Spectrum,* October 5, 1973). On the other hand, several key faculty and administrators interviewed indicated that the evaluations were "worthless," "junk," and of "poor quality." A *Spectrum* cartoon pictured the chairman of the faculty senate colleges committee throwing the evaluations in a garbage pail.

Perhaps the greatest surprise for college opponents came in the evaluation of College E. College A became rather aimless afer Fred Snell's departure and was terminated by the assembly. Its distinctive position in the university was assumed by College E. Indeed, the *Buffalo Courier Express* commented that "when critics express distaste and anger over . . . [the colleges], they most often cite examples form Colleges E and F" (November 25, 1973). In contrast, the evaluation of College E found its goals to be quite consistent with the Ketter goals. Six courses, including some of those criticized most widely around the university, were rated as very worthwhile. Instructors were rated highly in their "lecturing ability and ability to elicit student participation." The committee stated that "E" was addressing itself to areas of importance to the university and society, and behaving in a responsible manner. To those who felt "E's" practices repugnant—including the president, the vice president of academic affairs, the dean of undergraduate education, and the faculty senate chairman-elect, among orders—such conclusions were patently absurd and any report that could reach such a conclusion was "trashy."

The external evaluation was conducted in fall 1973, and it pointed to serious weaknesses and strengths in the colleges. The weaknesses included:

1. bad faith in regard to agreed-upon rules and procedures
2. lax standards in selecting instructors (compatibility issue 4)
3. tolerance of political advocacy (compatibility issue 3)
4. disregard for university standards regarding work and grading

## A Study of Fourteen Innovations

   (compatibility issue 4)
5. lack of adequate financial and faculty support
6. lack of healthy relations with the rest of the university.

The evaluation validated many of the allegations about the colleges which had been floating around the university. The strengths included:

1. motivation and enthusiasm
2. attention to slighted perspectives and values
3. sense of community
4. fostering of social awareness and involvement
5. experiential and interdisciplinary learning.

The evaluators felt that the strengths outweighed the weaknesses and urged a transformation of the colleges in a manner designed to eliminate the weaknesses and enhance the strengths. The transformation closely approximated a plan being prepared by the faculty senate subcommittee on the colleges, then headed by Jonathan Reichert, who replaced John Halstead.

Predictably, the colleges were disappointed and clung to the internal evaluation. The collegiate assembly complained that the external report was an attempt to impose more traditional norms and values upon the colleges. There were allegations that the external evaluators were unqualified to make the judgments they did, having spent approximately one day on each college. Furthermore, some were upset that two of the five evaluators were acquaintances of Jon Reichert. Ironically, similar charges had been made about the internal evaluation. Many of the people who had been unhappy with the inside evaluation thought the external report more "realistic" and "honest."

These reactions illustrate the fundamentally subjective character of evaluation. Acceptance of evaluation, regardless of the methods used, depends on the values and purposes of the recipient. Opponents of the colleges dismissed the favorable external evaluation, and proponents of the colleges disavowed the less favorable external evaluation. The evaluations gave opposing groups at Buffalo the fuel to continue to believe what they wanted to believe about the colleges.

## The Colleges: Continuing Institutionalization

No evaluation is perfect, and disbelief of the conclusions makes any flaws all the more apparent to the disbeliever.

The result, which should have been expected, was that there was not a unilaterally acceptable, ready-made formula for making the colleges compatible with the university. After the evaluation, there still remained serious compatibility problems, the elimination of which required major changes in the university or major changes in the colleges. The widespread awareness of the problem, combined with the massive nature of the incompatibility, necessitated a solution beyond the scope of imposing a few controls that would be acceptable throughout the university. As a result, S.U.N.Y.A.B. embarked upon a second institutionalization-termination of the colleges.

### Institutionalizing or Terminating the Colleges

Around the university the attitude toward the colleges was grim. President Ketter was disgusted. He told several people he was thinking of just ending the colleges. His administrative staff had been busy dreaming up the drastic schemes already discussed. All of the faculty senators interviewed reported abuses by the colleges in at least one of the four areas of incompatibility. By summer 1973, the mood of the host organization was somber.

It was under these conditions that Jonathan Reichert, associate professor of physics, was selected to head the faculty senate college committee. John Halstead resigned the committee chairmanship in spring 1973. Claude Welch, who was chairman of the senate nominations committee, remembered being told when he was dean that Reichert was an innovator or, rather, a successful institutionalizer of innovation at Case Western Reserve University. Reichert was a charismatic, friendly person, eloquent with a passion for bombast. He had the common mix of liberal perspective on society and moderately conservative outlook on the academy. Reichert was ripe for the challenge of chairing the college committee because his eye was on a future in academic administration. Before accepting the position, he conferred with the major academic administrators on their perception of the problem and the degree of latitude he would have in proposing a solution. He also sought assurances that the senate would give his committee the teeth to act decisively. With answers to his satisfaction, Reichert assumed the chairmanship of the colleges committee. He did so in time to have a say in the selection of the collegiate assembly director and to be a major force in shaping the external evaluation.

The faculty senate college committee was enlarged to include student representatives from the graduate student and undergraduate associations. Open hearings and meetings were held with people all over the university, both to discover the problems plaguing the colleges and to test possible solutions. By January 1974, a prospectus was prepared for consideration by the faculty senate. The Reichert prospectus, as it was known, looked much like the 1970 executive committee prospectus. Both were predicated upon boundary contraction by faculty-dominated committees lacking college membership. Each college had to conform to a new set of guidelines. The primary difference in the two prospectuses was that the Reichert document was tougher. It called for a more radical transformation of the colleges, as well as increased external control, but for complying with its terms colleges were being offered greater legitimacy and increased university resources. Reichert felt that only a tough procedure would establish the legitimacy of the innovation in the host organization.

The Reichert prospectus dissolved all of the existing colleges as of January 1975, and offered a procedure whereby the existing colleges could be considered for continuation in the interim. To continue, existing colleges were required to meet certain conditions that would be reviewed by the college chartering committee. This newly established committee was charged with creating, renewing, and dissolving collegiate units. It could consist of six faculty, two undergraduates, one graduate student, one administrator, and two college representatives to be appointed after the colleges were reconstituted. The vice president of academic affairs, the vice president of health sciences, the vice president for student affairs, the dean of undergraduate education, the dean of the colleges, and the chairman of the faculty senate colleges committee were made ex-officio members. All aspiring collegiate units would submit charters to the chartering committee and the committee would decide whether to approve, reject, modify, or delay the charter. The recommendation, which would include a term

## The Colleges: Continuing Institutionalization

of three to five years if favorable, would go to the president and dean of the colleges for action. Each charter was to include 14 specific items that would guide the chartering committee deliberations:

1. statement of intellectual purpose
2. statement of educational and pedagogical style
3. a description of courses
4. list of personnel and vitae
5. procedure for choosing future faculty
6. vita for the college master
7. evidence of ample faculty participation
8. statement of what constitutes affiliation with the colleges, rights, responsibilities, and privileges
9. procedure for choosing student members
10. statement of how two representatives would be chosen for a reconstructed collegiate assembly, renamed the collegiate council
11. statement of how future courses and instructors would be selected and evaluated
12. statement of budget process and fiscal controls
13. a description of internal governance
14. specification of duration of the charter and a statement of what would constitute fair, objective, and practical evaluation at the time the charter was reconsidered

Thirteen of the 14 items dealt primarily, if not exclusively, with compatibility concerns. Only item 14 could possibly be classified as profitability-oriented. However, its intent was unspecified and could just as easily have been compatibility.

After approval, a college was subject to immediate reconsideration for: failure to abide by the approved charter, loss without adequate replacement of key faculty or administrative officers, failure to follow university regulations, or insufficient student interest. Compatibility rationales outnumbered profitability rationales by a ratio of three to one. Only the last item was concerned with profitability, and that involved the evaporation of the need for which a college was created, as gauged by the loss of clientele.

## A Study of Fourteen Innovations

The prospectus identified the characteristics and operating procedures for individual colleges. The chief operating officer or master would have to be full-time university faculty member or suitably chosen alternative. The position would require at least a one-quarter to one-half time commitment for two years. The duties would involve long-range planning, budgeting, hiring of personnel, coordination of programs, and effective and democratic governance. Budgeting, personnel, curriculum, and staffing decisions of the individual colleges also required the approval of the dean of the colleges. Colleges could choose any form of internal governance that represented all concerned interests. Substantial participation by regular university faculty was expected. The collegiate budget would have to include funds for buying "release time" from departments for their faculty. Community resource people and graduate students would be permitted to join the colleges with college council recommendation and approval by the dean of the colleges. College courses could be either traditionally or pass-fail graded.

The roles of the dean of the colleges and the collegiate assembly were changed significantly. The dean would have to be at least a tenured associate professor in an established university department. He or she would have authority equivalent to that of a provost and would serve as the principal negotiator for funds and long-range planning with the university administration. The dean would have primary control in disbursement of funds to colleges and workshops. The duties would include an obligation to award merit increases to faculty from a college merit fund. Further, the dean would appoint college masters, approve college courses, and approve instructors subject to subsequent approval by the appropriate university authority. The dean would also serve on the major university committees and report to the president and vice president of academic affairs. He or she would make decisions and exercise the powers of office only after consultation with the college council.

The college council, which replaced the collegiate assembly, would consist of the master and a representative from each college. It would be chaired by the dean of the colleges and the chairperson of the faculty senate college committee would be an ex-officio member. The functions of the council would include advising the dean on all policy

## The Colleges: Continuing Institutionalization

matters; ensuring that each college adheres to its charter, reviewing course proposals, budget requests, and personnel recommendations; and, arranging the election of collegiate representatives to the faculty senate. The council could challenge the dean by a two-thirds vote, leaving the matter under dispute to be mediated by the faculty senate college committee.

The workshop requirement of the first Bennis prospectus was reinstated. Every college would have to begin as a workshop and serve a minimum of one semester in that capacity before being considered by the chartering committee for full status—a requirement that was waived for existing units. Workshops could be started by any group of faculty or students. It could offer noncredit seminars and other activities. After one semester, a workshop could offer courses for credit following approval by the dean and the Division of Undergraduate Education, but no workshop could exist for more than three semesters.

The prospectus was to serve as the colleges' constitution for four years. To aid in its implementation, the administration would be expected to make simple short-term and long-term funding commitments. It was noted that extra costs would be associated with the residential units, which would be expected to comprise about one-half of the colleges. The administration would also be expected to find methods by which release time could be purchased by the colleges in order to minimize the conflicts between the administration and the faculty. The administration was further asked to show a visibly positive attitude toward the colleges. It was also to encourage departments to provide faculty, especially senior people, and reward them for their participation. In addition, it was felt that the colleges should be represented on the Division of Undergraduate Education committee that would approve college courses.

The Reichert prospectus provided remedies in each of the four incompatible areas. With regard to compatibility issue 1, the power of the director was increased significantly. He or she became dean and was given provostal authority. The collegiate assembly was reconstructed and made advisory to the dean. With regard to compatibility issue 2, the reconstitution that made the collegiate assembly at least half faculty also changed the politics of the assembly, which was one of the conditions that led to the secession of Clifford Furnas College. Furthermore, the prospectus also recognized the differences between the residential and nonresidential colleges. With regard to compatibility issue 3, tougher procedures for course approval were instituted that combined increased external review with reconstitution of the assembly. With regard to compatibility issue 4, difficulties with experimental courses were solved by doing away with experimental courses. Insurance of university wide standards in courses also revolved about increased external controls. A pass-fail grading option was added. Significant faculty participation was required and new units were not permitted to offer credit courses.

The Reichert prospectus called for a boundary-contraction-via-resocialization mode of institutionalization for the colleges. It was based on an image of what the colleges should look like after they were resocialized. The college charters and supporting documentation were intended to indicate the degree to which the colleges had achieved resocialization. Failure to maintain resocialization would result in immediate revocation of the charter. Members of the Reichert committee indicated that it was possible that individual colleges might be terminated through chartering, but the primary aim of the prospectus was to transform or resocialize the collectivity of colleges, not to eliminate them.

According to the institutionalization-termination model, boundary contraction occurs under conditions of profitability and incompatibility. When given the definition of profitability, members of the Reichert committee indicated that the colleges as a whole were profitable. With regard to compatibility, numerous college incompatibilities were noted. The committee's belief in the incompatibility of the colleges was also shown in the emphasis upon compatibility in the 14 items designated for inclusion in the charter, and in the conditions established for revoking a charter. It was further emphasized in the Reichert committee's decision to restructure the colleges in such a manner as to eliminate the four major compatibility issues. In sum, the conditions of profitability and incompatibility associated with the Reichert committee's decision to resocialize the colleges were those hypothesized in the institutionalization-termination model.

The collegiate assembly reacted to the Reichert prospectus first

## The Colleges: Continuing Institutionalization

with a counter proposal, then with a minority report by the graduate student member of the Reichert committee who was a key Social Science College staffer, and finally with amendments to the prospectus. The colleges were particularly upset by the possibility of becoming a faculty clubhouse. Under the prospectus, they would be required to have faculty approval of courses, faculty instructors, faculty masters, and a faculty-dominated council. It was hard for long-time college staffers to accept the fact that they were being forced out of the colleges they had kept alive under adverse circumstances by a group that had, at best, deserted them in the past.

The prospectus went to the faculty senate in January 1974, and was the subject of four meetings stretching into March. The meetings were open to visitors who were even allowed to speak, though senate by laws permitted only senators to make motions. What was notable about the sessions was the senators' determination to change the colleges. The balance of power had shifted from the colleges and their supporters of 1969-1970 to the faculty. As the meetings were concluding, the college representatives who felt they had not been listened to stalked out en masse. The mass protest did not turn the tide in favor of the colleges as it had in December 1969. Quite the opposite occurred. Several senators who had been planning to offer liberalizing amendments became angered and scotched their plans. The only interesting outcome of the walkout was a fistfight between a college person and the undergraduate student association's vice president for academic affairs, a member of the Reichert committee, who tried to shut the meeting room doors to drown out student chanting. Not only was the student association vice president sympathetic to the prospectus, but so was the undergraduate student body president who vetoed legislation calling for a student wide referendum on the prospectus and congratulated Jon Reichert on a job well done.

Students had changed since the late 1960s. Daniel Yankelovich found a national turnabout in campus attitudes between the late 1960s and 1973. He found the campus rebellion dead and student rejection of the use of violence. Criticism of America as a sick society, of major societal institutions, and of the university decreased sharply. The new left had become a negligible factor on campus and the number of radical youth declined sharply. The gap between youth and mainstream adults had narrowed with respect to values, morals, and outlooks. There was a greater acceptance by college students of law-and-order requirements. Belief in the work ethic and the value of work education increased among the young. In fact, Yankelovich found a central theme on campus was how to find fulfillment within a conventional career (Yankelovich, 1974).

S.U.N.Y.A.B. reflected that change. During the week of November 11, 1974, *The Spectrum* ran a series on changes in Buffalo since the late 1960s. The transformation was best captured by four drawings depicting a man in the 1960s and 1970s and a woman in the 1960s and 1970s. The man of the 1960s with long hair and a scraggly beard carried a Molotov cocktail and held a clenched fist above his head. His counterpart of several years later had styled hair, in the place of the Molotov was a diploma, and sticking out of his clenched fist was a stack of dollar bills. The woman of the 1960s in a workshirt with loose disheveled hair carrier a brick and stood beside a broken window. A few years later she became smartly dressed and coifed, trading the brick for a book and standing beside an employment office window.

The number of students willing to go out and defend the barricades for the colleges was not very many. In contrast to 1970, a 1974 leaflet calling for student action by the Revolutionary Communist Youth seemed irrelevant and quite out of place. A student coalition was formed to fight the prospectus, but it got very little support. On February 8, 1974, a *Spectrum* editorial concluded that "most of this university's students seem too preoccupied with getting into law or medical school to care if the colleges die or not." In the end, students represented a pressure the faculty senate could and did discount. Fewer than 5 percent of the senators interviewed said they supported continuation of the colleges for fear of the consequences of terminating them.

In the end, the senate made changes in the prospectus, but they were more quantitative than qualitative in nature. Several people interviewed said they voted for the changes as a sign of cooperation or good faith in the colleges. In that sense there was accommodation to some college values, but only in one instance did the accommodation represent a substantive change in the prospectus. By a seven-

## The Colleges: Continuing Institutionalization

vote margin, each college was permitted to offer 10 percent of its courses on an experimental basis. A motion to increase the percentage to 25 percent was defeated. There were limits to which the senate would permit change. Motions to give the colleges parity with the faculty on the charter committee, to permit workshops to give credit courses, to diminish the planned faculty role in the colleges, and to limit charter revocation to deliberate acts were widely defeated. Similarly, proposals to toughen the prospectus also failed. A motion to increase the planned faculty role met a resounding defeat. The senate did alter the prospectus to permit college representatives to become members of the chartering committee immediately rather than after January 1, 1975. The powers of the dean were moderately increased relative to authorities external to the colleges, such as the dean of undergraduate studies and the vice president for academic affairs, in approving charters: the members of the chartering committee had to be mutually agreeable to the senate executive committee and the collegiate assembly; and the dean of the colleges was permitted to hire faculty. In the end, the prospectus, was approved with only one dissenting vote.

There had been a change in the senate's reasons for continuing the colleges. Eighty-eight percent of the faculty interviewed offered a constructive rationale associated either with Meyerson's original notion of centers of identification for students in the multiversity, or with the need for an experimental enclave in a staid university. In terms of profitability, the colleges were being preserved because they satisfied an organizational need, no longer because their termination threatened the satisfaction of more basic needs. However, it is important to realize that it was the idea of the colleges that was thought profitable, not their actual operation. The senators, with two exceptions, said they wanted to continue the colleges. The condition of profitability provided the rationale. At the same time, all of the faculty felt that the colleges as presently constituted needed to change. As noted earlier, every faculty senator interviewed mentioned at least one of the four compatibility issues as problems of the colleges. Even an individual who actively led the floor fight to liberalize the prospectus classified the colleges as "fuzzy" and said they needed to be shaken up. In his opinion, the liberalization was necessary only to insure flexibility after the chartering. Interestingly, 55 percent of the senate sample said they would not vote to abolish an academic unit until it proved it was worthy of elimination. This is synonymous with an innocent-until-proven-guilty stance, which goes a long way toward showing why universities have grown by adding new divisions and programs rather than by substituting the new for the old.

President Ketter approved the new prospectus in early April with three caveats. The first adjusted the prospectus to existing university policies or norms. The second made the arrangements of chartering unique to the college situation, so that existing mechanisms rather than ad hoc arrangements would be the procedure to follow in the future. The third made the senate dominant over the collegiate assembly in the chartering process, showing Ketter's commitment to a basic change in the colleges.

The faculty senate and President Ketter approved a plan to reinstitutionalize the colleges by boundary contraction via resocialization. The senators interviewed indicated that the colleges were incompatible with the personality of the university, but profitable. These are the hypothesized conditions for boundary contraction via resocialization.

What emerges most clearly in the approval of the institutionalization-termination plan is the development of political consensus at U.B. Where there had been polar groups in 1970 battling to impose conflicting definitions of university norms, values, and goals, there existed in 1974 a convergent definition of the university. The left-right faculty caucuses dissolved and students moderated their views on the university. U.B. had a strong president, perhaps slightly to the right of the faculty and students. The changes in political climate produced a strong centrist coalition. This permitted a more rational and open debate regarding the colleges, and produced the votes that eliminated the more liberal and more conservative amendments. The widespread sharing of a narrow range of norms, values, and goals relative to 1969 produced a much narrower definition of compatibility for the colleges.

The approval of the Reichert prospectus meant that the colleges, as a whole, had been labeled as needing resocialization. The implementation of the prospectus or the initiation of the chartering process was ultimately designed to select out the colleges that were not socialized

*The Colleges: Continuing Institutionalization*

successfully. According to the hypothesized institutionalization-termination model, successful resocialization would involve maintaining the level of profitability associated with the innovation, in this case the individual colleges, but eliminating the condition of incompatibility, which simply means showing that a college is not incompatible with the university.

## *Establishing the Chartering Committee*

By the end of April, the chartering committee held its first meeting. The faculty senate offered the collegiate assembly a list of nine nominees for the committee. After interviewing them, which angered some senators considerably, the assembly was unable to find six acceptable members. There was some dickering back and forth, and the colleges were forced to choose from a very slightly expanded list. Senate nominees chosen by Claude Welch's committee were intended to be people of varying sex and department who had formed no opinion of the colleges and would, as a result, give them impartial treatment. The faculty members ultimately selected for membership on the chartering committee were neither academic superstars nor institutional leaders. Two were full professors, one being a department chairman; four were associate professors; and one was an assistant professor. The nonstar quality, combined with the fact that they were selected by the colleges, made the chartering committee suspect among disbelievers.

The two collegiate assembly representatives were from College B and College F, the residential-nonresidential and political poles of the assembly. The two undergraduates appointed by the student association were very different. One was active in Women's Study College and the other was not associated with any of the colleges, but had gotten interested in them at the time of the senate meetings on the prospectus. The student government sought individuals who "were strong enough not to be coopted, but willing to compromise on the right issues." The graduate student association appointed a psychology doctoral student who had been very active in university governance, but uninvolved with the colleges. The administrative representative was the provost of the faculty of educational studies.

He was appointed to the committee by the vice president for academic affairs without consultation, but because the provost was so well thought of there was little criticism.

The final member of the committee was the dean of the colleges. That position was filled by 32-year-old Irving J. Spitzberg, Jr., a bright and self-confident lawyer with a Columbia, Yale, and Oxford education who had taught at the Claremont Colleges and Brown University. He had studied education abroad. Spitzberg was appointed at the time of the senate debates. Though he did not participate in the deliberations on the Reichert prospectus, he thought a fundamental change in the nature of the colleges imperative. Spitzberg, who chose a dean's role more consistent with that of provost than spokesperson, also lacked star quality and was appointed a nontenured associate professor in educational studies.

An important change in committee membership occurred during the summer of 1974, when Bernard Gelbaum "resigned" as vice president for academic affairs. Gelbaum was an academic law-and-order man whose hard line and lack of grace brought him increasingly under the fire around the university. "Impeach Gelbaum" buttons became quite fashionable and the student association president publically asked that Ketter remove him. His replacement, Acting Vice President Merton Ertell, came to the committee fresh.

The chartering committee was political internally and externally. The external political character was more interesting and subtle. Five members hoped to use the committee to further their careers. By doing well on the committee, they thought they could reap political hay. This sort of aspiration set the chartering procedure apart from either the 1970 or 1972 prospectuses. Participation in institutionalizing the colleges had changed from a potential or real threat in 1970 to a neutral activity in 1972 to a pursuit that might be rewarded in 1974. That, like the change in character of the faculty deliberations, was due to the crystallization of opinion on campus regarding the appropiate norms, values and goals of U.B.

Internally, the charter committee was divided at its extremes into pro- and anti-college groups with the majority in the middle. Most of the voting members of the committee came with slightly positive to slightly negative opinions of the colleges. At one extreme were two

## The Colleges: Continuing Institutionalization

student representatives who were determined to "save" the colleges; and at the other extreme were Charles Ebert, Jonathan Reichert, and Bernard Gelbaum, who were determined to see the colleges changed significantly. In the first few sessions of the committee, the groups jockeyed with one another in establishing the committee's procedures. Each side won a little and lost a little. Pro-college forces wanted to keep the meetings open to the public and tape record the discussions. As rumors about the colleges were flying thick and fast, it was felt that such a procedure would keep everyone honest. Nonetheless, for confidentiality, meetings were closed. A two-thirds vote was required to open a meeting. People desiring to observe at open meetings would have to register in advance with the committee secretary. The committee agreed to prohibit gossip or quotes from unnamed sources.

The anti forces, on the other hand, were granted only a minimal role in committee operation, as were all nonvoting members. They were neither permitted a vote at meetings, nor allowed to serve as chairperson. With regard to chairperson, the committee was kept open rather than committing itself to either side. An undergraduate moderate was elected to the position.

The pro-anti division created a surprising situation. Advocates on both sides were forced into stereotypical roles. The student supporters could not express their negative feelings about the more incompatible colleges because of the impact it might have upon the committee given their established role as defender. At the other pole, detractors were unable to express misgivings about the requirements of the prospectus for the same reasons. As a result, both poles became too extreme to exert leadership or significantly influence the committee.

A very simple but time-consuming procedure was developed for committee operations. The committee was divided into subcommittees, each with the responsibility of working with two to three assigned colleges. Each college would submit a charter with appropriate supporting documents which the subcommittee would review in detail. Comments would be solicited from interested parties in the university and the community at large. An open hearing would be held for each college. The hearing would last a maximum of 3½ hours: 1¼ hours for a college presentation, 1 hour for charter committee questions, and the remainder of the time for public discussion. The charter committee was required to submit its questions in advance. Colleges could defer questions subsequently formulated. After each hearing, the chartering committee would discuss the college. After all of the hearings and discussion sessions, the committee would make decisions on the fate of each college. The voting members of the committee would write one or more recommendations to President Ketter and each of the nonvoting members would write his own recommendations to the president. The committee began accepting charters in August 1974, and submitted its recommendations just prior to Thanksgiving.

Charter committee planning was highly formalized and emphasized procedure rather than substance. The committee drafted all kinds of procedures: charter committee rules and regulations, guidelines for applying for a charter, special rules for public hearings. The reason for all of that was the political nature and the political divisions of the committee. There was no consensus on what a college should be or how one would recognize excellence in a collegiate unit. In many respects, the committee appeared more divided than the university. That would be expected since the chartering committee was designed to represent the most diverse elements of the S.U.N.Y.A.B. community with respect to the colleges. As a result, the committee was only able to plan in terms of procedures to be followed. Formality was necessary to guard both the anti and pro factions against abuses by the other. This entailed spelling out agreed-upon procedures in the minutest detail.

## *Revamping the Colleges*

In 1974 there were 14 colleges. In the spring of that year, they described themselves as follows:

*College B*

   College B is a residential Collegiate Unit on the SUNYAB campus which focuses on the arts and humanities. Our students and faculty are drawn from every area of the University—the arts, humanities, social sciences, and natural sciences—but they all share an interest in the arts and in using the artistic perspective to make education a more

## College E

College E is a College which has defined itself not in terms of field or structural parts, but in terms of process: it is run as a cooperative. As such it has found continuing interest in revolutionary art, i.e., media; revolutionary science, i.e., parapsychology and yoga; and revolutionary social forms, i.e., minorities and white counterculture. (Became residential in 1974-1975.)

## College F

We feel that by dealing with the personal and making connection with the political we can make changes in our lives and the society around us.

## College H

College H is concerned about health in it broadest sense. It serves as a communication center, which opens up avenues for providing the best possible health care. The wholeness of a person's physical and mental being exists in concert with the state of the world in which he or she lives: the political climate, the social atmosphere, the economic situation. College H sees its programs as open to the entire community. We see this is an imperative because in a crisis state it is especially important to learn how we can become active determiners of our health behavior. The educational environment to be sought will be experimental. Education will not be confined to the classroom; rather students will have an opportunity to utilize their thoughts and ideas in the community. (Became residential in fall 1974.)

## College Z

The College Z program in Law begins with the assumption that the legal process in America as it is now constituted is experienced by most of the people it affects as incomprehensible and remote. Thus, in great part, the existence of the College program is predicated upon our attempt to discover and test new methods of creating legal awareness among the people of the community so that they will be able (at least minimally) to protect and defend themselves from illegal incursions upon their rights, to enable them to understand laws and proposed legislation and how it affects them, and thereby enable them to informedly criticize legislation and their legislators as well as initiate corrective action in the case of existing wrongs.

personalized and humane endeavor. The College offers both credit-bearing courses and non-credit workshops in an informal environment which provides a uniquely integrated educational experience.

## A Study of Fourteen Innovations

*Communications College*

It is the purpose of Communications College (Contemporary Crafts College) to provide an environment where the two opposing trends in art (the Fine Arts and the more immediate crafts) can come together. Students who participate will be taught the basic skills of the medium of their choice. Knowledge of the craft is initiated through the most obvious applications of the medium. Students are encouraged to develop their sense of design in a medium that will engage them in self-conscious expression. The craft areas taught are jewelry, ceramics, leather, enameling, and weaving.

*College of Mathematical Sciences*

The College of Mathematical Sciences is a community of students and faculty with interests that are mathematical. These interests vary from questions of theoretical interest to the applications of mathematics to medicine, biology, ecology, and the physical and engineering sciences. Though traditional education in mathematics has tended to emphasize the axiomatic development of mathematics the College wishes to emphasize another aspect—the study of concrete or practical topics and the development of these topics mathematically. Some College courses dwell on concrete or practical topics and encourage the student to express the truths these topics present and seek convincing arguments for their justification. (Became residential in Fall 1974.)

*New College of Modern Education*

Our College is examining and acting upon new theories of the process of education. We feel the present system of education fails to meet the needs of our contemporary society, and we are searching for better alternatives of theory and practice. Our studies range from new concepts of societal value systems and new theories of educational structures, such as "free schools," to new conceptions of the social conditioning process. Emphasis is placed on the practical application of the knowledge learned. Thus, students work in local educational experiments, examine their own personal educational processes, and contribute to the knowledge of others through film, video-tape, and journalistic media.

*Rachel Carson College*

The goals of Rachel Carson College are to provide students with the basic knowledge of environmental problems, to maintain an environmental action program, and to provide a service to the community. The faculty are drawn from biology, engineering, chemistry, sociology, international studies, and other departments. In addition several community people teach: an environmental lawyer, a city planner, a museum curator. Courses include several survey courses, courses in basic areas of environmental problems: energy and resources, population, law, nutrition, air pollution, land use. Several courses emphasize applying knowledge: environmental action, consumerism, field study of environmental impact. We hope to add next year a series of 1 credit hour outdoor skills courses in camping, sailing, canoeing, and rock climbing. (Became residential in fall 1974.)

*C. P. Snow College*

The demand for integrated, coherent courses on urban-related issues continues to increase on our campus. Our program is an attempt to complement the efforts of other urban programs in the University, as we seek to fill the gaps left by one-dimensional approaches. We try to tie together the skills and concepts learned in other disciplines into an action-oriented framework of research and clinic work on urban problems. We offer courses involved with urban systems, transportation planning, social planning and community reoganizing, urban economics, technological alienation and survival, planning methodologies, "grantsmanship," and urban law. Specific ongoing projects include the Housing Right Co-op, the Amherst Housing Survey, Behavioral Research in the Criminal Justice System, Auto Mechanics, Simulation Games, and some unique interfaces with law programs for supervised fieldwork in urban legal issues such as special housing courts and jury survey.

*Social Science College*

The purpose of this College is to bring people together to study radical social theory. We believe that such theory is necessary in order to understand American society. We reject the idea that societies can be understood through the use of the isolated and segmented disciplines and categories of orthodox social sciences. We believe that the development of a radical analysis of American society is a necessary part of the struggle to overcome the conditions which stifle human potential and prevent human liberation.

*Vico College*

Vico College represents an integrated, interdisciplinary approach to liberal education. Its staff is committed to education through intellectual confrontation with the critical ideas of Western culture. Through the College's *Core Courses* we focus upon the great texts of the past, from the Greeks through the 19th century, and accept the premise that the critical, moral, social and political crises of our own experience are, for the most part, perennial problems in modern dress. The students and faculty of Vico College are drawn from many disciplines; all of us agree that there is a need, in a large and fragmented university like S.U.N.Y.A.B., for a program which can integrate the diversity of educational experiences open to the student. (Became residential in fall 1974.)

*Women's Studies College*

Education in American universities is often the study of the culture and historical development of the middle and upper class white male. Neglected in the curriculum are the culture and struggles of groups, who out of their oppression, sought to change society. Women are one of these oppressed groups. We have been subjected to an educational system which has reinforced the stereotypic images of women as passive, dependent, unintellectual and unable to analyze and understand our own position in society. Education has not taught women the skills necessary to have a critical understanding of how society operates. We must therefore create our own education, an education that will begin to meet our needs as women; it will be an ongoing process to change the ways in which we think and behave. The Women's Studies College is run by and for the students taking Women's Studies courses and the people teaching them. Regular meetings are held throughout the year and everyone involved in the College is encouraged to participate.

*Clifford Furnas College*

Clifford Furnas College is a living-learning experience with about 300 students and a board of fellows drawn from U.B.'s best faculty. It's a smaller unit within the university. It's a place for the serious student. It's an attempt to integrate the students academic experience with his or her life out of the classroom. To this end informational learning is encouraged in an environment of good fellowship among students united in a common goal of obtaining something more out of the time spent in college.

The attitude of the colleges toward chartering varied between a view of the process as a nuisance to a view of the process as an inquisition. The colleges whose practices varied most widely from those of the university consistently described it as an inquisition. Though all of the colleges considered the evaluations that preceded chartering a form of harassment in view of the fact that they felt the good qualities pointed out were ignored, the colleges most consistent with the prospectus guidelines—Clifford Furnas and Vico Colleges—hoped chartering would result in a termination of the more radical

## The Colleges: Continuing Institutionalization

and incompatible colleges, leaving them more of the university's resources and a better reputation around S.U.N.Y.A.B.

The nature of the changes and the time commitment required to conform with the prospectus were so great for some colleges that they considered self-termination or moving outside the university. That was true of Women's Studies College, New College of Modern Education, and College Z. In the end, only College Z chose not to go through the chartering process. The "Z" program was strong and considered so around the university, so that several of its leaders felt that the lack of legitimacy resulting in continual evaluations and lack of funding troublesome, laborious, and uncalled for. The chartering requirement was the last straw. The leaders were a mobile group who had other interests and could make out well or better following other pursuits, so they chose not to participate in chartering. They felt the rest of the college at odds with their view of its purpose and not worthy of continuing, so they made sure the college closed.

In the case of College Z, a college that was incompatible with the prospectus, chose to give up rather than comply. Two indications of its incompatibility were that "Z" had no university faculty teaching courses during 1973-1974, and gave over 60 percent of its students A grades. The college had been praised by people all over the university, and its loss was lamented by even Jon Reichert. Several U.B. administrators, as well as charter committee members familiar with College Z, indicated that the college was profitable to the university because it offered a preprofessional program that students wanted—as indicated by high enrollments—in an area in which there were jobs. It also brought professionals back to the university for retooling in a time of tight enrollments and was popular in the local community. So College Z fit into the mode of being incompatible, but profitable. The compatibility could easily have been remedied, as several university faculty offered to participate in the college. But for the leaders of "Z" the association with the university had become unprofitable and they closed up shop. Because that was not true of Women's Studies College or New College of Modern Education, they chose to go through chartering.

The experience of College Z represents a refinement in the hypothesized institutionalization-termination model. Boundary contraction

## A Study of Fourteen Innovations

via termination, like all modes of institutionalization-termination, was postulated to be a host decision. "Z's" decision to voluntarily terminate shows that an innovation may itself choose institutionalization-termination by boundary contraction via termination. The innovation would be unable to self-select any other mode of institutionalization, since all others involve at least tacit consent or interaction with the host.

College Z sans leaders merged with C. P. Snow College, which had been reconstituted, and became the College of Urban Studies. Several units merged. Communications College, which had no university faculty on its staff, became part of College B. Rachel Carson College merged with an interdisciplinary graduate colloquium. Rachel Carson College had only five faculty out of a staff of 18 and had, on occasion, been accused of being activist to the extent of divorcing itself from scholarship. The graduate group, named the George Perkins Marsh Program, dealt with modern societies and international development. It had a core of dedicated faculty but no money or undergraduate students to teach. Rachel Carson College had some of each of the missing elements.

Merger permitted colleges that were incompatible with the prospectus to become compatible, and permitted strong programs to become stronger. For Communications College, there were no university faculty in its subject area. By becoming a subpart of "B," a college with a faculty, Communications College was able to maintain its integrity. For "B," an arts college, the addition of Communications College was a useful gain. The George Perkins Marsh Program could not itself have become a college since only established colleges were permitted to charter by the Reichert prospectus. By becoming a subpart of Rachel Carson College, chartering was made possible. For Rachel Carson College, merger saved the time and energy of recruiting faculty, which might have been difficult given previous conflicts with several science departments. For the remainder of "Z," which lacked faculty, it was too late to regroup and charter before the college fell apart, so joining Urban Studies permitted them to continue. For Urban Studies, like College B, the addition represented a coherent program in its subject area with a budget.

Three colleges radically transformed themselves to meet the chartering requirements. These included College E, New College of Modern

Education, and C. P. Snow College. All were grossly incompatible with the prospectus. "E" had two faculty members out of a staff of 59, New College had no faculty, and Snow had one faculty member. In terms of grades, the percentage of A's awarded varied from about 60 percent to 75 percent. Each of the colleges had a high turnover in personnel after the passage of the Reichert prospectus. The turnover occurred because staff were tired of fighting for continued existence or feared their college would not get through the chartering process. Some of the people who left were specifically mentioned by university faculty or administrators as the college's source of incompatibility with the university. College E became a "college of the poor" named after a black woman, Cora P. Maloney. Many of the old "E" people who wanted to stay around found the transformed college unpleasant for their tastes or were encouraged to leave. The number of faculty associated with the college increased to nine. New College became the College of Progressive Education, very few old staffers remained, and seven faculty joined the college. Governance was placed entirely in the hands of a faculty board. C.P. Snow, which became the College of Urban Studies, narrowed its mission and acquired 13 faculty members.

Radical transformation was a mechanism chosen by incompatible colleges after many staff members left. Unlike College Z, in these three cases a sufficient core remained or was able to be formed to sustain the college. For surviving members, chartering was carried out because it was felt that an important mission could be continued or because of salaries or rewards that would otherwise have been lost. For the survivors, continued participation in the college was based on profitability considerations of either an abstract or personal variety.

The remaining colleges changed in varying degree. The colleges incompatible with the prospectus attempted to remain substantially as they were before chartering was approved. They were Tolstoy College (College F) and Women's Studies College. Charles "Chip" Planck left "F" at the end of spring 1973 to work at farming. Charlie Haynie became head of the college. He appointed staff, approved courses, and pretty much ran "F" out of his hat. As Charlie Haynie changed, so did College F. The program at "F" was eclectic. Subject areas varied from education and community to male sex roles, gayness, and Polish culture. Despite changes in subject matter, an orientation toward anarchism remained constant. The method of study was inductive; beginning with individual experience, elements of repression and oppression would emerge and the student would eventually arrive at an anarchistic solution. The college staff argued that means were as important as ends, and decided to present the college to the chartering committee as it was. "F" sought to make cosmetic changes designed to comply with the letter of the prospectus, but not the spirit. A faculty master was appointed who would serve as "a cross between a constitutional monarch and a prime minister." Faculty were increased from one to eight, but it was felt that most would not be involved in policy discussions. Women's Studies College evolved a collective governance procedure that violated the prospectus in several ways, but, like "F," means were integrally associated with ends of the college. Women had to shape their own educations. The governance procedure, which was collective and involved two nonfaculty chairpersons, was part of the shaping process, as was the need to exclude men from several courses. In other respects, however, Women's Studies College complied with the charter requirements. Faculty involvement grew from four to nine, though there was little effort to recruit faculty. For both Tolstoy and Women's Studies, compliance with the prospectus would have been unprofitable for the colleges.

Two of the colleges changed very little. Clifford Furnas and Vico Colleges were both already compatible with the prospectus. Only 32.5 percent of the Furnas grades were A's, and only 22 percent of the Vico grades were A's. Their teaching staffs were 100 percent S.U.N.Y.A.B. faculty. These were the only two colleges that had active faculty masters prior to the prospectus, and most of the colleges' courses were cross-listed with departments. Nonetheless, each of the colleges made at least two changes: they increased the number of faculty involved and formalized governance procedures.

Those two changes were made by all of the remaining colleges as well. These included College B, Math Sciences College, College H, and Social Sciences College. These colleges differed from Clifford Furnas and Vico in that they expended more energy in seeking to

## The Colleges: Continuing Institutionalization

comply with the prospectus. With the exception of Social Science College, they really did not need to change that much. "B" (42.9 percent) and Math Sciences (63.6 percent) already had significant proportions of their staff composed of S.U.N.Y.A.B. faculty. Although more than 50 percent of "H's" staff was composed of community people, they had acceptable credentials. Social Sciences, which gave 58 percent of its grades as A and had only 7.5 percent of its staff composed of faculty, reorganized in grand style to meet the prospectus requirements. The number of Buffalo faculty on its staff increased from two to seven. These four colleges found that conforming to the prospectus would be more profitable than attempting to fight the prospectus or closing down. In three of the four cases it was because the changes were relatively minor. The fourth college, Social Sciences, feared that its previously bad reputation within the university was sufficient to scuttle the college if it did not change.

Despite differences in the approaches chosen by different colleges, there were similarities. The most important similarity was that all of the colleges except "Z" resocialized themselves to some degree in order to comply or appear to comply with the Reichert prospectus. Twelve of the 14 appointed S.U.N.Y.A.B. faculty as masters. Math Sciences appointed an advanced doctoral student as the administrative officer, but he was directly responsible to a faculty board. Women's Studies College was the only unit that violated the prospectus with regard to a master. As one dominant figure would have been inconsistent with the notion of collectivity, two individuals were appointed to coordinator positions in contravention of the prospectus.

Each collegiate unit added additional S.U.N.Y.A.B. faculty to its roster. The number of faculty associated with the colleges increased from less than 25 to 150. Some of this growth was deceptive. Several faculty lent their names to a college rather than their actual presence. A substantial number of the faculty interviewed had not even read the college's charter. In addition, the earlier number, which was presented to the chartering committee, included only faculty members teaching courses, while the second included all faculty associated with the colleges. To be sure, there was a very real increase in faculty, but not of the magnitude indicated.

## A Study of Fourteen Innovations

All of the colleges, with the possible exception of Women's Studies College, formalized their administrative procedures. Women's Studies already had a highly formalized operating procedure. What had once been satisfactory informal governing mechanisms, membership requirements, member's rights, and the like, were formalized to comply with the prospectus. Very often these changes were to the detriment of an existing collegiate atmosphere. In most cases they were downright fabrications or illusory changes, but the changes did make the colleges appear more like the university. Formalization caused many charter readers to remark that the colleges had changed into miniature departments. The charters seemed very much alike, in part because the content was so specifically spelled out, and in part because the documents were politically designed to gain the approval of the chartering committee and the president. As a result, more than half of the individuals who read the charters remarked upon the difficulty in remembering which charter was which.

The chartering also represented a universal headache for the colleges. It took away a lot of time and energy that might otherwise have gone into programming. In the less compatible colleges, the procedure was often collective, involving several writers and college wide review. In at least two of those units, courses were involved with the planning. In the more compatible colleges, chartering tended to be an activity of one or a few individuals. Students commonly chose not to participate. In both types of colleges there were numerous meetings devoted to planning, but there were more meetings in the less compatible colleges. Chartering made the less compatible units look like the more compatible. Unfortunately, the less compatible were doing a far better job than the more compatible at creating centers for student identification, which was the initial purpose of the colleges and one frequently cited by the faculty senate.

Nearly all faculty senators interviewed mentioned the need to get more faculty or faculty influence into the colleges. Several said that was the primary purpose for chartering. In the end, as was intended by the Reichert prospectus, that was the way chartering seemed to have been most successful. The increased involvement of faculty in the colleges represented diffusion of the innovation into the rest of the university. *Diffusion* was defined earlier as the spread of an innovation through the organization. A cross-section of college faculty were interviewed in order to understand why diffusion occurred.

First, it was found that faculty tended to choose colleges consistent with their interests and life-style, so there was compatibility. Interestingly, the less compatible colleges, which ultimately attracted smaller numbers of faculty, anticipated this, feeling they would find no recruits and be forced out of existence—some thought this was the goal of the chartering procedure. Several faculty said they joined because their department encouraged them to in order to increase the department's enrollments. Some faculty joined because the colleges offered subject matters or colleagues absent in their own departments. Other faculty said they joined because they felt flattered or needed when asked by a college to participate. Each of the rationales represented a form of self-interest profitability—that which would motivate an individual or subunit to adopt the innovation.

As postulated in the institutionalization-termination model, diffusion occurred under conditions of compatibility and self-interest profitability. In this instance, self-interest profitability was low. The rewards and incentives for participating in departments were much stronger. That is why all of the faculty said that college involvement was subordinated to departmental activities and why they remained so often at the periphery of the colleges.

## Chartering the Colleges

The chartering committee had the option of choosing either of the two positions in evaluating the colleges. It could render judgments on the success of the colleges in meeting the prospectus requirements, which would have been summative evaluation; or it could attempt to raise each of the colleges to a level of success necessary to satisfy the prospectus, which would have been formative evaluation. The committee followed the latter course. It did not specifically choose that course, but rather its character gravitated it in that direction. All members of the committee said they grew continually more impressed with the colleges as the committee progressed. They also thought the colleges satisfied an important campus need, which was profitability.

In addition, 15 members of the committee showed an inclination like that of the faculty senate for a philosophy of innocent until proven guilty—a college had to prove to the committee it was unfit in order to be terminated. President Ketter was also inclined to such an outlook. In any case, the combination of a positive attitude and a philosophy favoring continuance of the colleges resulted in the formative character of the chartering committee. It was a committee with a penchant more toward resocialization than termination, which would be expected in view of the generalized belief in college profitability. The dean of the colleges, because he was of the colleges and perceived by the committee as also of the university, was permitted to act as an intermediary between the committee and the colleges. At times he informed a college of the committee's attitude and the appropriate response; at times he negotiated with a college on behalf of the committee.

Much about the chartering process was illusory. The documentation submitted by the colleges was so voluminous that not more than three members of the chartering committee were able to get through all of it. More than half of the committee frankly admitted not knowing each of the colleges and others showed this to be true in passing on misinformation during their interviews. For example, it was not uncommon for committee members, when asked if they would be willing to teach in a college, to say that there was no college concerned with their particular field. In fact, one, and usually several, colleges dealt specifically with the topic. The colleges were unaware of the degree to which the committee misunderstood them, and changed more than they would have if they had been fully cognizant of the situation.

Similarly, the colleges changed less than their hearings or charters indicated. The degree of profitability of the colleges was exaggerated. For instance, one college brought a very large group of students to its hearing who idealized the college. This college had been unable to get students to participate in chartering and, in fact, was having trouble getting students to participate in its other activities, but this showing proved to the chartering committee that the college did an excellent job of meeting an organizational need and was, therefore, certainly profitable. The colleges changed substantially, but not to the extent the committee imagined.

## The Colleges: Continuing Institutionalization

The gap between the colleges and the committee was organizationally functional. It permitted the colleges to fill an organizational need—serving as an innovative enclave or center of identification for students. Transforming the colleges into departments would have precluded the need from being satisfied, as departments in the past failed at the twin tasks.

The gap was probably most apparent in the public hearings. The hearings were a stage with an audience composed of campus and local newspaper representatives who would inform the rest of the S.U.N.Y.A.B. community. It was here that the committee showed best what it was looking for: compatibility and profitability, with a decided emphasis on compatability that was quite consistent with the nature of a committee favoring resocialization over termination.

In the public and its private sessions, the chartering committee developed three unspecified criteria for compatibility: 1) a college had to conform to the prospectus, 2) a college had to have a positive attitude toward chartering, and 3) a college had to have had a good past history. The criteria for profitability was that a college had to fill a university need. This was primarily evidenced by demonstrating the need, establishing the uniqueness of the college program, having substantial enrollments, and having a large attendance at the public hearing. A secondary form of profitability involved improving the university environment in a general sort of way. That might mean bringing outside funding to the university or enhancing the S.U.N.Y.A.B. reputation nationally.

The chartering committee's emphasis upon these categories is shown in an analysis of the questions asked at the open hearings of four selected colleges.[2] Nearly three-quarters of the questions fell into one of the compatibility or profitability categories. The results were as follows:

1. Number of questions dealing with compatibility—38
   a. conformity to the prospectus—31
   b. attitude toward chartering—2

---

[2] Four colleges representing a cross-section of the units were studied indepth. The rationale and purpose for this are discussed in Appendix A, "Methodological Notes."

c. past history—5

The attitude of the college to chartering and the reaction of the committee were revealed in the tone and nature of the inquiry rather than in questions. In fact, at one open hearing a member of the committee became so enraged at a college's attitude that he momentarily stalked off.

2. Number of questions dealing with profitability—15
None of the four colleges were queried about secondary forms of profitability. Several others were, however.

3. Number of questions dealing with general information or other subjects—18
These questions dealt generally with a charter committee member's pet interest. For instance, Vico College, which specializes in the humanities, was asked, "How do you account for the interest of students from the science areas?" The only purpose of the question was to salve an individual's curiosity.

This analysis indicates several important things about the committee. First, 71 percent of all questions asked concerned the constructs of profitability and compatibility as defined in the institutionalization-termination model. Second, 2½ times as many questions concerned compatibility as profitability. In fact, more questions were concerned with general information than profitability. This illustrates that the chartering committee was far more concerned about the compatibility of the colleges than their profitability. It was most concerned about the degree of conformity with the prospectus. That constituted 44 percent of all questions asked and 82 percent of the compatibility questions.

Interestingly, the pattern of questions asked varied from college to college, as shown in the following example. Vico was a college that was profitable and very compatible with the university.[3] Most of its questions were of the general information variety; equal numbers

---

[3]The basis for the judgments on compatability and profitability of the three colleges will be explained shortly.

were concerned with compatibility as with profitability. In contrast, College F, which was dubiously compatible but profitable, had 5½ times as many compatibility as profitability questions addressed to it. The College of Progressive Education, which was unprofitable and dubiously compatible, had more than three times as many questions concerned with compatibility as profitability. This shows that the chartering committee's primary concern was with compatibility. Only after it was assured of a college's compatibility did it turn its attention in equal measure to the question of profitability.

## Determining Compatibility and Profitability

The colleges fared differently on the criteria associated with compatibility and profitability. What follows is a description of each college with regard to those criteria. This is done as a prelude to evaluating the success each college achieved at resocialization.

*College B*
A. Conforms to prospectus (+)

This is best summed up by the comment of one of the chartering committee members who said, "College B's charter proposal is quite consistent with the demands of the prospectus."

B. Attitude toward chartering (+)

College B outdid just about every other college in its attitude toward chartering. At its hearing, one student thanked Reichert for the prospectus and praised the document for its positive effect on the college. At the open hearing, a committee member commented that "the College seemed less defensive than some of the others have been."

C. Past history (+)

College B had no past bad deeds to atone for. When members of the chartering committee were questioned about qualms or opinions they had about the colleges, not one member had anything negative to say about College B's past. In fact, members of the chartering committee commented that College B "had a solid history." "had been a successful college," and "was not one of the colleges that chartering was created for." College B had been a victim of compatibility issue 2.

D. Profitability (+)

Chartering committee members were given the definition of profitability and were asked which colleges were profitable and which were not. They often pointed out a third group as exceptionally profitable colleges. With two exceptions, College B was classified as profitable. The exceptions were one classification as very profitable and one classification as unprofitable.

In addition, there was a consensus among chartering committee members that College B was unique. One student at the open hearing commented in a very moving fashion that "College B is a place where you can go and feel a sense of belonging. There are very few places in the university where one can get that feeling." Though its enrollments were not large, the College B public hearing was filled with students, which was commented upon several times in charter committee deliberations.

*Clifford Furnas College*

A. Conforms to prospects (−)

Clifford Furnas College would not agree to conform to the prospectus. The prospectus required that the college resume its place in the collegiate assembly successor body. At its hearing, Furnas' acting master said that under those conditions "it is possible that the College might not seek a charter." The chartering committee recommended a charter for Furnas "*contingent* upon the college's joining the College Council" (emphasis theirs).

B. Attitude toward chartering (0)

The attitude of Furnas College was neither positive nor negative. Different chartering committee members described the attitude as "haughty," "hubris," "didactic," "self-righteous," and "as if they were doing us a favor by participating."

*The Colleges: Continuing Institutionalization*

C. Past history (++)

The past was summed up in the chartering committee recommendation, which said, "Its history strongly suggests that it will enjoy continuing success." Chartering committee members continually remarked upon the past quality of the residential program. The Furnas standards of quality had been higher than the standards of the Reichert prospectus. Moreover, Clifford Furnas College had been a victim of compatibility issue 2.

D. Profitability (++)

Furnas was one of two colleges that more than six chartering committee members designated as exceptionally profitable. Furnas created a program that mirrored the intent of the original Meyerson plan. It built a home for the serious student. At its hearing, a continuous parade of students repeatedly gave testimony to Furnas' uniqueness and excellence. They demonstrated the need for such a college, too. A student told of his difficulty in finding a quiet place to study in the university. He was at his wits end until he found Clifford Furnas College, the home of the scholastically minded student. His impressions were reinforced by similar student accounts. Enrollments verified the emotions.

*College H*

A. Conforms with the prospectus (+)

The chartering committee credited College H with "an excellently prepared charter document, strong supporting documentation, . . . and adherence to the guidelines of the prospectus."

B. Attitude toward chartering (0)

"H," like most other colleges, was defensive about chartering in its open hearing. College H staffers acknowledged this in conversation, and chartering committee members whispered about it after the hearing. The defensive posture ruined what the charter committee described as "an articulate presentation at the open hearing."

C. Past history (+)

The minutes of the chartering committee of November 5, 1974, sum this matter up in two words: "solid record."

D. Profitability (+)

No one said College H was unprofitable, and a couple of people branded it exceptionally profitable. The chartering committee minutes of November 5, 1974, describe its focus as "unique." Enrollments were growing more rapidly than any other college. A secondary form of profitability was mentioned at least eight times by five different chartering committee members. It was felt that College H could bring both national attention and possible outside funding to U.B.

*Cora P. Maloney (College E)*

A. Conforms to prospectus (0)

Whatever the chartering committee suggested, Cora P. Maloney adopted. The chartering committee minutes of November 22, 1974, state that "the College has agreed to all the requests for changes made by the committee." Cora P. Maloney was willing to do anything to be approved by the committee. In fact, when asked for a minor revision in its charter, a college spokesman said, "Anything is O.K. We'll fix it up." Cora P. Maloney certainly did conform to the letter of the prospectus, but the eager willingness to do so made the committee suspicious. Moreover, because the college was only tangentially associated with the old College E, it was perceived by several charter committee members as new. New colleges were not permitted to charter. To this extent, Maloney presented an ambiguous case.

B. Attitude toward chartering (+)

Cora P. Maloney smiled, bowed, and scraped its way through chartering. It was not defensive or challenging of committee authority as other colleges had been. Chartering committed members commented that "it was the one college that knew how to show respect" and "(Maloney) was deferent to the point of lacking integrity."

*The Colleges: Continuing Institutionalization*

C. Past history (0)

Cora P. Maloney had no prior history. Though the college grew out of the old "E," it was an entirely new college. Nearly all of the College E staff were gone or going. One old "E" staffer said "I'm just hanging on for a little while until something else comes along." That person felt the remaining College E people were being pushed to the periphery of the college. In fact, Cora P. Maloney spokesmen disavowed College E at its open hearing. One charter committee member expressed the feeling of the others in saying, "the transformation from the old college E to the present Cora P. Maloney was so radical that it was almost impossible to recognize College E as its antecedent.

D. Profitability (+)

The majority of the chartering committee termed Cora P. Maloney profitable. It was felt to be unique. As it was brand new, there were no enrollments or many students to attend the open hearing. The lack of success of minority students at U.B. proved that there was a tremendous need for a living-learning unit that might aid them.

*Math Sciences College*

A. Conforms to prospectus (+)

Math Sciences was an uncontroversial college that conformed quite well with the prospectus. No doubts were expressed by any charter committee member.

B. Attitude toward chartering (0)

There were defensive moments at the Math Sciences open hearing. For instance, one staffer blasted a charter committee member, commenting that a remark he had made showed a "pedestrian attitude" toward math made by those with "near zero" knowledge. By and large, the attitude of the college was cooperative. The college attitude was not commented on favorably or unfavorably by the chartering committee.

C. Past history (+)

In the course of chartering committee discussions, there

were repeated references to the excellence of the Math Sciences program. Never was there a repudiation.

D. Profitability (+)

Math Sciences College was classified by a majority of the chartering committee as profitable. The college did an excellent job of getting minority students into math courses, according to two committee members who considered that an important need of the university. Several committee members classified the college as unique. There was no question about its enrollments.

*College of Urban Studies*

A. Conforms to prospectus (+)

One member of the committee commented that the charter application and present practice of the College of Urban Studies was consistent with the demands of the prospectus. No one else expressed doubts.

B. Attitude toward chartering (0)

There were no comments or reactions for or against.

C. Past history (0)

Urban Studies had a bad history with regard to compatibility issue 4, but all of those responsible had left the college. The only concern of the chartering committee was whether the college could "recover its momentum which was lost when the founders left the College." The best way to describe the committee's reaction to this college might be in the words of the committee member who said, "I have less familiarity with this college than I have with most others."

D. Profitability (+)

A majority of the chartering committee said that the College of Urban Studies was profitable. There were some questions about whether it duplicated other departments. The College Z program within Urban Studies and a community orientation were felt to be unique by several chartering committee members. Since Urban Studies had recently grown

*The Colleges: Continuing Institutionalization*

out of C. P. Snow College, enrollments were largely unknown.

*College of Progressive Education*
A. Conforms to prospectus (0)

The charter of the college conformed with the prospectus, but the chartering committee felt there was a rift in the college between the university faculty and some of its students who previously administered the college. Several members of the committee felt one of the students did not "seem qualified or capable of . . . a central role in the College." The faculty master of the college was planning to go on sabbatical in less than a year. Course quality was questioned by two charter committee members, and another suggested accurately that the college faculty were not fully committed. The short of it was that the college appeared to conform to the letter of the prospectus, but there were serious doubts about its conforming to the spirit.

B. Attitude toward chartering (0)

No reaction by committee members.

C. Past history (−)

Progressive Education had had a bad history. Its leaders were considered radical. The central member of the college had gotten his start at College A. Historically, no faculty had been associated with the college, and grading was the most inflated of all the colleges. These facts were known and the chartering committee was concerned about them. Questions about grading and instructor selection were asked at the open hearing. Progressive Education College had a weak record on compatibility issues 2 and 4.

D. Profitability (−)

Progressive Education was the college voted unprofitable by the vast majority of the chartering committee members (14). Enrollments were low and the chartering committee asked about that at the open hearing. The major difficulty, however, was that the department of social, philosophical, and historical foundations of education was planning to offer a similar program. This would have made the College of Progressive Education nonunique, unable to attract enrollments, and, more than that, unnecessary. The chartering committee members who felt the college unprofitable each mentioned one or more of those reasons.

*Rachel Carson College*

A. Conforms to prospectus (+)

The committee was satisfied with the college except for specific concerns about particular staff and the substance of certain courses. When those matters were cleared up, there was no further question of conformity with the prospectus.

B. Attitude toward chartering (0)

The chartering committee did not comment on this favorably or unfavorably.

C. Past history (+)

When other students were out trying to tear the university apart, Rachel Carson College was directing its students into constructive community environmental activities. This was commented on by a chartering committee member. There was a good feeling about Rachel Carson's previous history by a majority of the committee, though few seemed to know what it actually involved.

D. Profitability (+)

A majority of the committee rated Rachel Carson profitable. The two dissenting comments were that the college was exceptionally profitable and unprofitable. The college, according to the charter committee recommendation, "attracts large numbers of students." There was a widespread feeling among charter committee members that Rachel Carson College was unique and was a source of good publicity for the university.

*Social Sciences College*

A. Conforms to prospectus (0)

Like other colleges, there was a sense of ambivalence about

this college. The chartering committee recommendation reported that the "college has met all of the guidelines of the chartering process," but at the same time it pointed out that there were several major concerns, including a "vague image of ideological bias and putative denial of academic freedom." One member of the committee simply said, "I don't trust them."

B. Attitude toward chartering (0)

The college offered a great deal of information, but charter members in some cases expressed doubts about the spirit in which it was given. At its hearing, the college was quite defensive. Three chartering committee members brought that up repeatedly.

C. Past history (−)

The committee's lack of trust and the negative feelings about academic or ideological bias were a result of the past. Social Sciences College was weak on compatibility issues 2, 3, and 4 — particularly 3. The previous history of the college was discussed earlier in the chapter.

D. Profitability (+)

A majority of the committee described Social Sciences College as profitable. The uniqueness of its perspective on analysis in the social sciences was generally the reason why. Those who classified the college as unprofitable did so for reasons of redundancy or because they did not recognize the need that the college satisfied.

*Tolstoy College (College F)*

A. Conforms to prospectus (0)

Most of the faculty and administrators on the chartering committee said they could not understand College F. There was a strong feeling that a college that could not be understood could not be compatible with the prospectus. There were feelings, supported by college statements, that changes in the college — a new master, faculty participation, and the like — might only be a ruse. This was discussed earlier in the chapter. College F used its first open hearing to present student poetry, perform human relations exercises, and turn committee questions around. The college presented an affective and experimental face to the cognitively and academically oriented charter committee. At least half of the chartering committee had a negative reaction to the hearing. When "F" learned the chartering committee's reaction, it requested a second hearing. A closed hearing between the college and the committee was arranged. At that time the college was not represented by a group of students and community people who dominated the first hearing, but rather by well respected U.B. faculty. The college faculty translated the College F mission into "academese," and conformity to the prospectus became clear. One of the primary spokesmen for the college at the first meeting described the second meeting as similar to going to your relatives with your parents. Your relatives take you more seriously because your parents are with you. The master began exerting a more dominant role in the college, and the other faculty became more intimately involved after repeatedly announcing their commitment in public. The faculty "F" sought to "coopt" profoundly changed the college. The fact of the matter was that College F's old staffers tried to create an image of continuity with past practices and compliance with the prospectus. The chartering committee did not know which to believe. Neither did President Ketter, who made the college go through a third hearing in the presence of his administrative staff. He questioned the degree to which "F" had really changed. The fact of the matter was that College F had changed significantly, but few in the college were willing to accept the fact that they had changed. The chartering committee and the president had ambivalent feelings about College F. He questioned the degree to which "F" had really changed. The fact of the matter was that College F had changed significantly, but few in the college were willing to accept the fact that they had changed. The chartering committee and the president had ambivalent feelings about College F.

## The Colleges: Continuing Institutionalization

B. Attitude toward chartering (0)

Just as the committee and president were unable to gauge whether the college had conformed to the prospectus, so they were unable to decide whether the college was trying to hoodwink them. This conflict came clearly to the surface when a portion of a homosexual student's biography, which was produced in a College F class, was read. The biography was graphic in sexual and fecal description. The reader, a principal in the chartering process, commented to the committee that College F will laugh at us in public, not only behind our backs as at present, if we accept this material for chartering. Another in the room replied that one of the university's most eminent scholars regarded the work as scholarship. The president and the chartering committee were never able to discover what was illusion and what was fact.

C. Past history (−)

The history of College F was discussed previously. When asked about their skepticism regarding College F, almost half of the chartering committee members attributed it to past history. College F was criticized with regard to compatibility issues 2, 3, and 4.

D. Profitability (+)

A bare majority of the chartering committee categorized College F as profitable. The rationale was always associated with uniqueness or the large turnout at its first hearing. Low enrollments in the college were a serious concern.

*Vico College*

A. Conforms to prospectus (+)

There was no doubt of that. No charter committee member ever questioned Vico's conformity with the prospectus.

B. Attitude toward chartering (−)

Vico faculty were proud of their accomplishments, so proud that they tended to demean the other colleges and to treat the chartering committee condescendingly. The chartering committee never forgot its shabby treatment. Whenever Vico was discussed, words like "haughty," "self-satisfied," "nasty," and "blow-hard" were likely to follow.

C. Past History (++)

The feeling of one member of the chartering committee was that Vico was a solid conservative college with a strong history behind it. Several charter committee members linked the histories of Furnas and Vico Colleges. Both were composed entirely of faculty, sought serious students, and offered tough programs. One student member of the chartering committee quipped that the differences between Vico and the English department was that Vico had a more rigorous program. Vico had been a victim of the abuses associated with compatibility issue 2.

D. Profitability (+)

Vico was considered profitable by a majority of the members of the chartering committee. At odds with that assessment was the fact that Vico lacked enrollments and, as a result, was occasionally described as a faculty clubhouse. Few students came to its hearing. The committee long debated whether the college was unique. By the end of the proceeding, all but three members considered it profitable and an equal number considered it unique.

*Women's Studies College*

A. Conforms to prospectus (−)

Women's Studies College did not comply with the prospectus. It had two chairpersons who were not considered suitable alternatives to a U.B. faculty member. Because men were excluded from some courses and its charter used the word *women* generically (thereby technically excluding all men), there were repeatedly expressed qualms about academic freedom violations of both teachers and students. Discrimination against men, generic use of the world *women,* and the lack of a faculty master were specifically cited in the charter committee recommendation. The fact that undergraduates taught some Women's Studies' courses was a concern to several charter committee members. One charter committee member remarked that Women's Studies College "raised serious and fundamental educational issues as well as important conflicts with regard to the prospectus."

B. Attitude toward chartering (−)

Women's Studies College was very negative about chartering. Three hundred vocal people attended its public hearing. Speakers and charter committee members were awarded for their comments with sustained applause or loud booing. This was the incident that provoked a charter committee member to stalk off. Another member who appeared very even-tempered tapped his foot in anger throughout the hearing. Most of the chartering committee members brought up this hearing in their evaluation of the utility of an open hearing. Subsequently, Women's Studies refused to accept the suggestions or demands of the chartering committee and instead called demonstrations to fight the committee and later the president.

C. Past history (0)

The discussion of Women's Studies was so present-oriented that most charter committee members had not formed an impression of its past.

D. Profitability (++)

Women's Studies College was the other college that six committee members classified as exceptionally profitable. Their comments were reflected in the committee recommendation. The college was praised for being "the largest Women's Studies College in the nation." It was felt "that the work of the college [was] known and appreciated nationally." Complementing the college's richness in secondary profitability was its primary profitability. women's Studies College was over subscribed in enrollments and unique in the university. For better or worse, the open hearing proved the dedication and enthusiasm of its students.

## A Study of Fourteen Innovations

Table 4.1 summarizes the performance of the individual colleges: + equals positive performance; 0 equals neutral or uncertain performance; − equals negative performance; and, multiple signs equal exceptional performance. The compatibility total is a summary of the net valence of positive and negative factors associated with any one college. It offers a sense of the ambience of the college, not a summary measure of its compatibility. The different indicators were certainly not of the same importance, given that almost half of the charter committee's public hearing questions dealt with compliance to the prospectus. The other two compatibility considerations—prior history and attitude toward chartering—were more indicators of the degree to which a college could be believed and the vigor with which evaluation should be pursued. There were only two colleges—Furnas and Women's Studies—that did not satisfy the letter of the prospectus, and those colleges had compiled with the substance. Interestingly, the colleges whose rating were "0" met the letter, but there were doubts about their substantive satisfaction.

Table 4.1 The Chartering Committee's Assessments of the Colleges

| College | Compatibility | | | Total | Profitability |
|---|---|---|---|---|---|
| | Prior History | Attitude Toward Chartering | Meeting Prospectus Requirements | | |
| College B | + | + | + | 3+ | + |
| Clifford Furnas | ++ | 0 | − | + | ++ |
| College H | + | 0 | + | 2+ | + |
| C. P. Maloney | 0 | + | 0 | + | + |
| Math Sciences | + | 0 | + | 2+ | + |
| Urban Studies | 0 | 0 | + | + | + |
| Progressive Education | − | 0 | 0 | − | − |
| Rachael Carson | + | 0 | + | 2+ | + |
| Social Sciences | − | 0 | 0 | − | + |
| Tolstoy | − | − | 0 | 2− | + |
| Vico | ++ | − | + | 2+ | + |
| Women's Studies | 0 | − | − | 2− | ++ |

With this background, the chartering committee made its decisions and the nonvoting members wrote recommendations to the president. The opinions of the two groups were quite similar. Although the nonvoting members tended to be harder on the college—they recommended slightly fewer colleges for charters and in general supported charters of shorter duration. The colleges not recommended were those viewed as marginal by the voting members of the committee. The difference in outcomes resulted from a higher standard for compatibility among the nonvoting members and a greater level of suspicion of the degree to which the colleges actually changed, frequently based on gossip, prior experience, or unnamed sources within the college.

President Ketter read the recommendations and documentation on the colleges, which consisted of 13 plump looseleaf binders; accepted letters from inside and outside the university; and then initiated a second miniature version of the chartering committee proceedings with a group of his core advisors and the dean of the colleges. The procedure was a step removed from the colleges so that they would be unable to interfere. It occurred because the chartering committee had a soft image. It also occurred because the president really could not believe that the colleges had changed as much as the committee said they had. At the Ketter sessions the same subjects, questions, and concerns raised in the chartering committee were reaired, though more candidly and overtly. In the end, President Ketter took the same position as the chartering committee, but combined that with the nonvoting members' shorter charter durations and interim evaluations for most units. External controls were again imposed rather than a less accepting mode of institutionalization. Units of dubious compatibility were given a shorter tether rather than being terminated. *Dubious*, in this instance, referred to units that complied with the letter of the prospectus, but were thought to have missed the spirit. The questions that arose with dubious colleges were with regard to credibility, not substance.

Ketter's verdicts fell into three categories, all involving boundary contraction: 1) resocialization approved—the manner in which a college was resocialized was accepted; 2) resocialization negotiated—an acceptable form of resocialization was arranged via active negotiation between the host and the innovation. The innovation was not as

## A Study of Fourteen Innovations

instrumental in setting the criteria for its resocialization under "resocialization approved"; and, 3) termination—the innovation was not permitted to continue.

Table 4.2 Resocialization Approved

|  | Compatibility | Profitability |
|---|---|---|
| Three-year charter |  |  |
| College B | 3+ | + |
| Three-year charter with review of specific practice in 18 months |  |  |
| College H | 2+ | + |
| Mathematical Sciences College | 2+ | + |
| Rachel Carson College | 2+ | + |
| Vico College | 2+ | + |
| Three-year charter with *in toto* review in 18 months |  |  |
| Cora P. Maloney | + | + |
| College of Urban Studies | + | + |
| Two-year charter with *in toto* review in 12 months |  |  |
| Social Sciences College | − | + |
| Two-year charter with *in toto* review in 12 months and redraft charter |  |  |
| College F (Tolstoy College) | 2− | + |

The compatibility and profitability scores in Table 4.2 were taken from Table 4.1. As hypothesized, the decisions showed that both profitability and compatibility (at least to the letter of the prospectus) were required for approval of resocialization. Though the compatibility scores of Social Sciences and Tolstoy Colleges appear negative in Table 4.2, both were shown to have complied with the letter of the Reichert prospectus, which is to say that neither was found to be incompatible with the norms, values, and goals of S.U.N.Y.A.B. Successful resocialization, as measured by approval, meant that a college had to retain its profitability and eliminate its previous incompatibility. A college did not have to prove it was compatible, only that it was not incompatible. The greater the compatibility total, the longer the charter duration and the fewer the external controls imposed in the post-chartering period. Marginally compatible units in this atmosphere of innocent-until-proven-guilty were accepted as resocialized for limited periods and under tight scrutiny.

The fact that Social Sciences College and College F were approved as resocialized showed that the emphasis of the chartering process

## The Colleges: Continuing Institutionalization

was on selecting out the colleges that had definitely not met the demands of the prospectus, as opposed to screening in those that definitely had met the demands of the prospectus. The latter is a more rigorous procedure that would be expected of a summative evaluation emphasizing termination. The former is indicative of a formative evaluation emphasizing resocialization. This is not to say that Social Sciences College and College F were not scrutinized closely. College F, which had the lowest rating on total compatibility of all colleges as revealed in Table 4.1 was examined more vigorously than any other college. No other college had three hearings. In contrast, College B— with the highest total compatibility rating—was barely discussed by the president or the chartering committee, and was rushed through the proceedings in a hail of praise. College F's "negative attitude toward chartering" and "negative past history" caused it to be evaluated far more painstakingly than Cora P. Maloney College, which had the same rating on "meeting the prospectus requirements." Social Sciences College, which had a negative rating only on "past history," was also treated more harshly than Cora P. Maloney, though better than "F" despite the same rating on "meeting the prospectus requirements."

Table 4.3  Termination

|  | Compatibility | Profitability |
|---|---|---|
| College of Progressive Education | 0 | − |

As hypothesized in the institutionalization-termination model, the conditions of unprofitability and dubious or marginal compatibility resulted in the termination of a college. Progressive Education was marginal in compatibility in the same way that Social Sciences College and College F were. The difference between the colleges was that Progressive Education was also unprofitable (see Table 4.3). As a result, it would appear that unprofitability would be the important element in termination.

Table 4.4  Resocialization Negotiated

|  | Compatibility | Profitability |
|---|---|---|
| Women's Studies College | 2− | ++ |
| Clifford Furnas College | + | ++ |

## A Study of Fourteen Innovations

Units that were exceptionally profitable (Table 4.4) were given leeway with regard to departures from the prospectus. The terms of compatibility were more flexible and determined more by the college, but the substance of the prospectus still had to be satisfied. Unlike the other colleges, Clifford Furnas was given until fall 1975 to join the collegiate council, which began in January; and Women's Studies was allowed to have two non-Ph.D.'s head its college, providing one was called administrative officer. Initially, Women's Studies courses were permitted to exclude men if such exclusion was approved by the division of undergraduate education. A resolution procedure rather than a definitive policy was offered. By fall 1975, all Women's Studies courses were opened to men. The demand that Women's Studies College redraft its charter was changed to a demand that it clarify the use of *women* as a generic term. The debate between the president's office and Women's Studies continued on and on with periodic threats to terminate the college. As such, it appears that an unwillingness to become compatible leads to termination. This should not be construed as inconsistent with the institutionalization-termination model. Members of the chartering committee who thought Women's Studies was profitable were asked: If the college refused to adopt the changes required, would it still be profitable? The majority answer, with three understandable exceptions, was no. The rationale was that so much time and energy would be spent in keeping the college in line that it just would not be worth having. Extreme incompatibility and unwillingness to adhere to prescribed directions for becoming compatible result in unprofitability, in that the deviating innovation begins to draw too heavily on scarce institutional resources.

### *Epilogue*

When all the dust settled, Jonathan Reichert was the big winner. In spring 1975, he was elected chairman of the faculty senate, a traditional path to an administrative career at S.U.N.Y.A.B. Reichert was rewarded by his colleagues for personally ending collegiate incompatibility.

The reward for having stopped being compatible were far less. Almost one-sixth of the faculty senate interviewees unsolicitedly expressed doubts about the degree to which the colleges had actually changed

## The Colleges: Continuing Institutionalization

and the rigor of the chartering commission. One voting member of the chartering committee wrote to the president describing the inadequacies of the colleges, the chartering committee, and the chartering process. The president, other administrative officers, and several nonvoting members of the committee also expressed doubts about the process and its outcomes. There was a big difference between being permitted to continue existing in the university, not being terminated, and being accorded autonomy and thought a legitimate and integral part of the university. The colleges would have to earn this. Until that time they could certainly not expect the promised resources: merit money and tenure for staff, increased budgets, release time for a large portion of faculty from their departments, and so on. Dickering with departments for release time for the masters was a major chore. The colleges were made by the university to haggle with the student government over dormitory space during summer 1975.

The situation came to a head in spring 1975 when New York State retrenchment in higher education resulted in a multi million-dollar cut in the Buffalo budget. That, combined with an 8 percent inflation rate, meant a monumentous budget reduction to the university. The faculty union asked that the colleges' budget be cut before academic departments were slashed. A special administrative budget-cutting committee created to deal with the crisis initially recommended that the college budget be cut by $200,000 to save departmental faculty. The vice president for academic affairs refused such a drastic cut and instead reduced the college budget by $25,000, or 6 percent. In contrast, the academic area cut the most was the social sciences, which lost only 2 percent of its budget. To get extra resources under these conditions, the colleges would have to prove they were better than existing academic departments. The colleges had transformed themselves with the promise of a greater portion of university resources; for their efforts they got a little more than survival.

The university, on the other hand, got a better deal—the colleges were successfully resocialized. So said a group of three outside evaluators in June 1978.

## A Study of Fourteen Innovations

The Colleges have survived a critical infance during which their very survival was at time in doubt. The most serious concerns that were expressed about them have been resolved. They have at least made a start towards meeting the obligations to which they are committed, to satisfy certain essential needs of undergraduate education and service to the community which are not otherwise met. They have developed a mode of collegiate government which seems to work well. They have created a sense of neighborhood for groups of students. They have made a beginning towards involving larger numbers of faculty members in their activities. They have taken elements of the University to the community: neighborhoods, minorities, women, problems of the environment; and they have generated community interest in the University as well. In trying to get a measure of how much all of this amounts to, we bore in mind the setting in which this took place: the turbulent founding year, the physical expansion and fragmentation of the campus, the shortage of money, the increasingly conflicting loyalties of the faculty to their professions versus their University. Most of these problems are now endemic to all universities, and so we are sensitive to the context in which Buffalo has been able to bring the Colleges to their position today: we think it is a remarkable accomplishment [Arnaud, Arthurs, and Chandrasekhar, 1978].

# PART THREE

# CONCLUSIONS

CHAPTER 5

# *How and Why Innovation Fails*

The aim of this volume is to discover how and why innovation fails. Toward that end, a model of the institutionalization-termination process of innovation was tested in a study of the colleges at the State University of New York at Buffalo. The task of this chapter is to analyze the findings of that study.

The institutionalization-termination model was shown to be valid in a study of 14 innovations.[1] Each of the four modes of institutionalization-termination was isolated in the course of the study, and the conditions of profitability and compatibility postulated for each were shown to be correct. Boundary expansion via diffusion occurred under conditions of compatibility and self-interest profitability. Boundary expansion via enclaving occurred when the innovation was compatible and generally profitable. Boundary contraction via resocialization occurred under conditions of profitability and incompatibility. Boundary contraction via termination occurred when the innovation was unprofitable and incompatible. It is likely that it would occur under conditions of compatibility and unprofitability, as unprofitability was shown to be the key determinant. No other forms of or alternatives to boundary expansion and boundary contraction were discovered.

---

[1]Bear in mind that this conclusion is based on a single case study. It is possible that the model is valid for only S.U.N.Y.A.B. Furthermore, it is possible that there are exceptions to the model, though none were located in this study.

155

## Conclusions

### Why Innovation Fails

According to the model, *innovation failure* is defined as a premature decline in the planned level of impact or influence of an innovation on the host organization. Some innovations, such as compensatory education programs, are planned only as innovative enclaves. There is never any intention of diffusing the innovation. Other innovations, like the colleges at Buffalo, are intended for diffusion. Enclaving for the colleges represented a decline in status. Martin Meyerson and the Ketter committee planned the colleges to be a major feature of the university. They were to be expanded vastly beyond their modest beginnings, which was quite a contrast with the Stern prospectus goal of limited enclaving. This is to say that the position an innovation holds can only be judged successful or unsuccessful relative to its planned goals. On the other hand, no innovation is created with the hope of boundary contraction, that is, resocialization or termination. If termination is planned, it is a goal only after the innovation has fulfilled its purpose. Under other circumstances, termination would be considered premature or a sign of failure. The two modes of boundary contaction would then normally represent a decline in status for an innovation.

The range of possibilities for an innovation—from extreme boundary expansion to extreme boundary contraction—represents a continuum from total diffusion to complete termination. Termination, resocialization, enclaving, and diffusion are ideal types or points on the continuum, varying from substantial impact by the innovation on the host to substantial impact on the innovation by the host. The emphasis in boundary expansion is upon impact by the innovation on the host while boundary contraction concentrates upon host impact on the innovation. The treatment of the colleges at Buffalo—between the Stern prospectus which sought boundary expansion via enclaving and the Reichert prospectus which advocated boundary contraction—showed how very close boundary contraction and boundary expansion really are. Though the colleges were technically being enclaved, the continued evaluations encouraged the colleges to conform or become more compatible with the university if they were to get a good rating. This involved an informal renunciation of some of their past behavior and the adoption of some university-valued traits, which amounts to a weak form of resocialization. All of this is to say that at their edges, the four modes of institutionalization-termination begin to meld together, as do boundary expansion and boundary contraction, to form a continuum.

Movement down the continuum always constitutes failure if it occurs before the innovation has accomplished its purpose. Passage of an innovation downward in institutionalization-termination stages involves an institution wide decision and is marked by a formal degradation ceremony. After the Stern prospectus, which represented downward movement for the collegiate units, colleges were forced by the university administration to conform to a series of demands. The winners were allowed to make the rules for the losers. After the Reichert prospectus, which was a sign of further downward movement, the colleges were made to go through a public hearing that bore a certain similarity to a criminal court trial, while the chartering committee and presidential review were not dissimilar from a parole board. In any case, the colleges were forced to acknowledge the fact that they had been vanquished, and rightly so, for they were bad. This follows from the description of boundary contraction in Chapter 2.

In contrast, passage upward from the institutionalization-termination stage-to-stage from termination to diffusion is informal and occurs in an unit by unit and in a person-by-person fashion rather than involving the whole oganization. This was true in the diffusion of the colleges among S.U.N.Y.A.B. faculty and departments. Should the colleges rise from their current resocialized position to one of boundary expansion via enclaving, this would involve simply a change in attitude by individuals and departments regarding profitability, not a formal ceremony. And that, in fact, appears to be exactly what is now happening.

With three factors in mind—the definition of *failure*, that institutionalization-termination is a continuum, and that movement down the continuum represents failure—the question of why an innovation fails can now be answered. Failure results from an innovation's decline in profitability, compatibility, or both. *Compatibility* was previously defined as the degree of congruence between the personality—norms, values, and goals—of an innovation and its host. Indicators of compatibility were found to be the attitude of the innovation toward the host, the past history of the innovation, and the actual congruence of the innovation and host norms, values, and goals. The first two indicators are fudge factors that indicate the degree of examination and amount of suspicion and distrust appropriate in evaluating the innovation's compatibility with the host.

*Profitability* was previously defined as the degree to which an innovation satisfies the organizational, group, and personal needs of the host. Several different indicators of profitability were discovered. Two forms of profitability were identified as well: positive and negative profitability. *Negative profitability* exists when it is desirable to continue an innovation because treating it in any other manner would undermine already satisfied organizational, subunit, or individual needs. The likelihood of arson and campus unrest were the source of negative profitability at Buffalo in 1970. *Positive profitability* exists when an innovation is desirable in itself, and that is a stronger form of profitability. Indicators include clients, enthusiasm, uniqueness, reputation, money, outside funding, and the like.

Compatibility is a screen for measuring the organizational inappropriateness and dissatisfaction related to boundary change associated with an innovation. Profitability is a measure of the satisfaction and effectiveness of an innovation in meeting organizational needs. A decline in compatibility means that an innovation has become less appropriate and more unsatisfactory for the host. Similarly, a decline in profitability indicates that an innovation is less satisfactory and less effective.

Compatibility and profitability are the twin wheels that run the institutionalization-termination model. As compatibility declines, innovations move from boundary expansion to boundary contraction, specifically resocialization. Under normal circumstances resocialization is that brand of boundary contraction reserved for dealing with incompatibility. An innovation that attempts to serve as an alternative to the host rather than a supplement would always be extremely incompatible. Refusal to become a supplement would constitute unwillingness to become compatible. The members of College E, that preceded Cora P. Maloney College, sought to create a college that would serve as an alternative to the university. They realized that failure to become a supplement to the university would mean termination, so many key staffers left. The same was true of the College of Modern Education. Extreme incompatibility and an unwillingness to become more compatible means that the host organization is required to spend a good deal of time attempting to curb "inappropriate" behavior by the innovation. Curbing the innovation begins to take so much time that the host organization is unable to satisfy its more basic needs, which makes the innovation unprofitable and termination is the result. In such instances, unprofitability is the cause of termination; incompatibility is only an indirect cause. The negotiations between Women's Studies College and President Ketter ebbed back and forth. Women's Studies College rewrote its charter in early summer 1975, but not to the satisfaction of the president. He felt that the charter was incompatible and that the college was getting to be too much trouble, so he refused to sign the charter—which amounted to termination. Fortunately for Women's Studies College, it was very strong in the profitability realm and that saved it from termination and allowed instead a resumption of negotiations of the college's future. The basic facts in the case point to a link between profitability and compatibility, such that when an innovation becomes too incompatible, it then becomes unprofitable.

A decline in profitability, like a decline in compatibility, moves an innovation from boundary expansion to boundary contraction, except that unprofitability results in termination rather than resocialization. Termination is the variety of boundary contraction associated with unprofitability. Profitability would seem to be more important than compatibility in innovation success. This is not surprising in that it is likely easier to eliminate the dissatisfaction associated with incompatibility than to generate the satisfaction associated with profitability. The importance of profitability is shown in that the colleges at S.U.N.Y.A.B. with high profitability were given greater latitude with regard to compatibility than less profitable colleges. This is especially interesting in that it occurred during boundary contraction via resocialization, which is concerned chiefly with compatibility. The importance of profitability is perhaps best underlined by the behavior of S.U.N.Y.A.B. faculty. Faculty chose to participate more heavily in departments than the colleges because departments were more profitable. This was true even of faculty members who felt the colleges

## Conclusions

more compatible with their personal life-styles than their departments. Profitability is of concern to both the innovation and the host. As was indicated, an innovation must be profitable to the host, but the host must also be profitable to the innovation. For example, the College of Progressive Education was terminated by the host for being unprofitable, while College Z decided to terminate itself because it found the host unprofitable. Similarly, many old college people left their colleges because they felt that continuing a relationship with the host to be unprofitable. A reciprocal relationship between the host and the innovation was not found for compatibility, however.

The answer to the question, Why innovation fails? would then be because it is either unprofitable or incompatible. The degree of failure is greater if it is unprofitable.

### How Innovation Fails

Institutionalization-termination decision-making is a political process. This is so because institutionalization-termination occurs in times of strife and is concerned with creating laws that will resolve the issues leading to the strife and thwart its future occurrence. In any law-making procedure, some people win and others lose; that is, laws are vehicles for controlling behavior, so that any law will limit the behavior of some individuals. Even in a society that chooses to make murder a crime, there must be some people who gained fame, fortune, and power because of their success at murder. Such people lose the source of their livelihood—they are the losers.

The law-making procedure of institutionalization-termination decision-making looks much like our national system of law-making. There were operating subcommittees that reported to a legislature, in this instance the Buffalo faculty senate. The faculty senate laws were subject to the approval or veto of the executive, the president of the university. There were also lobbies, pressure groups, and procedures for appealing unjustly perceived laws. Lacking in the process was the U.S. system of checks and balances. The legislature was only advisory to the president and the body of appeal was the faculty senate, the same group as the legislature. The senate was probably the accepted appeal body, both because of its collective expertise and because it was more representative of the university than the executive. The rationale for the differences in U.S. and S.U.N.Y.A.B. law-making was that the university is a community of scholars where it is assumed that the most reasonable ideas will prevail. The elaborate network of checks and cross-checks would seem unnecessary in such an environment. As the university has become more a mirror of society in recent years, its legal machinery has become more and more elaborate, perhaps someday achieving the complexity of that of the society. Certainly litigation at the university is booming. A 1978 survey by the Carnegie Council found that law suits were up at three out of four of the nation's most prestigious research institutions—the Yales, the Harvards, Michigans, and Berkeleys of the country. By the way, the elaborate machinery of institutionalization-termination is unlikely to exist in many other types of organizations.

The form of institutionalization-termination selected by the host is determined by people and times. In times of plenty, the planned mode of institutionalization for the colleges was boundary expansion via diffusion. In times of steady state, the actual mode of institutionalization was boundary contraction. Similarly, the form of institutionalization that was selected varied from Martin Meyerson to Robert Ketter. The desired form of institutionalization-termination varied from faculty senate chairman to faculty senate chairman. Good times as opposed to bad times, and innovators like Meyerson in contrast to consolidators like Ketter, tend to favor more generous terms of institutionalization-termination. The reasons were explored in Chapter 3.

In any case, the university appears a rather generous organization in its reluctance to terminate innovations. The attitude of innocent-until-proven-guilty, which permits an innovation to continue until it proves it is unworkable, rather than being made to prove itself worthy of continuing, was found to be widespread at S.U.N.Y.A.B. The outcome of such an attitude, however, is continued skepticism in the host regarding the innovation after institutionalization-termination. In order to increase its share of university resources, an innovation must then prove it is a legitimate activity of the host. At steady-state S.U.N.Y.A.B., the colleges were being required to prove they

## Conclusions

are better than existing departments to get their fair share. This is quite surprising. Normally one would expect a sense of legitimacy to precede the decision not to terminate an innovation.

Two characteristics of university organizations might explain the prevalence of the innocent-until-proven-guilty philosophy. First, the university has no obviously measurable criteria for success. For instance, a company that makes pens can see if a new product increases monetary profit. If it does, or has the potential to do so, it is profitable; if it does not, it is unprofitable. This is a bit simplistic, but the university has nothing even remotely approaching such a measure. Its goals are abstract and so are its measures of profitability. As a result, it is harder for a university to justify the termination of a program or activity.

Second, the modern or practiced concept of academic freedom makes justification of termination even more difficult. Academic freedom has come to be the right of faculty to teach in strict privacy and to do their research in isolation. In fact, student course evaluations have been criticized by faculty for violating their academic freedom. The problem then is that autonomy has become popularly linked with academic freedom, encouraging existing programs and activities simply to continue because scrutiny of any sort is inappropriate.

Nonetheless, colleges and universities do practice boundary contraction and sometimes even termination, but likely at a lower rate than other organizations. The degree to which a host organization is capable of making a negative institutonalization-termination decision is dependent upon the degree of internal solidarity with regard to shared orientations—norms, values, and goals. As campus wide shared orientations coalesced at S.U.N.Y.A.B., institutionalization-termination grew harsher and harsher even though the colleges were more tame in later years. The greater and more widespread the host divisions, the more rancorous the institutionalization-termination and the less likely a permanent solution will be reached. In such an environment, multiple modes of institutionalization-termination are proposed and gain constituent backing. The 1970 institutionalization of the colleges that occurred on a campus divided over norms, values, and goals was characterized by rancor, temporary solutions, and support for a multitude of institutionalization-termination solutions. Interestingly, there is never total agreement. Even in 1974, when agreement was rather widespread, several modes of institutionalization occurred at the same time. While the colleges were being subjected to boundary contraction, boundary expansion was also occurring. The reason is that there were administrative subunits and individuals within the host organization whose needs differed from the rest. But, as would be expected, boundary contraction—which coincided with the more commonly shared orientation—rather than boundary expansion was the predominant fate of the colleges.

In instances of political division, the innovation is given an increasingly important role in negotiating an institutionalization-termination solution. Institutionalization-termination becomes a matter of negotiating an acceptable solution. The colleges were more influential in 1970 in prospectus development and acceptance than in 1974, when the campus was more united. The actual negotiation process can best be seen in the discrepancy between the 1970 faculty poll favoring strong controls on the colleges and the vote of the faculty senate for the lenient Stern prospectus. Under conditions of political division, more emphasis is placed on control procedures than an innovation substance because there is little common ground between the most extremely divided groups. Procedures can be agreed upon more easily than the substance of an innovation. The 1970 Stern prospectus was concerned primarily with procedural aspects of the colleges, such as the number of credits a student could take per term, the procedures for approving experimental courses, and so on. This was not nearly as true of the Reichert prospectus, which demanded considerable faculty involvement and ended the experimental course option. When there are political divisions, extremists are able to decide the course of institutionalization-termination, but are ineffective or excluded under conditions of political solidarity. Dissident elements of the faculty and student body had to be appeased during 1970 institutionalization-termination or there was a danger of unrest being resumed. In 1974 extremist elements were ineffective both during the faculty debates and in the chartering committee. Under all circumstances institutionalization-termination results in greater formalization of innovation procedures such as governance, hiring,

## Conclusions

and the like; but under conditions of political division, the degree of formalization is less. The colleges became more formalized under the Reichert prospectus than the Stern prospectus. This is because greater host solidarity results in greater scrutiny of the innovation and less in-fighting within the host.

Despite the conditions under which institutionalization-termination occurs, it may be repeated several times. If, as mentioned, it occurs in a politically divided host, it is more likely to be repeated at least once after the host stabilizes; however, even in a nonpolitically divided host, changes in times and personnel, host and innovation, can trigger another institutionalization-termination phase. The difficulty with repeated institutionalizations is that they are a drastic and gross way of adjusting the relationship between an innovation and the host. They are very time-consuming, require months to be completed, and necessitate a mobilization of host membership.

An easier mechanism is regulation. This involves controlling the flow of host resources to the innovation, the internal procedures of the innovation, and the autonomy of the innovation from the host. Both the Stern and Halstead prospectuses advocated boundary expansion via enclaving. By means of regulation, the status of an innovation under any mode of institutionalization-termination can be increased or decreased. The Halstead document, by imposing greater regulations, brought the colleges closer to boundary contraction.

Regulation is a function of the host. It has the advantage of being quick, razor-edged, and lacking in the machinery that makes institutionalization-termination cumbersome. Regulation increases as an innovation is perceived to be either decreasingly profitable or decreasingly compatible, which means that the innovation is perceived in some way to be illegitimate by the host. The lack of legitimacy is signaled through the recognition of innovation abuses. The imposition of regulations always serves as an organizational boundary-marker pointing out unacceptable or illegitimate behavior. In this manner regulations, like institutionalization-termination, can help to clarify boundaries. In fact, the amount of regulation which consists of rule-making and enforcement increases as the quality and quantity of innovation abuses are perceived to increase. Regulation began at Buffalo as a half-hearted effort by administrators, and became increasingly tough, wider in scope, and greater in amount as time passed. The enforcement of regulations is selective. For instance, departments at Buffalo were not punished for failing to have their courses approved as were the colleges. When the number of regulations increases sufficiently, they are incorporated into a new institutionalization-termination document. The Halstead prospectus was such a document.

As regulation increased, the colleges at Buffalo complained louder and more often about violations of their autonomy. As with institutionalization-termination appeals, the faculty senate served as the ultimate judge of the correctness of the regulations. The senate was an excellent body for carrying out that function in that it had to guard itself against the executive as well. To permit the executive to overstep his or her boundaries with regard to the innovation was to invite similar activity with regard to the faculty. All organizations do not have such established and readily available appeal procedures. The university is a particularly democratic organization.

When the host—through institutionalization-termination or regulation—required changes of the colleges, they usually reacted to the demand by complaining and complying. Most innovations develop a desire to continue and are dependent on the host for sustenance. At times, accepting a change meant the loss of characteristics associated with the purpose for creating the college. For instance, some colleges had created academic communities for students or excellent centers of identification, yet were reorganized in a manner that undermined those communities. Such changes sometimes resulted in a continuation of the position formerly held by an innovation on the institutionalization-termination continuum rather than a decline.

Innovations were found to have complied with the host in three ways. They included: piecemeal change, holistic change, and merger. Two ways of not buckling to the host were encountered as well. Some colleges took a passive stance, choosing simply to stay as they were. In all cases such a decision was ultimately reversed or subject to negotiation—it was never a successful solution. The more successful way of refusing to comply with host demands was by self-termination. The only college that was incompatible with the university that did not change significantly was College Z, which closed.

*Conclusions*

The failure of an innovation involves several steps:

1. A need is perceived by the host for institutionalization or termination of the innovation after its trial period. If the innovation is successful, an institution wide and formal institutionalization-termination process does not occur. Under such conditions, informal institutionlization-termination and regulation are sufficient to align the innovation with the host.
2. One or more plans for institutionalization-termination are formulated and one is approved.
3. The plan is implemented and initiated.
4. The innovation is subsequently regulated by the host as perceived necessary. The process is repeated as many times as necessary, with the innovation moving down the boundary expansion-boundary contraction continuum with each repetition.

CHAPTER 6

# *Implications: A Literature Review*

Chapter 1 boldly proclaimed that a great deal is known about innovation. A few tantilizing morsels were dangled before the reader. But to be quite candid and to provide a rationale for writing this book, it was pointed out that there are also serious gaps in our knowledge. So far this volume has attempted to fill a few of these holes — at least that was the hope for Chapters 2 through 5. With that done, it's now time to pull together what we knew at the outset and what we learned in the course of this book.

In the quest to discover why innovation fails, this volume emphasized two related subjects — organizations, universities in particular, as locations for innovation and innovations themselves. For the remainder of this chapter each will be examined in turn. The three purposes for doing this are: 1) to see if the institutionalization-termination model presented in Chapters 2 to 5 is consistent with the existing literature on innovation and change; 2) to see if the existing literature adds any further explanation to the institutionalization-termination model; and, 3) to see if the institutionalization-termination models adds any "explanatory power" to the existing literature. This entails a research review of sorts — a review of major findings in the literature rather than a review of the full range of publications of the subject. The procedure will be to present conclusions from key research pertaining to colleges and universities as well as organizations in general, and to examine the implications in terms of the institutionalization-termination model.

*Conclusions*

Let's begin with organizations since that is how this book began. The author is aware that "consistency is the hobgoblin of little minds," but argues in turn that symmetry in defense of scholarship is no vice.

*Organizations*

Aside from innovation, and perhaps change, organization is the key concept of this volume. The term was prominent in each of the last five chapters, and detailed (some might say minute) attention was given to the case study organization, the State University of New York at Buffalo. The irony is that organization is a relatively unimportant part of the institutionalization-termination model. It is what might be called "a given."

The model starts with the organization. Regardless of its variations, there is no change in the model. It is the innovation that must vary. No matter what the nature of the organization, the innovation must be compatible and profitable with it if the innovation is to succeed. Otherwise, failure is always the consequence. As a result, this discussion of organizations can do little in the way of confirming or disconfirming the model. What it can do, though, is to amplify and elaborate upon both the current literature on organization and change, and the institutionalization-termination model.

The fact of the matter is that innovation is more likely to occur in some types of organizations than others. Shepard (1969) refers to the extreme examples of this phenomenon as "Innovation-Resisting and Innovation-Producing Organizations." At the risk of laboring the obvious, these are the organizations at opposite ends of the resistance continuum. There are certain systematic differences between them, three in particular. And that is the subject matter that this discussion of organizations will deal with.

*1. Innovation Resistance Is Related to Organizational Stability*

This is the finding of JB Lon Hefferlin (1969). He examined the correlates of innovativeness or, as Hefferlin called it, dynamism in, of all places, colleges and universities. His research, published under the title *Dynamics of Academic Reform,* involves a study of a representative sample of 110 colleges and universities. Hefferlin found instability to be the critical ingredient for the innovation producing organization. He reported that colleges without graduate programs—and thus more chance for instability or change—had a greater rate of change than universities. Academic reform was also more prevalent at colleges and universities with changing faculties owing to expansion and turnover, low rates of tenure, junior staff members influential in educational policy-making, rotating department chairpersons, and trustees and educational leaders oriented more toward change than stability. Student-centered institutions—that is, colleges and universities financially dependent on attracting students and their tuition money—and those located in metropolitan areas also exhibited a proclivity for change, due, as were other factors, to greater instability.

Hefferlin's thesis goes beyond the institutionalization-termination model. The kind of college he describes as innovative is one that might be classified (using the language of the model) as lacking in rigid boundaries. Owing to changing leadership, a changing staff, a changing marketplace, a changing environment or locale, and the absence of a static graduate school ethic, such schools are more flexible and open. If we analogize an organization's boundaries to the belt holding up a pair of pants, we might say that Hefferlin's colleges are circumscribed by a loose belt with a few extra notches for breathing room. If the wearer of such a belt puts on a few extra pounds, the belt need not be adjusted. Similarly, if an organization departs from its norms, values, and goals a small amount, no change need be made in its boundaries if the boundaries are flexible or nonrigid. To a certain extent boundary expansion occurs automatically. It is just a matter of taking up the available slack.

Dropping the belt analogy (to the pleasure of the author and most certainly the reader), *flexible boundaries* means there is greater likelihood of boundary expansion when an organization is faced with an innovation. The opposite is true of rigid boundaries. In that case, it is more likely that innovation differences with the host will be perceived as deviant, resulting in boundary contraction. Under such conditions, innovations are unlikely to be adopted or to persist if already adopted. All of this is to say that in stable or rigid organizations, innovations are more likely to be perceived as incompatible, unprofitable, or both.

*Conclusions*

It is interesting to note, though, that rigid boundaries do not necessarily make for a stuffy or traditional organizaton. Burton Clark (1970) sends this message via his book, *The Distinctive College,* a study of the "organizational sagas" of three innovative colleges—Antioch, Reed, and Swarthmore. Each was a school that struck out on its own to achieve a nontraditional or exceptionally innovative mission. Such endeavors are always subject to what John Weingart and I have called the centripetal force of inertia. That is, all kinds of forces inside and outside the organization press to make it more like traditional organizations of its type. The only protection for such organizations is rigid boundaries. In the case of Clark's three colleges, this meant a small, little-changing core of personnel; a little-changing program; clearly articulated clientele and financial support groups; a student subculture for socializing entering students to appropriate norms, values, and goals; and a true ideology. In combination, these elements preserved the three experiments. At the same time, they ruled out other types of innovation, which more than likely would have been the traditional practices of other institutions. For the three colleges, such practices would indeed have represented innovations, but undesirable ones from the point of view of their innovative missions. And that is the function of boundaries—to preserve the status quo. It seems quite reasonable to think that the more the status quo is valued or the external environment feared by an organization, the more rigid its boundaries.

*2. Innovation Resistance Is Related to a Variety of
   Organizational Variables*

Hage and Aiken (1970, chapter 2) offer an awfully good summary of the principal organizational variables that most past researchers have said influence the innovation-producing or resisting qualities of an organization. Bear in mind, however, that this research is not without its critics. For instance, Zaltman, Duncan, and Holbek (1973) argue that the relationships postulated by Hage and Aiken do not hold throughout the innovation process, but rather at particular stages. Their criticism appears apt and similar criticisms of this variety may be wholly justified, but they do not diminish the value of the Hage and Aiken work for our present discussions. What Hage and Aiken

## Implications: A Literature Review

offer the reader are postulates concerning the likelihood of change associated with seven different organizational variables. So far as the weight of present research is concerned, it supports Hage and Aiken, provided the postulates are taken to refer to general tendencies or directions for change or innovatoin. The postulates do not necessarily apply to particular organizations, specific periods of time, and definitely not to each of the individual stages of the innovation process. The Hage and Aiken postulates are:

> The greater the formalization (i.e., the greater the degree of codification of jobs, the greater the number of rules specifying what is to be done, and the more strictly rules are enforced), the lower the rate of organizational change.

> The greater the complexity (i.e., the greater the number of occupational specialities of an organization and the greater the degree of professionalism of each), the greater the rate of organizational change.

> The higher the centralization (i.e., the smaller the proportion of jobs and occupations that participate in decision-making and the fewer the decision-making areas in with they are involved), the lower the rate of organizational change.

> The greater the stratification (i.e., the greater the disparity in rewards such as salaries and prestige between the top and bottom ranks of an organization), the lower the rate of organizational change.

> The higher the volume of production (i.e., emphasis on quantity versus quality in organizational outputs), the lower the rate of organizational change.

> The greater the emphasis on efficiency (i.e., concern with cost or resource reduction), the lower the rate of organizational change.

> The higher job satisfaction (i.e., between organizational morale), the greater the rate of organizational change.

These seven postulates flow directly from the institutionalization-termination model. The first three postulates are matters of compatibility and the next four are concerned with profitability.

## Conclusions

With regard to compatibility, it is not surprising that increased formalization reduces change. This is the phenomenon just discussed —rigid boundaries. The more rules, jobs, or other aspects of organizational life that are codified, 1) the more rigid are organizational boundaries 2) the more limited the range of acceptable norms, values, and goals, and 3) the less likely innovation is to persist.

Complexity and centralization are opposites in terms of compatibility. Complexity increases the number of autonomous decision-makers or decision-making units in an organization. That is the essence of specialization and professionalization. By definition, centralization reduces both the number of decision-makers and decision areas. As regards compatibility then, complexity tends to increase the range of acceptable norms, values, and goals of an organization by increasing both the number of people whose opinions matter and the number of areas in which those opinions matter. Centralization does just the opposite and thereby reduces the range of acceptable norms, values, and goals. This means that the complex organization is likely to have a wider range of acceptable norms, values, and goals than the less complex organization. And the centralized organization is likely to have a narrower range of acceptable norms, values, and goals than the less centralized organization. So as complexity increases, the likelihood of an innovation being incompatible with the organization declines. As centralization increases, the likelihood of incompatibility increases. The result is more boundary expansion in the more complex organization and more boundary contraction in the more centralized organization.

Let's turn now to profitability. Stratification or wide disparity in the distribution of rewards from the top to bottom of an organization must certainly discourage innovation. Decision-makers tend to be people in the higher echelons of an organization, and for them innovation is threatening. It involves jeopardizing their status. To change things requires risking their goodies to some degree. That is unprofitable, and unprofitability always leads to boundary contraction. Were decisions made by people at the bottom of the organizational hierarchy, the likelihood of innovation would undoubtedly rise.

Productivity and efficiency are examples of a narrow range of profitability. Recall that profitability is defined as the degree to which an innovation satisfies adopter needs. If the potential adopter of an innovation either has no need because productivity and efficiency are high, or defines the need very narrowly in terms of productivity or efficiency alone, the likelihood of innovation is significantly reduced —most potential innovations will appear unprofitable.

Finally, job satisfaction is a very basic need. Until that need is satisfied, it is highly unlikely, as mentioned earlier, that solutions to more advanced needs will be sought. This also reduces the potential for innovation. Most innovations will appear unprofitable.

By way of conclusion, one might say that established organizational characteristics—like complexity, centralization, formalization, stratification, efficiency, productivity, and job satisfaction—dictate the degree to which innovation in general will be compatible and profitable with an organization. The likelihood of innovation incompatibility is increased in an organization that is low in complexity and high in formalization and centralization. Universities, by the way, tend to be high in complexity and low in formalization and centralization. The likelihood of innovation unprofitability is increased in an organization that is low in job satisfaction, efficiency, and productivity. Here again universities have the opposite mix of characteristics. Accordingly, institutions of higher education might be classified as low in innovation resistance relative to organizations in general.

*3. Innovation Resistance Is Related to Organizational Character*

Organizational character, the gestalt or total complexion of a particular organization, is one of those topics that is best explored by careful study of a specific organization, so we will fall back on the university here.

The 1960s and early 1970s produced a flurry, probably closer to an avalanche, of publications about the organization of American colleges and universities. It was a transitory interest spurred largely by student unrest. And with the apparent return of quiet to the nation's campuses, this brand of research has become passe, though the rise of collective bargaining and faculty unionism in recent years have kept some interest in the subject alive and a trickle of literature in the pipeline.

## Conclusions

The legacy of this effort is a hodgepodge of the good, the bad, and the ugly. What stands out are a variety of alternate descriptions of the university as an organization. Particularly noteworthy are John Millett's (1962) characterization of the university as a collegial organization in his book *The Academic Community,* Herbert Stroup's (1966) depiction of the university as a bureaucratic organization in his volume *Bureaucracy in Higher Education,* and J. Victor Baldridge's (1971) portrayal of the university as a political organization in his case study of New York University entitled *Power and Conflict in the University.*

Each description seemed to bear a grain of truth. The image of the collegial organization is readily apparent in the decision-making of college faculties, who collectively determine the promotion of staff and the direction of educational policy. This would be an apt description of the way the Buffalo faculty senate performed in the case study. The picture of the university as a bureaucracy is observable in the hierarchical ordering of university personnel with a chain of command that includes department chairpersons, division heads, school deans, academic vice presidents, presidents, and trustees. Indeed, the lack of such organization was considered one of the failings in the case study colleges by the State University of New York at Buffalo. The political portrait of the university was confirmed daily in the newspaper accounts of campus unrest in the late 1960s. It was certainly one of the most prominent features of the Buffalo case study. The fact of the matter is that each of these descriptors does an excellent job of characterizing some aspects of college or university organization, but none describes it fully. In general, they call to mind the parable of the blind men and the elephant. Each blind man touched a different portion of the animal and took that for the whole. Just as the elephant is not a snake as the blind man who touched its tail said, so the university is not wholly a bureaucratic, collegial, or political organization.

With the hope of building a better elephant, it's useful to consider just what went wrong with past writings. Several things come immediately to mind. The Millett and Stroup volumes are essays intended to describe the university as a particular type of organization, rather than to impartially assess the organizational character of the university. Both authors were quite successful in their endeavors. They convincingly demonstrated that a number of college activities are governed by a single form of organization, but neither book, nor both taken together, provides the basis for a comprehensive theory of the entire university as an organization.

The Baldridge thesis grows out of a solid research base, but the research is of the type that David Riesman has called "firehouse research—the alarm bell rings, the researcher slides down the greased pole, rushes to the fire, and begins collecting data" (Keniston, 1973, p. xv). In Baldridge's case, the fire alarm was a cornocopia of assorted troubles at New York University. His research was concerned with how these troubles were resolved. His case study is remarkably good, but his conclusions suffer from weaknesses germane to all firehouse research. To change metaphors in midstream, Baldridge took a snapshot when what was needed was a motion picture. His snapshot caught only a portion of the university and caught it at only one moment in time. It missed the organization in its entirety and it missed the historical perspective. The current organization of higher education is a product of almost 350 years of evolution in which the university has grown by increasing the number and kind of activities in which it engages. The snapshot of recent troubles fails to capture the rich pattern of elaboration, change, and interaction of the old with the new that have provided the continuity over time of college and university organization.

In short, current literature about the university as an organization has had three basic weaknesses:

1. It has failed to consider the university as a whole, dealing instead with selected activities.

2. It has failed to regard the university as a historical entity, focusing instead upon the university at a single moment in time, usually a time of crisis.

3. It has failed to regard the organizational character of the university as pluralistic, emphasizing instead a single type or form of organization.

In the next few pages an alternate analysis or typology of the university as an organization will be offered. It grows directly out of the past writings and seeks to improve upon them by responding to

*Conclusions*

the weaknesses that have just been pointed out. The typology is historic in origin. It is based upon the three functions that comprise the mission of American institutions of higher learning—teaching, research, and service. The typology offers a comprehensive analysis of higher education organization since all of the activities associated with colleges and universities in this country have grown from the teaching, research, and service functions, and are to the present day designed to support and pursue those functions. Finally, the product of the typology is pluralistic in its depiction of college and university organization.

## A Typology of University Organization

The mission of the American university has not always been trifunctional. The earliest American college, established in 1636, was a single-purpose institution and that purpose was teaching. Only gradually over the next 275 years did American colleges grow to include the research and service functions. The growth occurred by expansion rather than substitution. That is, colleges adopted new functions one at a time by adding them to their existing function or functions rather than by substituting the new function for the old. Different schools adopted the new functions and the activities associated with them in different ways, and the newly adopted functions and activities were emphasized in varying degree at different schools. The typology that follows draws upon these differences, based as it is upon institutions that, for a time, emphasized one function far more greatly than others. The typology describes the forms of organization that govern university and college activities emphasizing each of higher education's primary functions and combinations thereof.

### Activities Associated with the Teaching Function

We think of teaching as a cooperative endeavor, a communion of sorts between student and teacher, student and student, and teacher and teacher. Expressions like *living* and *learning* are intimately associated with it. Accordingly, activities associated with the teaching function of universities tend to be organized in a collegial or communal manner. This, according to John Millett (1962, p. 235),

## Implications: A Literature Review

... presupposes an organization in which functions are differentiated and in which specialization must be brought together in a harmonious whole. But this process of bringing together, of coordination if your will, is achieved not through a structure of superordination and subordination of persons and groups, but through a dynamic of consensus.

The key elements of the Millett definition are differentiation of function, a sense of wholeness, nonhierarchical structure, and consensus of opinion. They are all found in the American colonial college and its predecessor, the medieval college. Both were exclusively teaching institutions. The colonial college was small in size, populated by a homogeneous group of people, and modeled after the Cambridge colleges in England. It has been described as "a large family sleeping, eating, studying, and worshipping together" (Rudolph, 1962 p., 88). The roles in this family were differentiated. The faculty acted as moral guardians or parents, and the students, who were often considerably younger than contemporary college students, were treated as children. The family was nonhierarchical. There were no faculty ranks and no administration to speak of. The sense of wholeness and consensus of opinion grew out of a shared religious commitment. College presidents were ministers, the majority of faculty were ministers, and until the middle of the eighteenth century, 50 percent of the students became ministers after graduation (Brubacher and Rudy, 1976, pp. 8, 10).

The continental medieval college was larger than the colonial college, but similarly communal.[1] The University of Paris, for instance, was divided into "nations," four cooperative and nonhierarchical groups, that were crcatcd to protect faculty and students who were strangers in foreign university towns and to provide them with classroom space, dormitories, and other forms of assistance including burial service. The larger size of the medieval college made reaching a consensus more difficult for it than the colonial college. However, consensus was reached, but only because daily life at these "self-governing and self-respecting" institutions was much consumed by meetings (Haskins, 1967, p. 50).

---

[1] For a brief description of the medieval college and "nations," see Schachner.

## Conclusions

*Activities Associated with the Research Function*

When people think of research, the image that comes quickly to mind is the philologist, looking like Monte Wooley, laboring alone late at night in his ill-lit room, hunched over a partially legible ancient manuscript with magnifying lens in hand; or the solitary scientist, played by Paul Muni, feverishly mixing chemicals as dawn's early light streams through his small laboratory window. Research tends to be individual or small-group work, and the university activities associated with it are anomically or atomistically organized. This form of organization, not previously discussed, has frequently been attributed to the university by angry parents, politicians, and law officers, but it has not been incorporated into the serious organizational literature. *Anomic organization* is a state of relative normlessness that exists when individual desires predominate in a college rather than commonly agreed-upon norms. *Anomic* is too strong a term, being inimical to the notion of organization, but gives a sense of the entropy associated with the research mission of the university. *Atomistic* is perhaps the better term.

In any case, atomistic organization provides an apt description of life at Johns Hopkins University, America's first research university, which was founded in Baltimore in 1876. Hopkins had both a teaching and a research function, but the emphasis was decidedly upon research. For example, the first entering class included 54 graduate students and only 12 matriculated undergraduates (Hawkins, 1960 p. 90). Hopkins was built firmly on the foundation of the German research university. The two key concepts of *lernfreiheit*, which granted students the right to attend school when they wanted and the ability to take whatever courses they wished, and *lehrfreiheit*, which gave faculty the right to teach and publish research of interest regardless of findings, were imported directly from Germany. At Hopkins the commitment to *lehrfreiheit* meant that faculty and departments were given the freedom to design their own courses and workloads. The commitment to *lernfreiheit* gave students the freedom to take whatever programs they chose. The result of the new freedoms was "extreme specialization" by faculty, the development of "semi-autonomous" departments, and an individually isolated student body (French, 1946, pp. 45, 335). Meetings of the entire Hopkins faculty were "rare and without authority" (Hawkins, 1960, p. 213). The first Johns Hopkins president "compared the members of the university to a hive of bees each storing up honey in a narrow cell unobserving and unobserved" (pp. 308-309). An assistant commented that most Hopkins men had "little real knowledge of what others are doing" (p. 309).

*Activities Associated with the Service Function*

When people complain about the long lines, having to go from office to office for information, and speaking to supervisor after supervisor, more often than not they are talking about the university service function. Activities associated with it tend to be organized in a bureaucratic fashion. Herbert Stroup (1966, p 14) defines bureaucracy:[2]

> as a large-scale organization with a complex, but definite social function. It consists moreover, of a specialized personnel and is guided by a system of rules and procedures. In addition, a carefully contrived hierarchy exists in which the social function of the burearcracy is carried out impersonally.

All of the elements of the Stroup definition can be found in the most well-known American experiment in service that originated at the University of Wisconsin in 1904. Charles Van Hise, then president of the university, declared that the entire state of Wisconsin was the campus of the university. The service function involved the university with the state legislature, local government, civic groups, and the office of the governor. Numerous faculty applied their scholarly expertise to state problems. The service function also encouraged the university to extend education into the community through the development of off-campus study and off-campus courses. As part of this effort the university sent renowned faculty to teach short, popularized courses in the large towns and cities, offered technical and how-to-do-it instruction on campus, and established large

---

[2]Stroup will be used as the source here rather than Max Weber, the father of bureaucracy, since Stroup deals specifically with institutions of higher education. Moreover, the Stoup definition obviously grows out of Weber's work.

*Conclusions*

extension and correspondence programs. The service effort was so broadly conceived that one Wisconsin booster went so far as to say that the cow was one of the by-products of higher education in Wisconsin "for the university saved the dairy industry" (Rudolph, 1962, p. 364). As a result of the commmitment to the service function, the University of Wisconsin became a larger and more complex organization.[3] New services were added and the university was reorganized into schools which were subdivided into departments. The university also became more hierarchical in structure. The faculty meeting declined in prominence and the power of high level administrators increased. Furthermore, specialization of roles grew as the number of middle management deans proliferated. Given the massive growth of staff and activities associated with the service mission, rules, regulations, and impersonality grew more abundant as well.

*Activities Associated with Multiple Functions*

Activities associated with multiple functions are often politically organized. According to Baldridge, political organization involves strategic conflict in which campus interest groups are, at the same time, struggling with one another and cooperating. The essence of political organization is "negotiation and the exchange of advantages and favors." The objective of participation in political organization is to "wring concessions and advantages" from the college or university community without destroying it (Baldridge, 1971, pp. 203-204).

Political organization differs from the other three forms of organization in that there is no historic ideal type from which it descends. It occurs only when there is conflict within a college or university about which forms of organization or whose opinion should govern activities that serve more than one of the teaching, research, or service functions. Activities with multiple functions are likely to result in conflict because the research, teaching, and service functions call for three different form of governance that make competing and irreconcilable demands upon college personnel. Atomistic, collegial, and bureaucratic organization each cede decision-making power to differ-

---

[3]For a discussion of changes at Wisconsin as a result of the service function, see Curti and Carstensen (1949, p. 105-107).

ent campus groups. Atomistic organization grants the individual student and faculty member the power to make decisions. The voice of each is the voice that counts. Collegial organization grants decision-making power to a collectivity of students and faculty, with no one individual able to make decisions for the entire group. It is the collective voice that matters. Bureaucratic organization places differing amounts of decision-making power in the hands of different campus groups. However, it is the voice of the person at the top that is heard. This means the chief administrator, who is not given any decision-making power in atomistic organization, is given the most power in bureaucratic organization. Quite an interesting situation!

For this reason, when the people in a college community disagee about the nature of an activity and the form of decision-making that should govern that activity, the community divides into smaller competing groups. Each group is composed of people with shared definitions of how the disputed activity should be construed, and each applies pressure to have its definition of the situation accepted by the entire community.

*Putting It All Together*

The typology, then, indicates that four forms of organization operate simultaneously in American colleges and universities. Three-collegial, atomistic and bureaucratic organization-govern the activities historically associated with higher education's primary functions of teaching, research, and service, respectively. The fourth form of organization, political organization, although associated with activities that serve more than one of the three functions, is not necessarily the form of organization for all multiple-functioned activities that colleges pursue. Colleges avoid political organization by agreeing to stress one of the multiple functions that an activity involves rather than the others. Thus, while all or most institutions of higher education tend to at least dabble in teaching, research, and service, different types of colleges and universities place different emphases on each. The community college emphasizes the service function, the liberal arts college emphasizes the teaching function, and the research university emphasizes the research function.

Colleges also avoid political organization by subdividing multi-

## Conclusions

functional activities and organizing different parts of the activity in different ways. With regard to courses, for instance, doctoral dissertation guidance, which emphasizes research, might be organized atomistically while introductory or survey courses, which emphasize teaching, are often organized collegially.

Nonetheless, universities are always politically organized. It is the degree of political organization that varies. At Buffalo, for instance, political organization appeared to be the dominant form of organization during 1969-1970. Despite the obvious harmony on campus in 1974, there was still political organization, but it was so small as to be discountable as a force in governing the university.

Similarly, the mix of the four organizational forms would be expected to vary from college to college. This is so because different colleges pursue slightly different activities, have different functional emphases, and probably classify the activities they engage in somewhat differently with respect to teaching, research, and service.

In a like manner, the mix of the four organizational types at any one university would be expected to vary with time. For example, after the U.B. merger with the State University of New York, there was an organizational change to match the change in mission. In its transition from a local, private service university under Clifford Furnas and the presidents preceding him to a public university stewarded by Martin Meyerson, the organizational character of U.B. decreased in the degree to which it was bureaucratic and increased to the extent it was anomic.

*Innovation or Organizational Character*

Enough said about universities for the moment. Despite their unique characteristics as organizations (see Perkins, 1972), several conclusions can be drawn from the discussion about organizational character in general and about resistance to innovation in particular.

The character of a specific organization is a product of its history and the various organizational forms or types of which it is composed. The character of the university, for example, was said to be a product of nearly 350 years of history and four organizational types (bureaucratic, anomic, collegial, and political organization). In the university's case, the organizational types were mission-related and may be in other organizations as well.

The character of few, if any organizations, can be accurately described as being wholly of one type. Even if one type appears

## Implications: A Literature Review

dominant, other types generally exist in its shadow. By the way, the four types found in the university are not exclusive. Other types, such as coercive organization, may be found in different organizations, such as prisons.

The mix of types in a particular organization will likely vary with time, circumstance, and organizational mission.

As organizational character changes, so does the innovation-producing or resisting character of that organization. The reason is that each organizational type incorporates a different level of innovation resistance. For example, collegial organization builds in a high level of innovation resistance through its decision-making process. Decisions are based on consensus. Consequently all or most people must agree to adopt an innovation. Even if the majority favor an innovation, a minority can veto it. Ironically in such organizations, once an innovation is adopted, it persists practically forever since a consensus is needed to terminate it. In contrast, anomic organization incorporates a low level of innovation resistance to small innovations. Only the consent of a single individual is necessary to adopt an innovation. For larger innovations, resistance is greater. Since each member of the organization is autonomous, it is difficult to get agreement on organizationwide innovations. The situation is not dissimilar from trying to grasp sand—it trickles away grain by grain.

Given the mix of organizational types in most organizations, different activities and decisions within an organization are likely to be governed, at least to a small extent, by different organizational types, as was the case in the university. This means that innovation resistance is likely to vary throughout an organization.

As a consequence of the mix of organizational types, the individuals and groups that are involved in decision-making throughout the organization will vary. The reason is that each organizational type, as shown in the university, invests decision-making in the hands of a different assortment of people. The result is a certain variation in the standards of compatibility and profitability used throughout the organization. The less visible the innovation and the fewer people or groups involved, the wider the variation is likely to be. This is so because the fewer the actors involved in decision-making, the less likely they are to be representative of the organization.

The conclusion that would have to be drawn from this discussion is

*Conclusions*

that an organization is not a monolithic whole. This is especially the case in large complex organizations. Standards of compatibility and profitability may vary somewhat throughout the organization, which means that innovation resistance is likely to vary throughout the organization as well. While boundary expansion and innovation acceptance may be the response to an innovation in one part of an organization, boundary contraction and innovation rejection may result throughout the rest of the organization. With this happy news in mind, it is time to consider the innovation side of the ledger.

*Innovations*

Chapter 1 described the literature on innovation as extensive—that might be called the calm and understated assessment. In actuality, the publications verge on the incomprehensible by their sheer number, cutting across the fields of agriculture, anthropology, business, economics, education, history, psychology, sociology, the sciences, the professions, and most other subjects that one can think of.

For the sake of the current discussion, three types of literature need to be distinguished from the rest of the morass: 1) the literature on innovation characteristics and innovation success, 2) the literature on how to carry out successful innovation or change, and 3) the literature on obstacles to innovation success. This, in sum, is the literature most germane to the institutionalization-termination model, so this is where our discussion will begin, looking at each of the three types in turn.

*1. Literature on Innovation Characteristics and Innovation Success*

Innovation characteristics literature is comparable to the organizational variable literature already discussed. It is concerned with the specific features of an innovation—any innovation—that enhance or detract from its likelihood of being adopted or persisting. It is important to note that adoption and persistence are the most common measures of innovation success, which is different from the definition associated with the institutionalization-termination model, where success is defined negatively as the absence of downward movement on the institutionalization-termination continuum prior to the innovation's

## Implications: A Literature Review

accomplishment of its purpose. The implications of this will be discussed later.

Current research varies considerably on the number, even the substance, of the characteristics that determine an innovation's success or failure. Zaltman and his colleagues (1973) are at the high end of the spectrum suggesting some 19 attributes. Many of the suggestions are new and there is little evidence in the literature to demonstrate their validity.

Nonetheless, if one surveys the literature as Rogers and Shoemaker (1971) have done, basing their conclusion on more than 1500 empirical and nonempirical studies, five critical characteristics emerge: *relative advantage* ("the degree to which an innovation is perceived as being better than the idea it supercedes"); *compatibility* ("the degree to which an innovation is perceived as consistent with the existing values, past experience, and needs of the receiver"), *complexity* ("the degree to which an innovation is perceived as relatively difficult to understand and use"), *trialability*, elsewhere called *triability* and *divisibility* ("the degree to which an innovation may be experimented with on a limited basis"), and *observability*, also called *communicability* ("the degree to which the results of an innovation are visible to others").

Rogers and Shoemaker (pp. 350-352) say the following relationships exist between these characteristics and innovation success.

"The relative advantage of a new idea, as perceived by members of a social system, is positively related to its rate of adoption." Sixty-seven percent of the empirical studies examining relative advantage support such a conclusion.

"The compatability of a new idea, as perceived by members of a social system, is positively related to its rate of adoption." Again, 67 percent of the empirical studies examining the characteristic confirm the relationship.

"The complexity of an innovation, as perceived by members of a social system, is not related to its rate of adoption." Previous studies show only slightly more than chance relationship between adoption and complexity. Fifty-six percent indicate a positive association.

"The trialability of an innovation, as perceived by members of a social system, is positively related to its rate of adoption." This is sup-

*Conclusions*

ported by 69 percent of the empirical studies.

"The observability of an innovation, as perceived by members of a social system, is positively related to its rate of adoption." Seventy-eight percent of the empirical studies of observability support such a conclusion.

At first blush, there does seem to be a certain disparity between the Rogers and Shoemaker conclusions and the institutionalization-termination model. Rogers and Shoemaker find four characteristics —relative advantage, compatibility, trialability, and observability— to be positively related to innovation success, while the model indicates that success is a consequence of only two characteristics— compatibility and profitability.

On further examination, this numerical disparity disappears. It should be noted that Rogers and Shoemaker are concerned with the adoption of innovation in contrast to the institutionalization-termination model which deals solely with the period after they are adopted. In Chapter 2, it was pointed out that the decision to institutionalize an innovation is much the same as the decision to adopt or initiate and implement one. But there are important differences as well. That is, the adoption of an innovation also involves the prior two steps or stages of 1) recognizing the need for an innovation, and 2) the planning and formulating of the innovation itself. And this accounts for at least two of the characteristics omitted in the institutionalization-termination model—trialability and observability.

Trialability is a matter that precedes the decision to adopt an innovation, but becomes inconsequential thereafter. It is concerned with the ability of an organization to try an innovation on the installment basis. There is a certain risk in trying anything new. If it doesn't work, there is some comfort in knowing that the situation is reversible without undue harm to the organization. Recall that this was one of the major drawbacks mentioned for holistic change. If it fails to work, there is nothing left. Be that as it may, once an innovation is in place, holistic or not, the question of trialability becomes moot. It is, as a result, a subject not even considered in the past adoption period.

As for observability, this is a concern largely of the second stage of the institutionalization-termination process—planning and formulating a solution. If an innovation is unobserved and, as a result, unknown, it is quite unlikely to be thought of as a solution to the organization's need. Observability is, for this reason, a critical innovation characteristic during the preadoption period. During the postadoption period, observability remains a concern of the innovator, but it is a concern of a different sort. It becomes a matter of rumor control, making sure that the rest of the organization has an accurate picture of the innovation. And this, though apparently a problem of observability, is more fundamentally an issue of compatibility and profitability. That is, preventing the innovation from appearing incompatible or unprofitable. Observability is by no means a necessary innovation characteristic in terms of insuring success during the postadoption period. In fact, in the case in which an innovation is actually incompatible or unprofitable, it would be advantageous from the point of view of the innovator for the innovation not to be observed by the rest of the organization.

This leaves Rogers and Shoemaker with two characteristics—relative advantage and compatibility—and the model with two characteristics—profitability and compatibility. The two sets are much the same. Relative advantage is a measure of profit. Rogers and Shoemaker (1971, p. 139) describe it as an indicator of the intensity of reward or punishment resulting from the adoption of an innovation.

Disparities in the definitions of the characteristics are, however, instructive. As for compatibility, both Rogers and Shoemaker, and the model are referring to precisely the same phenomenon-the fit between an innovation and the organization. The difference in definitions here is trivial. It can be chalked up to the model's reliance on traditional sociological terminology, and Rogers and Shoemaker's use of a more popular phraseology.

The situation is similar for profitability and relative advantage. Both are measures of gain, material and nonmaterial, based on the perceptions of the adopter. Profitability is a sharper concept to the extent that it relies upon the needs of the adopter rather than the generalized notion of betterment. This difference allows for finer discrimminations of the concept of profitability into general, self-interest, negative, and positive forms.

*Conclusions*

To summarize then, the innovation characteristics associated with the institutionalization-termination model are consistent with the existing literature on innovation characteristics and innovation success. The construct of profitability, however, may represent a refinement over the more commonly used concept of relative advantage.

*2. Literature on How to Carry Out Successful Innovation or Change*

These writings, collectively called the literature of planned change, are a jumble of theories, research of varying quality, folk wisdom, reminiscences, and snake-oil remedies that are intended to help the potential innovator understand what steps must be taken to enhance the likelihood of an innovation's success. Four schools or ways of thinking about planned change can be identified, however. They might be called the rational school, the human problems or human relations school, the power school, and the eclectic school, which includes each of the other three and the kitchen sink, too.

The *rational school* emphasizes change through research and utilization of knowledge and other expert resources. The most familiar names associated with it are probably Everett Rogers and Ronald Havelock. The philosophy of the school rests on several basic assumptions:

> One fundamental assumption is that men are rational. Another assumption is that men will follow their rational self-interest once this is revealed to them. A change is proposed by some person or group which knows of a situation that is desirable, effective, and in line with the self-interest of the person, group, organization, or community which will be affected by the change. Because the person (or group) is assumed to be rational and moved by self-interest, it is assumed that he (or they) will adopt the proposed change if it can be rationally justified and if it can be shown by the proposer(s) that he (or they) will gain by the change [Chin and Benne, 1969, p. 34].

The emphasis is decidedly upon enlightened self-interest and gain. For this reason, the rational school might be described in the language of the institutional-termination model as the profitability school. It seeks to increase the likelihood of innovation by raising the perceived profitability of change.

## Implications: A Literature Review

The *human problems or human relations school* is therapeutic or educational in orientation and brings about change through alterations in the personality and motivations of organizations, groups, and individuals. Among the well-known members of this school are Rensis Likert, Warren Bennis, Ronald Lippitt, Chris Argyris, Walter Sikes, F. J. Roethlisberger, and Douglas McGregor to mention just a very few. The assumptions made by the human relations school about the world are, not surprisingly, quite different form those of the rational school.

> [The human problems or human relations school holds that] patterns of action and practice are supported by sociocultural norms and by commitments on the part of individuals to these norms. Sociocultural norms are supported by the attitude and value systems of individuals— normative outlooks which undergird their commitments. Change in a pattern of practice or action, according to this view, will occur only as the persons involved are brought to change their normative orientations to old patterns and develop commitments to new ones. And changes in normative orientations involve changes in attitudes, values, skills, and significant relationships, not just changes in knowledge, information, or intellectual rationales for action and practice [Chin and Benne, 1969, p. 34].

This, to be sure, is the compatability school. By changing the norms and values of the people in an organization, the human problems/relations school hopes to increase the likelihood of innovation success.

The *power school* brings about change by means of coercion. It holds that those with less power will comply to the will of those with more power. Consequently, decision-making elites are often capable of imposing the changes they wish. The political model of organization advanced by J. Victor Baldridge, which was discussed earlier, is an outgrowth of this school, but is a more civilized and democratic version in which competing coalitions are substituted for competing elites.

All three of the schools examined so far—the rational school, the human problems/relations school, and the power school share something in common. They all have poor track records—each is incomplete. The rational school neglects innovation compatability; the human problems/relations school neglects innovation profitability;

and, the power school ignores both. The power schools, by the way, has the worst track record. The problem is that planned change as dictated by the power school "has a remarkable tendency to solve one set of problems only to generate another set; to give advantage to one group, but to disadvantage another; to eliminate one structural strain, but to create another (Baldridge, 1971, p. 96). As Lindquist (1978, p. 9) perceptively notes, "Losers of today's battles do not give up. They mount a new demand." Change may get adopted in this manner, but it is unlikely to persist. The example of New College at the University of Alabama, discussed in Chapter 2, which was established by the president of the university despite faculty objections, is a truly exceptional exception.

The limitations of the three schools may explain why the fourth, the *eclectic school*, is currently in vogue. It is a pragmatic school lacking in the ideology of the others. It goes with what works. Perhaps in its most ideal sense, the eclectic school can be described as seeking to overcome the weaknesses of the others by combining their strengths along with other successful change strategies. The result, unfortunately, too often comes out looking like a recipe put together by a committee, and there are enough such recipes to make an impressively sized cookbook.

To save the reader the trouble of purusing such a volume, several of the recipes (Bennis, 1973; Conrad, draft; Lindquist, 1978; and Martorana and Kuhns, 1975) have been collapsed or synthesized. The result is a new 12-ingredient recipe for successful change. The details of its derivation can be found in Appendix B; a shorter version is offered here:

1. Create a climate, even a demand, for change
2. Diminish the threat associated with innovation and avoid hardline approaches
3. Avoid being timid
4. Appreciate timing
5. Gear the innovation to the organization
6. Engage in information dissemination and evaluation
7. Communicate effectively
8. Get organizational leaders behind the innovation

## Implications: A Literature Review

9. Build an active base of support
10. Establish rewards
11. Plan for the postadoption period
12. Other[4]

To be quite candid this recipe, like much of the eclectic literature, is a confusion of procedures (e.g., engage in information dissemination and evaluation), goals (e.g., build an active base of support and get organizational leaders behind the innovation), postures (e.g., avoid being timid), and innovation stages (e.g., item number 1 points out the importance of the first stage of the innovation process—recognition of need—and item 11 cautions not to forget the final stage). Nonetheless, the two determinants of the institutionalization-termination model—profitability and compatibility—are prominent throughout. Compatibility is a theme in items 1, 2, 4, 5, 8, and 9. And profitability is directly touched upon in items 1, 2, and 10. This recipe, then, is consistent with the institutionalization-termination model in emphasizing the importance of compatibility and profitability in innovation success. However, it does not make it clear that these are the only criteria for success; neither, on the other hand, does it preclude that possibility, as no other determinant leaped forth from the recipe.

By way of conclusion, it might be said that the literature on planned change indicates that profitability and compatibility are probably both necessary if an innovation is to succeed. The lack of success of the rational, human problems/relations, and power schools may be a consequence of the neglect by each of compatibility, profitability, or both. The currently more popular eclectic school was found to include both profitability and compatibility prominently among its prescriptions for innovation success.

### 3. Literature on Obstacles to Innovation Success

The publications in this area are much like those on planned change, particularly as concerns quality and character. The most significant difference is that the obstacle literature approaches the

---

[4]"Other" is a miscellaneous category for one-of-a-kind statements that numbered only 3 out of a total of 56 coded. See Appendix B for further explanation.

## Conclusions

issue of successful change from the opposite direction; that is, the problems an innovation must overcome if it is to succeed.

The literature here tends to be of two sorts—that dealing with organizations and larger social systems in general, and that concerned with particular types of organizations. In the next few pages an example of each will be examined.

As for organizations in general, one of the most thoughtful pieces of writing is an article by Godwin Watson (1969) entitled "Resistence to Change." In it, he identifies five obstacles to innovation within existing social systems. They are:

1. *Conformity to norms*

    "Members of organizations demand of themselves and of other members conformity to institutional norms . . . because norms are shared by many participants they cannot easily change; (p. 493). Watson points out that conformity or rejection of the nonconformist are the usual outcomes.

2. *Systemic and cultural coherence*

    No innovation can be considered an island unto itself. Changes in one part of an organization will necessitate changes throughout the organization. But "innovations which are helpful in one area may have side effects which are destructive in related regions" (p. 494).

3. *Vested interests*

    "The most obvious source of resistance is some threat to the economic or prestige interests of individuals" (p. 495).

4. *The sacrosanct*

    "The greatest resistance concerns matters which are connected with what is held sacred. . . . The closer any reform comes to touching some of the taboos or rituals in the community, the more likely it is to be resisted" (p. 495).

5. *Rejection of outsiders*

    "Most change comes into institutions from 'outside.' . . . A major problem . . . is to secure enough local initiative and participation so that the enterprise will not be vulnerable as a foreign importation" (p. 496).

These obstacles are problems that persist throughout the innovation process—from the time a need is first recognized to the time an innovation is institutionalized or terminated. All five barriers can be

## Implications: A Literature Review

be described as potential problems of incompatibility or unprofitability. Conformity to norms, protecting the sacrosanct, and rejection of outsiders are all matters of incompatability. The first two obstacles are concerned with preserving the existing norms, values, and goals of an organization, and the third involves rejecting that which is inconsistent with an organization's personality.

Unprofitability is the trouble with the other two barriers—vested interests and systemic and cultural coherence. As mentioned in the discussion of organizational stratification, for individuals and even subunits that are well endowed relative to the rest of an organization, most change is threatening. It is for this reason that vested interest makes innovation unprofitable. As for systemic and cultural coherence, recall that in Chapter 2 profitability was said to be a measure of whether an innovation both satisfies the need for which it was created and whether it positively or negatively affects the rest of the organization. What Watson describes as the coherence barrier is actually a case of innovation that has a negative effect on the remainder of the organization. It is in this sense an unprofitable innovation.

Before offering any conclusions about Watson's work, let's turn to the literature on barriers in a particular type of organization. And for the sake of novelty, make that organization a university. Once again the best source is Hefferlin (1969). He first notes five obstacles common to innovation success in all types of organizations, universities included:

1. Organizations are inherently passive. This means "they exist for the routinization of behavior," preserving the status quo (p. 10).

2. Voluntary organizations attract members who agree with their activities. That is, "organizations are self selective" and recruit members "who appear compatible with them" (p. 10).

3. Organizations tend toward institutionalization and ritualism. This is quite similar to Watson's notion of the sacrosanct.

4. Organizations that are livelihoods for people tend to come to exist only as livelihoods for those people. Here Hefferlin is concerned with the problem of vested interest.

5. Maintenance of institutional,effectiveness or achievement is only one problem that organizations must face in order to survive. Other problems take precedence over it. This refers to the question of timing noted in the literature on planned change.

*Conclusions*

All of Hefferlin's five barriers, like Watson's, can be described as problems of innovations being potentially incompatible or unprofitable with their host organizations. There is even some overlap in the two men's analyses. In any case, item 4 on Hefferlin's list deals with possible unprofitability and all of the rest are concerned with incompatibility.

What makes Hefferlin's (1969) work unique is the next seven barriers he proposes. These are barriers peculiar to the university. They include the following:

1. The purposes and support are basically conservative. Hefferlin describes colleges and universities as devices essentially for the "perpetuation of culture" with a "long tradition of custom and precedent" (p. 13). Innovation is not especially compatible with such an organization.

2. The educational system is horizontally fragmented. This means that colleges are wedged between secondary education and graduate school, both of which dictate what colleges should do. Hefferlin says modification of college programs beyond accepted boundaries "would be as risky as for a typewriter manufacturer to market typewriters with an arrangement of keys different from that of the standard keyboard" (p.14). Consequently, universities might be described as organizations with a very narrow range of acceptable norms, values, and goals.

3. Within higher education, institutional reputation is not based on innovation. That is, "the accepted roads to academic prestige and advancement are not those of unconventionality" (p. 15). So innovation is considered a rather unprofitable endeavor.

4. Faculty members have observed their vocation for years as students before joining it. Socialization runs deep within the university and innovation that runs against the grain is more likely to be thought of as deviant.

5. The ideology of the academic profession treats professors as independent professionals. This means both variation in the norms, values, and goals within a university, and impressive power of passive resistance among members. Establishing the compatibility of an innovation is no picnic under these conditions.

6. Academics are skeptical about the idea of efficiency in academic

## Implications: A Literature Review

life. Hefferlin refers here to the rejection of educational measurement by many faculty. In such an organization, common needs are hard to demonstrate and varied standards of profitability abound.

7. Academic institutions are deliberately structured to resist precipitant change. Procedures for approving change are elaborate and slow. A relatively large number of people and groups tend to participate, so that an innovation is likely to be subjected to quite an assortment of varied standards for judging profitability and compatibility.

As pointed out in their descriptions, each of these seven barriers, like those examined before them, are profitability and compatibility related. What is remarkable though, particularly given the context of this book, is Hefferlin's distinction between the barriers to successful innovation in universities and those of organizations in general. The university barriers all follow from the organizational barriers. Each is a specific case of the general rule. It is as if the organizational prototype had been applied to the university. It had not, by the way. The similarity merely confirms one of the basic tenets of the social sciences. A specific organization, like the university, is supposed to be different from all other particularistic organizations, but if social research is to have any meaning it should be exactly like all other organizations in general.

This has been a bit of a digression, and it is necessary to return to the principal concern of the moment—the literature on barriers to innovation success. So far as the institutionalization-termination model is concerned, this literature is consistent with the notion that innovations which are compatible and profitable with their organizations tend to succeed; and those that are not fail. All of the barriers described by Watson and Hefferlin could be fully accounted for in terms of the constructs of compatibility and profitability alone. The terms *barrier* and *obstacle* may be misnomers, however. The elements identified by Hefferlin and Watson might better be thought of as innovation limiting factors. That is, they are the items that determine the kinds of innovations an organization cannot adopt. To this extent they are right on the boundary. They are natural snags. If an innovation is to trip over an organizational crack, the barriers identified are simply the most likely spots.

## Conclusions

By necessity the discussion to this point has been somewhat diffuse, concentrating in turn on discrete portions of the literature on innovation and change. It is now time to pull together all of the various pieces and see just what they add up to. Recall that there were three stated purposes for this chapter:

1. to see whether the institutionalization-termination model is consistent with the existing literature on innovation and change,

2. to see whether the institutionalization-termination model adds any explanatory power to the existing literature, and

3. to see whether the existing literature adds any explanatory power to the institutionalization-termination model.

As to the first purpose, the institutionalization-termination model was consistent with all of the literature examined, including the innovation and change literature on both institutions of higher education and organizations in general. This should not be interpreted to mean that the model was proven correct or valid, however. It simply means that no literature was discovered that is at odds with the model. It means additionally that the findings of the literature examined on innovation characteristics and innovation success, planned change and innovation success, and barriers to innovations success could all be explained in terms of the model.

The institutionalization-termination model has three basic elements: *a process* involving boundaries, boundary contraction, and boundary expansion; *a series of outcomes* including diffusion of innovation, enclaving of innovation, resocialization of innovation, and termination of innovation; and, *a switch or control mechanism* for making the model work—innovation compatibility and profitability. To prove the model valid, each of the elements would have to be shown to be accurate as well as the hypothesized relationships between them. This is an impossible assignment if the means selected for its accomplishment is the existing literature of innovation and change. And this brings us to the second purpose of this chapter.

The existing literature on change is structured differently from the model. It emphasizes *the switch* and *the outcomes*. *The process* tends to be ignored. The focus of the research on *the switch* and *the*

## Implications: A Literature Review

*outcomes* is also different from that of the model. As for *outcomes,* the current literature speaks generally of only two possibilities — success and failure. *Success,* as noted earlier, is defined primarily in terms of innovation adoption and persistance. Failure is nonadoption or nonpersistence.

The situation with *the switch* is just the opposite. The possibilities seem nearly limitless with some researchers talking of a score or more factors determining the innovation outcome.

To this extent the institutionalization-termination model does add explanatory power to the literature on innovation and change. First, it offers a needed explanation of *the process* whereby innovation success and failure occur. In so doing, it makes the phenomenon of innovation more comprehensible.

Second, the model specifies a very few variables — two to be precise, compatability and profitability — that determine innovation success and failure in the postadoption period. These variables alone were found to be all that was necessary and sufficient to explain failure and success on the basis of the literature examined. The model might then be described as adding parsimony to existing explanations of innovation success and failure. By so simplifying, relationships that were formerly hidden have become more obvious. For example, it became possible to offer a hypothesis for why only the eclectic school of planned change might be successful. Moreover, in concentrating on only two variables, it has also been possible to develop one of them further than it had already been developed in the existing literature. Profitability, as noted previously, is more sharply defined in the model than the more commonly used construct of "relative advantage," which is comparable in meaning. Profitability was also found to be a more complex phenomenon than previously indicated. That is, different types of profitability were found to exist — positive profitability, negative profitability, general profitability, and self-interest profitability. This shedding of additional light on profitability has the potential to make the innovation process more understandable to its students and perhaps its practitioners.

Third, the institutionalization-termination model ties innovation success to the purpose for which the innovation was intended. This is an advance over gearing success to adoption and persistence. By way

## Conclusions

of example, the Buffalo colleges were adopted and persisted; yet they were by no stretch of the imagination a success in their early years. The reason is that the colleges were intended to be diffused throughout the university but remained only an isolated enclave. In terms of the goals for the colleges, their position constituted failure. However, if success were measured by persistence, they would have to be called successes, which flies in the face of reality. The model's contribution here is in providing a more relative, innovation based definition of success.

Fourth, the model goes beyond the rather gross concepts of success and failure with regard to the outcomes of the innovation process. It specifies four outcomes and a continuum of results varying from total innovation impact on the host organization (innovation diffusion) to total host impact on the innovation (termination). The lack of research on outcomes has been a serious gap in the innovation literature. Particular outcomes such as diffusion have been well documented (Rogers and Shoemaker, 1971). The others—enclaving (Leeds, 1969), resocialization (Kennedy and Kerber, 1973), and termination (Erikson, 1966)—are also discussed in the literature, but they have not been linked as possible and continuing consequences of the innovation process.

Fifth and finally, the model offers a complete explanation for what occurs during the innovation process and why. This has not been characteristic of the innovation literature.

With regard to the third and last purpose of this chapter, the existing literature makes an important contribution in terms of understanding the role of the organization in innovation success and failure. The model, as observed, treats the organization as a given. It has no formal place in explaining the success or failure of a particular innovation. In the final analysis this is still the case. However, the organization cannot be ignored. The literature makes clear that as a rule organizations vary in the degree to which they resist innovation. In terms of the model, this means that some organizations are more prone to respond to innovations with boundary contraction and others with boundary expansion. Hefferlin's study on organizational stability showed that organizations with flexible boundaries are more likely to respond with boundary expansion. Such organizations have built

## Implications: A Literature Review

in relatively wide ranges of compatibility and possibly even profitability. In contrast, the Hage and Aiken (1970) review of organizational variables indicated that organizations with a narrow range of acceptable norms, values and goals, or a restricted definition of profitability, are more likely to respond with boundary contraction.

The literature on organizational character also showed that compatibility and profitability standards within an organization vary with times, circumstances, and the issues being considered. Moreover, organizations are likely to have at least some deviation in compatibility and profitability standards throughout. This means that resistance to innovation will vary across organizations as well, and that innovation may be easier in some parts of an organization than others. The variation also indicates more fundamentally that in some organizations, the unit of analysis might better be a subunit or part of the organization than the whole, depending on the size and nature of the innovations, not to mention the organization.

The existing literature also makes clear that there is probably variation in the factors that determine the outcome of each of the four stages of the innovation process. Zaltman et al. (1973) made this statement directly and Rogers and Shoemaker (1971) provided additional evidence in pointing out innovation characteristics—observability and trialability—that were necessary for innovation adoption, but not in postadoption persistence. Accordingly, there may also be times in the innovation process when compatibility and profitability are not critical, but there is as yet no evidence to suggest such a conclusion.

In short, the very important contribution of the existing literature was in pointing out the variations associated with innovation—variation in organizations, variation within organizations, and variation throughout the innovation process.

APPENDIX A

# *Methodological Note*

The purpose of this note is to describe what went into Part Two of this book, "A Study of 14 Innovations," and why it was done. Part Two was intended to: 1) shed light on a subject that had not received adequate attention in the past; 2) fill in the flesh and bones of the innovation model presented in Chapter 2 by paying in-depth attention to the institutionalization-termination stage of the change process; 3) test the innovation model of Chapter 2 and lay the groundwork for future research; and, 4) observe the dynamic character of innovation over an extended period.

The research approach best fitting this bill is the case study. It allows the researcher to obtain a feeling for the environment being studied. The reseacher can immerse him or herself in a culture and learn the life and language of the people living in it. The case study thereby enables a researcher to explore ongoing processes as well as outcomes. It also offers the flexibility necessary for in-depth exploratory research. The case study often allows the researcher a choice in regard to the duration and scheduling of time in the field, and usually a choice of research techniques, including questionnaires, tests, interviews, observation, and document studies. The researcher also has the opportunity to investigate as many different questions as desired, including new questions developed in the course of the research, the chance to formulate and test answers to the questions while still in the field, and the possibility of exploring potential dead ends without loss.

*Appendix A*

Along with all of these advantages, the case study offers one serious liability. It is not typical or generalizable; that is, every research setting is different from every other, so that whatever is discovered in one setting is not necessarily applicable to any other. As a result, the case study is not a vehicle for discovering universal truths, which is unfortunate because that is the goal of the social sciences. However, it can aid in that process by laying a solid foundation for future research. The careful choice of the case study to avoid obvious and unwanted uniqueness, and the specification of known limitations inherent in the particular case are helpful.

Other research methods lack this basic disadvantage, but no other incorporates as many needed advantages as the case study without significantly increasing the time and monetary investment required. As a result, this investigation utilized the case study approach. The setting was an organization with 14 similar innovations, undergoing the institutionalization-termination process for the second time. The fact that all of the innovations were of the same type and existed in a single organization is terribly important in interpreting the results of the case study. The use of a single organization means that differences in the organizational response to the innovations are attributable to differences in the innovations, not to variations in the organizations being examined. The study of one type of innovation means that differences in organizational response are a result of substantive differences among the innovations, not mere variations in their type.

The organization studied in this case was the State University of New York at Buffalo and the innovations were experimental colleges collectively and imaginatively called "the colleges." The rationale for studying this organization was a personal interest and familiarity with universities, combined with the proximity of that particular school and its excellence as a setting for this study. Where else could one find a single organization in the midst of institutionalizing more than a dozen identical innovations?

For the purposes of this research, Buffalo's experimental colleges were an excellent type of innovation to study. They had neither the problem of being too small nor too big. A small or piecemeal innovation such as a new course rarely involves the whole organization, but usually only a subunit such as an academic department or at most an

## Methodological Note

academic division. Nonetheless, the institutionalization-termination process should be the same in all cases, only occurring on a lesser scale. However the reduction in scale means that the process can involve as few as two individuals—the department chairman and the innovator—which tends to make it more informal and less subject to observation.

On the other hand, big or holistic innovations such as that described at Brown complicate and impede the clarity of the institutionalization-termination process. Because the innovation supplants large portions of the organization, the organization and innovation become enmeshed and individually indistinct. Although the dynamics of the process should again be the same, the situation is too blurred to study in the detail desired. The experimental college or innovative enclave represents a middle range innovation that is distinct from the organization, but sufficiently large to involve the entire organization in a formal and, therefore, observable institutionalization-termination decision.

Before going on to describe the study, it would be useful to recap briefly the events that transpired at Buffalo. To start with, the colleges were traditionally a group of independent undergraduate subunits with diverse interests and areas of study; some were residential, others were not. Each of the colleges offered an assortment of theme-related courses, but none were degree-granting. The colleges operated under the purview of the faculty senate, which was advisory to the president of the university. The senate is the universitywide legislative body through which the faculty of the university make their opinions known. In April 1974 the senate drafted a new operating prospectus for the colleges, which dissolved all of the existing units as of January 1975, but provided a procedure whereby the 14 existing colleges could be approved in the interim. A universitywide committee called the chartering committee, also advisory to the president of the university, was created. Each college interested in continuing past January was required to submit a charter or constitution and a mass of supporting documentation to that committee. The content of the material was minutely specified. Based upon the constitution, documentation, and a public hearing for each college, the chartering committee recommended to the president that each charter

*Appendix A*

be accepted, rejected, modified, or delayed. In January 1975, after reading the committee's recommendation, nonvoting members' recommendations, college documents, and after holding his own meetings, the president made decisions on each college.

The chartering process was a resocialization measure; however, some colleges chose not to go through chartering or were rejected, which is termination. The combination of the two added up to a study of boundary contraction, but that was not all that occurred. There was, surprisingly, boundary expansion as well.

This was the second time the colleges were institutionalized. The first instance was in 1970 when the colleges en masse were institutionalized through boundary expansion via enclaving. The reasons for the 1970 institutionalization were the same as those responsible for the 1974 chartering, but the colleges were not the same. At that time there were 15, only nine of which were among the 14 colleges of the second institutionalization.

In short, the situation provided an excellent opportunity to test the model discussed in Chapter 2. Each of the four hypothesized forms of boundary contraction and boundary expansion were part of the Buffalo case study. This made possible a test of whether the conditions of profitability and compatibility postulated for each were correct. Further, this permitted an examination of whether there were other forms of boundary expansion and boundary contraction, as well as alternatives to boundary contraction and boundary expansion.

## *The Study*

The institutionalization-termination of the colleges at Buffalo was a decision involving much of the university community. As such, a research methodology appropriate for the study of collective decision-making was necessary. Two methods have been popular. One is Floyd Hunter's reputational method, in which knowledgeable community members are asked to name the major power holders in the community and the roles of the named individuals are investigated with regard to community decisions. The other approach is Robert Dahl's decision-making method, in which the individuals involved in making decisions are viewed as the influential people. Hunter's method is founded

## Methodological Note

on the assumption that decision power is concentrated in an elite; that is, one group of people have a disproportionate amount of power and make or influence the outcome of community decisions. The emphasis of this method is upon studying the elite. Dahl's method views the power to make decisions as situational and diffuse; that is, different groups and individuals may be involved in any given decision.

For this study, the decision-making method was adopted for two reasons. First, the focus of the study was upon decision-making — institutionalization-termination decision-making. It was concerned more with understanding the innovation (the rationale, process, and results of decision-making ) and the roles of individuals and groups in decision-making, than with discovering the individuals with the most power in decision-making. Second, the reputational method relies upon survey research while the decision-making method utilizes the case study. The need for case study was previously stipulated.

The actual study of the institutionalization-termination of the colleges at the State University of New York at Buffalo was conducted from August 1974 to January 1975. In order to break the research into more manageable pieces, institutionalization-termination decision-making was divided into three phases: conditions prior to institutionalization-termination, institutionalization-termination 1, and institutionalization-termination 2.

The study of the conditions prior to institutionalization-termination involved an examination of the first three stages of the innovation process, from the time the organizational need was first recognized through the time institutionalization-termination 1 commenced. S.U.N.Y.A.B. had a very rich cache of documentation for researching this period. This included catalogues, memos, reports, position papers, vitae, program evaluations, committee minutes, accreditation studies, college self-studies, personal papers, school newspapers, and local newspapers. This material was supplemented by interviews with the principals of the period. These interviews were designed to fill in gaps, resolve conflicts, and simply provide flavor to the documentation.

The study of institutionalization-termination phases 1 and 2 involved an examination of each of the steps in the decision-making process, which has already been outlined, and the impact of the decisions. Far more time was spent on the 1974 institutionalization-

## Appendix A

termination—it was followed from start to finish. When this research began, the first institutionalization-termination was already five years in the past. It was reconstructed by means of document study and interviews. The documents were the same as those just mentioned, plus faculty senate materials. There were also interviews with the 1969-1970 college students and staff and with S.U.N.Y.A.B. faculty and administrators who were involved in the decision.

For the second institutionalization-termination, 50 percent of the 96-member faculty senate were interviewed; all of the members of the chartering committee were interviewed and all of the committee's activities were observed; the president and his advisors were observed and many were interviewed; and, key individuals involved in the chartering of each of the colleges were interviewed. In addition, four colleges that were both representative of a cross-section of the 14 subunits and exemplary of differing responses to the chartering requirement were researched in depth. Three were involved in both institutionalization-terminations. In these four colleges, at least half of the current core membership was interviewed, as were previous core members when possible, and meetings and chartering activities were observed. The in-depth study of a small number of colleges was necessitated by personal time constraints and the overlapping activity schedules of different colleges. Documentation utilized to study institutionalization-termination 2 included faculty senate minutes and tape recordings of meetings; faculty senate, chartering committee, and college reports, minutes, memos, personal papers, position papers, subcommittee minutes, correspondence, proposals, statements of procedure, and charges; college charters and supporting documentation; the nonvoting chartering committee member reports; the president's correspondence and reports; a demographic study of each of the 14 colleges' and local and university newspaper articles. The greater depth of study of the second institutionalization served to formulate the questions and substance involved in the investigation of the first.

The entire study made use of three research techniques—interviewing, observation, and analysis of documents. One hundred and thirty-two people were formally interviewed, and many more participated through informal discussions. (Table A.1 provides a breakdown of the status of the interviews.) Formal interviews were, with several

## Methodological Note

exceptions, open-ended and conversational, lasting between a few minutes and four-and-one half hours, but based upon a common inventory of topics or concerns. (Interview schedules can be found in Tables A.2 to A.4) The exceptions were interviews with individuals knowledgable about historical periods in the life of one or more colleges. These interviews were not based on a common inventory. The activities of all of the parties in the second institutionalization-termination were observed, except those of the faculty senate. It was not possible to attend the senate deliberations, but recorded tapes of these sessions were heard. College activities were explored largely, though far from exclusively, in the four in-depth study colleges. The sheer mass of documentation was overwhelming, organizationally unnecessary, and ecologically unfortunate, but a boon for this study.

After collecting the mass of data, the next step was making sense of it. This involved organizing the data into smaller and more manageable topics, and linking the topics in a manner designed to produce an understandable whole. The whole was then both examined for evidence confirming or disconfirming the institutionalization-termination model, and sifted through for data that might further develop the model.

Table A.1   Status of the 132 Interviewees*

| | |
|---|---|
| College Personnel (staff and active students) | 67 |
| State University of New York at Buffalo administrators | 12 |
| State University of New York at Buffalo faculty | |
|    Faculty senators | 50 |
|    Nonfaculty senators | 39 |
| State University of New York at Buffalo Student Association | |
|    Undergraduate Student Association | 4 |
|    Graduate Student Association | 2 |

*Many interviewees fit into more than one category.

## Appendix A

Table A.2  Charter Committee and Selected Administrators Questionnnaire

This is the general questionnaire that was administered to members of the chartering committee and selected administrators active in the chartering procedure:

1. How and why did you get involved with the chartering committee? Were you aware of all of the work that would be required?
2. What are your feelings regarding the collegiate prospectus?
3. What do you view as the purpose of chartering?
4. In light of 3, what is the relationship between the committee and the colleges, and the committee and the university?
5. How do you think the open hearings worked out?
6. How has serving as a representative of a particular university constituency affected your role on the committee?
7. Have you gotten to know the individual collegiate units well?
8. Do the charters accurately reflect the colleges?
9. How has the chartering process changed the colleges? Desirable-undersirable?
10. Describe your concept of what a collegiate unit should be?
11. How have you used this conception in making decisions about the colleges? Describe with reference to Vico College, College B, College F, and the College of Progressive Education (the case study colleges).
12. How has participation on the committee affected your view of the colleges?
13. Has the committee operated as you expected it would? Desirable?
14. Do you feel uncomfortable about any of the colleges you voted on? Why?
15. What were the strengths and weaknesses of the chartering process? How would you change it?
16. What do you expect to happen now?
17. (Read definition of *profitability*.) Using this definition how would you classify each of the collegiate units you examined?
18. *(For administrators)* What will now be the financial future of the colleges? Can they be expected to achieve the status of departments?

Table A.3  College Personnel Questionnaire

This is the general questionnaire that was administered to the personnel in both case study and non-case study colleges.

1. How long have you been involved with your college?
2. Why did you become involved with your college?
3. Describe your involvement with the college.
4. Would you like to be more involved with the college?
5. If yes, what prevents you from being more involved in the college?
6. What was your reaction to the recent chartering procedure your college went through?
7. How were you involved in the chartering process?
8. What was the impact of chartering upon your college?
9. Do you think your college charter reflects the actual operation of your college?
10. *(For university faculty)* What is the attitude of your department toward your participation in the college?
11. *(For university faculty)* How will your participation be regarded in terms of future promotion, tenure, or salary increment?
12. *(For university faculty)* What impact has participation in the college had upon your departmental activities?

## Methodological Note

Table A.4  Faculty Senate Questionnaire

This is the general questionnaire that was administered to members of the faculty senate.

1. Are you familiar with the colleges at Buffalo?
2. Why did you vote in favor (only one individual voted against) of the Reichert prospectus, which prolonged the life of the colleges?
3. Under what conditions would you vote to terminate a university program?
4. What evidence would you require?
5. (Read definition of *profitability*.) Using that definition, how would you classify the colleges at Buffalo collectively? Individually?
6. If you know, what is the attitude of your department toward participation in the colleges?

APPENDIX B

# A Synthesis of Theories on Planned Change

In an attempt to understand the common features of what is referred to in Chapter 6 as the eclectic school of planned change, the prescriptions for change of colleges and universities by Bennis (1973), Conrad (draft), Lindquist (1978), and Martorana and Kuhns (1975) were analyzed. Together the authors offered 58 statements about how change should occur. These statements can be grouped into 12 discrete categories:

1. Create a climate, even a demand, for change
   —create a climate for change (Conrad)
   —create a need for change (Conrad)
   —encourage active openness (Lindquist)
   —create demand (Martorana and Kuhns)
2. Diminish the threat associated with innovation and avoid hard-line approaches
   —know when to compromise (Conrad)
   —serve as a compromiser (Conrad)
   —deemphasize the importance of change (Martorana and Kuhns)
   —build on existing concerns (Martorana and Kuhns)
   —develop legitimacy (Martorana and Kuhns)
   —avoid threatening (Martorana and Kuhns)
   —compromise and coopt (Martoran and Kuhns)
   —provide reassurance (Martorana and Kuhns)
   —use trial balloons (Martorana and Kuhns)
   —use a frontman (Martorana and Kuhns)
   —carry out a hidden agenda (Martorana and Kuhns)
3. Avoid being timid
   —don't settle for rhetorical change (Bennis)
   —confront opposition (Martorana and Kuhns)
   —outflank opposition (Martorana and Kuhns)
   —control internal organization (Martorana and Kuhns)

## A Synthesis of Theories on Planned Change

4. Appreciate timing
   - allow time to consolidate gains (Bennis)
   - appreciate timing (Martorana and Kuhns)
5. Gear the innovation to the organization
   - know the territory (Bennis)
   - guard against crazies (Bennis)
   - don't allow those opposed to appropriate issues such as standards (Bennis)
   - establish the compatibility of the change (Conrad)
   - appreciate environmental factors (Martorana and Kuhns)
   - respect the past (Martorana and Kuhns)
   - determine obstacles (Martorana and Kuhns)
   - obtain an overview (Martorana and Kuhns)
6. Engage in information dissemination and evaluation
   - encourage interpersonal and informational linkage (Lindquist)
   - build in evaluation (Martorana and Kuhns)
7. Communicate effectively
   - recruit with honesty (Bennis)
   - communicate and publicize proposal (Conrad)
   - control communication (Martorana and Kuhns)
8. Get organizational leaders behind the innovation
   - exert administrative leadership (Conrad)
   - initiate, guide, and involve influential leaders (Lindquist)
   - utilize opinion leaders to persuade others (Martorana and Kuhns)
9. Build a base of active support
   - build support among like-minded people (Bennis)
   - involve those who are affected (Bennis)
   - involve a wide range of faculty (Conrad)
   - combine initiative with involvement (Conrad)
   - build coalitions (Conrad)
   - build faculty support (Conrad)
   - encourage ownership (Lindquist)
   - aim for personal commitment to change among participants (Martorana and Kuhns)
   - create power blocks (Martorana and Kuhns)
10. Establish rewards
    - emphasize the benefits of the innovation for faculty (Conrad)
    - build an effective structure of rewards and resources (Conrad)
    - build in material and psychic rewards (Lindquist)
11. Plan for the postadoption period
    - make adjustments throughout the implementation period (Conrad)
    - choose an appropriate mechanism for administering the program (Conrad)
    - select key people for administering the program (Conrad)
    - select personnel for decision-making positions (Martorana and Kuhns)
12. Other
    - plan for how to change as well as what to change (Bennis)
    - incorporate an explicit implementation plan into the proposal (Conrad)
    - organize for implementation (Conrad)

# Bibliography

Arnaud, D., Arthurs, A., and Chandrasekhar, B. S. "Report of External Evaluation Committee for the Colleges." June 1978 (unpublished).
Azumi, K., and Hage, J. *Organizational Systems*. Lexington, Mass.: Heath and Co., 1972.
Baldridge, J. V. *Power and Conflict in the University*. New York: Wiley, 1971.
Bennis, W. *The Leaning Ivory Tower*. San Francisco: Jossey-Bass, 1973.
― ― ―. "Prospectus for the Colleges." State University of New York at Buffalo, 1969.
Bennis, W., Benne, K. D., and Chin, R. *The Planning of Change*. New York: Holt, Rinehart, and Winston, 1969.
Bradner, L., and Straus, M. "Congruence Versus Profitability in the Diffusion of Hybrid Sorghum." *Rural Sociology* 24 (1959): 381-383.
Brubacher, J. S., and Rudy, W. *Higher Education in Transition*. New York: Harper & Row, 1976.
*Buffalo Evening News, The*. Buffalo, N.Y.
*Buffalo Courier Express, The*. Buffalo, N.Y.
"Califano Cautions Against Education Dependence on U.S." *Higher Education and National Affairs*. August 25, 1978, p. 1.
Carnegie Council on Policy Studies in Higher Education. *More Than Survival*. San Francisco: Jossey-Bass, 1975.
Cheit, E. F. *The New Depression in Higher Education*. New York: McGraw-Hill, 1971.
Chickering, A. W. Halliburton, D. Bergquist, W. M. and Lindquist, J. *Developing the College Curriculum: A Handbook for Faculty and Administrators*. Washington, D.C.: Council for the Advancement of Small Colleges, 1977.
Chin, R., and Benne, K. D. "General Strategies for Effecting Changes in Human Systems." In the *Planning of Change*. Bennis, W. G., Benne, K. D., and Chin, R., eds. New York: Holt, Rinehart, and Winston, 1969.

## Bibliography

Clark, B. R. *The Distinctive College: Antioch, Reed, and Swarthmore.* Chicago: Aldine, 1970.

Cohen, A. K. *Deviance and Control.* Englewood Cliffs, N. J.: Prentice-Hall, 1966.

Conrad, C. "Initiating and Implementing Changes in General Education." (Draft).

Corson, J. *The Governance of Colleges and Universities.* New York: McGraw-Hill, 1975.

Corwin, R. *Reform and Organizational Survival.* New York: Wiley, 1974.

Coser, L. *The Functions of Social Conflict.* New York: Free Press, 1956.

Curti, M., and Carstensen, V. *The University of Wisconsin: A History, 1848-1925.* Madison, Wis.: University of Wisconsin Press, 1949.

Czernin, F. *Versailles 1919.* New York: Capricorn Books, 1964.

Dahl, R. *Who Governs? Democracy and Power in an American City.* New Haven, Conn.: Yale University Press, 1961.

Dalton, G. W., and Lawrence, P. R. *Motivation and Control in Organizations.* Homewood, Ill.: Irwin-Dorsey, 1972.

Davis, F. J., and Strivers, R. *The Collective Definition of Deviance.* New York: Free Press, 1975.

Emery, F. E. *Systems Thinking.* Middlesex, Great Britain: Penguin Books, 1972.

Erikson, K. *Wayward Puritans.* New York: Wiley, 1966.

Faris, R. E. L. *Handbook of Modern Sociology.* Chicago, Ill.: Rand McNally, 1964.

Filstead, W. J. *An Introduction to Deviance.* Chicago, Ill.: Markham Press, 1972.

--- . *Qualitative Methodology.* Chicago, Ill.: Markham Press, 1972.

Finkelstein, M. "Statistical Portrait of the Colleges." State University of New York at Buffalo, 1974.

Flacks, R. "The Liberated Generation: an Exploration of the Roots of Student Protest.'" In Baldridge, J. V. *Academic Governance.* Berkeley, Calif.: McCutchan Publishing Corp., 1971.

Flexner, A. *Medical Education in the United States and Canada.* Boston: D. B. Updike, 1960.

Fliegel, F., and Kivlin, J. "Farm Practice Attitudes and Adoption Rates." *Social Forces* 40 (1962): 356-370.

French, J. C. *A History of the University Founded by Johns Hopkins.* Baltimore: Johns Hopkins University Press, 1946.

Glenny, L. A. "Nine Myths, Nine Realities: The Illusions of Steady State." *Change* (Winter, 1974-1975): 24-28.

Glenny, L.A.; Shea, J. R.; Ruyle, J. H.; and Freschi, K. H. *Presidents Confront Reality from Edifice Complex to University Without Walls.* San Francisco: Jossey-Bass, 1976.

## Bibliography

Gouldner, A. "Cosmopolitans and Locals: Toward an Analysis of Latent Social Roles -I." *Administration Science Quarterly* 2 (December, 1957): 281-306.

Grant, G., and Riesman, D. *The Eternal Dream*. Chicago; University of Chicago Press, 1978.

Griliches, Z. "Hybrid Corn: An Exploration in the Economics of Technological Change." *Econometrica* 25 (1957): 501-522.

Gross, E., and Grambsch, P. V. *Change in University Organization, 1964-1971*. New York: McGraw-Hill, 1974

Gross, N., Giacquinta, J. B., and Bernstein, M. *Implementing Organizational Innovations*. New York: Basic Books, 1971.

Gusfield, J. *Symbolic Crusade*. Urbana, Ill.: University of Illinois Press, 1963.

Hage, J., and Aiken, M. *Social Change in Complex Organizations*. New York: Random House, 1970.

Halstead, J. "Memo to Faculty Senate Executive Committee and the Incoming College Committee." State University of New York at Buffalo, June 25, 1973.

--- . "Prospectus for the Colleges." State University of New York at Buffalo, 1972.

Hammond, P. E. *Sciologists at Work*. Garden City, N.J.: Doubleday Anchor Books, 1967.

Haskins, C. H. *The Rise of Universities*. Ithaca, N.Y.: Cornell University Press, 1967.

Havelock, R. G. *Planning for Innovation Through Dissemination and Utilization of Knowledge*. Ann Arbor Mich.: Institute for Social Reserach at the University of Michigan, 1969.

Hawkins, H. *Pioneer: A History of Johns Hopkins University*. Ithaca, N.Y.: Cornell University Press, 1960.

Heald, H. "Meeting the Increasing Demand for Higher Education in New York State." Albany, N. Y.: 1960. Unpublished

Hefferlin, JB. *Dynamics of Academic Reform*. San Francisco: Jossey-Bass, 1969.

Heirich, M. *The Spiral of Conflict: Berkeley, 1964*. New York: Columbia University Press, 1970.

Hunter, F. *Community Power Structure*. Chapel Hill, N.C.: University of North Carolina Press, 1953.

Johnson, D. B. "Erosion of Innovation in Higher Education." Ph.D dissertation, University of Minnesota, 1969.

Keniston, K. *Radicals and Militants: An Annotated Bibliography of Empirical Research on Student Unrest*. Washington, D.C.: Heath, 1973.

Kennedy, D. B., and Kerber, A. *Resocialization: An American Experiment*. New York: Behavioral Publications, 1973.

Kerlinger, F. N. *Foundations of Behavioral Research*. New York: Holt, Rinehart, and Winston, 1964.

*Bibliography*

Kerr, C. *Uses of the University*. New York: Harper Torchbooks, 1963.
Ketter, R. "Martin Meyerson Advisory Committee Report." State University of New York at Buffalo, 1966.
Kohlmeier, L. M. *The Regulators*. New York: Harper & Row, 1969.
Ladd, D. R. *Change in Educational Policy*. New York: McGraw-Hill, 1970.
Leeds, R. "The Absorption of Protest: A Working Paper." In Bennis, W., Benne, K. D., and Chin, R., *The Planning of Change*. New York: Holt, Rinehart, and Winston, 1969.
Lemert, E. M. *Human Deviance, Social Problems, and Social Control*. Englewood Cliffs, N.J.: Prentice-Hall, 1967.
Levine, A. *Handbook on Undergraduate Curriculum*, San Francisco: Jossey-Bass, 1978.
Levine, A., and Weingart, J. *Reform of Undergraduate Education*. San Francisco: Jossey-Bass, 1973.
Lindquist, J. *Strategies for Change*. Berkeley, Calif.: Pacific Soundings Press, 1978.
Lippitt, R., Watson, J., and Westley, B. *The Dynamics of Planned Change*. New York: Harcourt, Brace, 1958.
Maguire, L., Temkin, S., and Cummings, C. P *An Annotated Bibliography on Administering for Change*. Philadelphia: Research for Better Schools, Inc., 1971.
Mann, F., and Neff, F. W. *Managing Major Change in Organizations*. Ann Arbor, Mich.: Foundation for Research on Human Behavior, 1961.
March, J. G., ed. *Handbook of Organizations*. Chicago: Rand McNally, 1965.
Martorana, S. V., and Kuhns, E. *Managing Academic Change*. San Francisco: Jossey-Bass, 1975.
Maslow, A. H. *Motivation and Personality*. New York: Harper & Row, 1954.
Mayhew, L. B. *How Colleges Change: Approaches to Academic Reform*. Stanford, Calif.: ERIC Clearinghouse on Information Resources, Stanford Center for Research Development in Teaching, 1976.
Merton, R. *Social Theory and Social Structure*. New York: Free Press, 1957.
Meyerson, M. "Address to the Faculty Senate." State University of New York at Buffalo, November 28, 1966.
Middle States Association of Colleges and Schools. "Report on State University of New York at Buffalo," Boston: Middle States Association of Colleges and Schools. 1972.
Miles, M., ed. *Innovation in Education*. New York: Teachers College Press, 1964.
Millett, J. D. *The Academic Community*. New York: McGraw-Hill, 1962.
*Monthly Reports*. State University of New York at Buffalo, September, 1966.
Palola, E. G., and Padgett, W. *Planning for Self-Renewal*. Berkeley, Calif.: Center for Research and Develoment in Higher Education, 1971.
Parsons, T. *The Social System*. New York: Free Press, 1951.

## Bibliography

Perkins, J. *The University as an Organization*. New York: McGraw-Hill, 1972.

Pressman, J. L., and Wildavsky, A. B. *Implementation*. Berkeley, Calif.: University of California Press, 1973.

Reichert, J. "Prospectus for the Colleges at the State University of New York at Buffalo," 1974

*Reporter, The*. State University of New York at Buffalo,

Rheinehold, R. "Brown University Trend: Back to Old Curriculum," *New York Times*, February 24, 1974, p. 47.

Rogers, E. *Diffusion of Innovations*. New York: Free Press, 1962.

Rogers, E., and Havens, A. E. "The Impact of Demonstrations on Farmers' Attitudes Toward Fertilizer." Wooster: *Ohio Agricultural Experiment Station Research Bulletin*, 891 (1961):

Rogers, E., and Shoemaker, F. F. *Communication of Innovations*. New York: Free Press, 1971.

Rossberg, R. "Prospectus for Colleges by Faculty Senate Educational Policy Committee." State University of New York at Buffalo, 1970.

Rudolph, F. *The American College and University: A History*. New York: Random House, 1962.

*San Francisco Chronicle*. San Francisco, California.

Sarason, S. *The Creation of Settings and the Future Societies*. San Francisco, Calif.: Jossey-Bass, 1974.

Schachner, N. *The Medieval University*. New York: Barnes and Company, 1962.

Scott, J. W., and El-Assal, M. "Multiversity, University Size, Quality and Student Protest: An Empirical Study." In Baldridge, J. V. *Academic Governance*. Berkeley, Calif.: McCutchan Publishing Corp., 1971.

Selznick, P. *TVA and the Grassroots*. Berkeley, Calif.: University of California Press, 1949.

Shepard, H. "Innovation-Resisting and Innovation-Producing Organizations." In Bennis, W. G., Benne, K. D., and Chin, R., eds., *The Planning of Change*, New York: Holtz, Rinehart, and Winston, 1969.

Sikes, W., Schlesinger, L., Seashore, C. *Renewing Higher Education from Within*. San Francisco: Jossey-Bass, 1974.

Smelser, N. *Social Change in the Industrial Revolution: An Application of Theory to the Lancashire Cotton Industry*. Chicago: University of Chicago Press, 1959.

Smith, P. "The Need for Change." State University of New York at Buffalo, November 26, 1972.

*Spectrum*. State University of New York at Buffalo, Buffalo, New York.

Spicer, E. *Human Problems in Technological Change*. New York: Wiley, 1967.

State University of New York at Buffalo, "Self-Study for the Middle States

*Bibliography*

Association of Colleges and Schools." 1972.

Stern, R. "Prospectus for the Colleges Written by Faculty Senate College Committee." State University of New York at Buffalo, 1970.

Stroup, H. *Bureaucracy in Higher Education.* New York: Free Press, 1966.

Tönnies, F. *Community and Society.* New York, N. Y.: Harper Torchbooks, 1957.

Up the Colleges Committee. "Prospectus for the Colleges." State University of New York at Buffalo, 1970.

Vroom, V. *Methods of Organizational Research.* University of Pittsburg Press, 1967.

Watson, G. " Resistance to Change." In *The Planning of Change.* Bennis, W. R., Benne, K. D., and Chin, R. (ed.). New York, N. Y.: Holt, Rinehart, and Winston, Inc., 1969.

Webb, E., Campbell, D., Schwartz, R., and Sechrest, L. *Unobtrusive Measures.* Chicago: Rand McNally, 1971.

Weber, M. *The Theory of Social and Economic Organization.* New York, N. Y.: Free Press, 1947.

Yankelovich, D. *The New Morality: A Profile of American Youth in the Seventies.* New York, N. Y.: McGraw-Hill, 1974.

Zald, M. N., and Denton P. "From Evangelism to General Service: The Transformation of the YMCA," *Administration Science Quarterly*, 8 (1963), p. 214-234.

Zaltman, G., Duncan, R., and Holbek, J. *Innovations and Organizations.* New York, N. Y.: John Wiley and Sons, 1973.

# Index

Academic freedom: autonomy linked to, 162; compatibility issue of, 96-97, 101, 103, 110
Academic quality, compatibility issue of, 97-101, 103-104, 110. *See also* Faculty; Grading system
Aiken, M., 6, 7, 8, 170-171, 199, 214
Alabama, University of, New College at, 20-22, 190
Alternatives, supplements distinct from, 52, 158
American Telephone and Telegraph, college degrees from, 6
Antioch College, innovation at, 170
Argyris, C., 189
Arnaud, D., 150-151, 212
Arthurs, A., 150-151, 212
Atomistic organization, 178-179, 180-181, 182
Autonomy, 84-85, 91, 93, 162, 165
Azumi, K., 212

Baldridge, J.V., 174, 175, 180, 189, 190, 212
Barth, J., 58
Bazelon, D., 58
Benne, K. D., 188, 189, 212
Bennington College, as new college, 4
Bennis, W., 31, 32, 46, 51, 53, 55-56, 58-59, 60, 65-68, 70, 74, 75, 77-80, 84, 109, 189, 190, 210-211, 212

Bergquist, W. M., 212
Bernstein, M., 214
Berte, N., 21
Borst, L., 45, 46, 48
Boundaries: blurring of, 80; concept of, 12; convergence of, 14-15, 16; flexible and rigid, 169-170; incidents marking, 87-88; and innovation, 12. *See also* Boundary contraction; Boundary expansion
Boundary contraction: concept of, 14-15, 19-20, 24-25; continuing, 89, 96, 106, 110, 114-115, 123-124, 127, 147, 148-149; and innovation failure, 155, 156, 157, 158, 159, 161, 163. *See slso* Resocialization; Termination
Boundary expansion: concept of, 14, 19-20; continuing, 89, 128-129; and innovation failure, 155, 156, 157, 161, 163, 164. *See also* Diffusion; Enclaving
Bradner, L., 16, 212
Brandenburg, R., 56
Bressler, M., 6
Bridges, E., 71
Brown University, curriculum change at, 3, 5, 7, 9, 203
Brubacher, J. S., 177, 212
Buffalo, 69, 70, 71, 73, 79, 84
Bureaucratic organization, 179-180, 181

California, University of, at Berkeley: Center for Research and Development in

## Index

Higher Education at, 57; mass education at, 4; post-riot administration at, 31, 34-35, 43
California, University of, at Los Angeles, mass education at, 4
California, University of, at Santa Cruz, cluster colleges at, 4
Cambridge University: cluster idea at, 4; collegial organization of, 177
Campbell, D., 217
Carnegie Council on Policy Studies in Higher Education, ix, 55, 57, 161, 212
Carstensen, V., 180 $n$, 213
CAx02 ("Conflict and Change in the Local Community"), 49-51, 52, 68, 69, 74
CF302 ("Social Change in America"), 71-73, 74
Chandrasekhar, B.S., 150-151, 212
Cheit, E. F., 54, 212
Chickering, A. W., 212
Chin, R., 188, 189, 212
Chisolm, L., 55
Claremont Colleges, cluster arrangement of, 4
Clark, B. R., 170, 213
Clifford Furnas College (College D), 143; continuing institutionalization at, 95, 96, 98, 102, 110; described, 122, 126; evaluation of, 134-135, 145, 148-149; initiation-implementation stage of, 46, 48, 52, 53; institutionaliazation-termination stage of, 80, 83
Clustering, concept of, 4
Coffman, L., 22
Cohen, A. K., 213
College A, 139; initiation-implementation stage of, 46, 48-54; institutionalization-termination stage of, 64-65, 67, 68-74, 80, 82, 83, 84, 85, 86-87, 90, 103
College B: continuing institutionalization at, 95, 100, 115; described, 118-119, 126-127; evaluation of, 133-134, 145, 147, 148; initiation-implmentation stage of, 46, 48, 52, 53; merger with, 124
College C, initiation-implementation stage of, 46, 47
College D. *See* Clifford Furnas College
College E. *See* Cora P. Maloney College
College F. *See* Tolstoy College

College H: described, 119, 126-127; evaluation of, 135-136, 145, 147
College Z: described, 119, 138; incompatibility of, 123-124, 127, 160, 165
Colleges: evaluation of, 102-105; institutionalization continuing in, 89-151; new, innovation through, 4-5; organization and administration issues in, 92-94, 101, 108, 109, 126, 128; as organizations, 176-184; outcome criteria lacking for, 162; stages of innovation in, 29-88
Collegial organization, 176-177, 180-181, 182
Collegiate assembly: compatibility issue of, 94-96, 101, 109-110; functioning of, 76, 84, 85-86, 87, 90, 94-96, 110-111
Collegiate concept, 36-38, 40-41, 66-67
Communications College, 47; described, 120; merger of, 124
Compatibility: and academic freedom, 96-97, 101, 103, 110; and academic quality, 97-101, 103-104, 110; and college organization and administration, 92-94, 101, 108, 109, 126, 128; and collegiate assembly, 94-96, 101, 109-110; criteria for, 131-132; defined, 17, 19; examples of, 21, 22-23, 24; and innovation failure, 157-158, 159; in institutionalization-termination stage, 15-25; and literature review, 171-172, 187, 189, 191, 193, 195, 197; and research bias, 17; at State University of New York at Buffalo, 79-88, 92-101, 107, 109-110, 123, 125, 126, 128, 129, 133-149
Conrad, C., 190, 210-211, 213
Contraction. *See* Boundary contraction
Cora P. Maloney College (College E): continuing institutionalization of, 94, 98-99, 100; described, 119, 124-125, 145, 147, 148; evaluation of, 103, 136-137; initiation-implementation stage of, 46, 48, 158; institutionalization-termination stage of, 84
Corson, J., 213
Corwin, R., 8, 213
Coser, L., 65, 213
Cummings, C. P., 8, 215
Curti, M., 180$n$, 213
Czernin, F., 213

## Index

Dahl, R., 204-205, 213
Dalton, G. W., 213
Dannieli, J., 58
Davis, F. J., 213
Decentralization, 45, 53, 61, 64, 92
Denton, P., 217
Diffusion: concept of, 14, 19-22; continuing, 89, 128-129; and innovation failure, 155, 156, 157, 161, 163
Duncan, R., 7n, 170, 185, 199, 217

Eberhard, J., 55
Ebert, C., 84-85, 98-99, 100, 117
El-Assal, M., 34, 216
Emery, F. E., 213
Enclaving: concept of, 14, 19-20, 22-23, 79; innovation by, 5; and innovation failure, 155, 156, 157, 163, 164
Enrollment: reasons for decrease of, 56; trends in, 33, 55-57
Erikson, K., 8, 12, 198, 213
Ertell, M., 116
Evaluation: of colleges, 102-105; summative and formative, 129-130, 148
Expansion. *See* Boundary expansion
Expertise, role of, 50

Faculty, and experimental colleges, 41, 51, 58-59, 63-66, 82, 98, 99, 100, 123, 125, 126, 127, 159-160, 208
Faris, R. E. L., 63, 213
Farrell, M., vii
Fentiman, L. C., ix
Filstead, W. J., 213
Finkelstein, M., 213
Flacks, R., 34, 213
Flexner, A., 29, 213
Fliegel, F., 16, 213
Ford Venture Fund, 21
French, J. C., 178, 213
Friedenberg, E., 58
Funding, 57-58, 150
Furnas, C., 30-35, 38, 40, 182

Gelbaum, B., 93, 94, 96, 100, 101, 116, 117
George Perkins Marsh Program, formation of, 124

Giacquinta, J. B., 214
Glenny, L. A., 56, 57, 213
Goals, defined, 11; of State University of New York at Buffalo, 32-34, 40-41, 60-63, 92, 97, 98, 99-100, 102-103. *See also* Norms, values, and goals
Good, R. J., 71
Gould, S., 72, 84
Gouldner, A., 31n, 214
Grading system, at experimental colleges, 42, 51, 86-87, 98, 99, 123, 125, 126, 127
Grambsch, P. V., 214
Grant, G., 8, 214
Griliches, Z., 16, 214
Gross, E., 214
Gross, N., 214
Gusfield, J., 8, 214

Hage, J., 6, 7, 8, 170-171, 199, 212, 214
Halliburton, D., 212
Halsey, A. H., 39
Halstead, J., 90-91, 101, 102-103, 104, 105, 164, 165, 214
Hammond, M., 45, 46, 47-48
HammoH., 177, 214
Havelock, R. G., 188, 214
Havens, A. E., 18, 216
Hawkins, H., 178, 179, 214
Haynie, C., 49, 125-126
Hays, D., 55
Heald, H., 33, 40, 214
Hefferlin, J. L., viii, 6, 168-169, 193-195, 198, 214
Heirich, M., 31, 214
Hobbs, W., vii
Hochfield, G., 100
Holbek, J., 7n, 170, 185, 199, 217
Holistic innovation: concept of, 5-6; at State University of New York at Buffalo, 41, 43
Hopkins, M., 50
Host organization: boundaries of, 13-14; and compatibility, 157-158, 159, 162; concept of, 9; and profitability, 160; regulation by, 164-166
Huddleston, J., 45, 46, 47
Hunter, F., 204-205, 214
Hutchins, R. M., 30

## Index

Illinois, University of, Chicago Circle, transfer credits not accepted at, 100
Initiation-implementation stage: concept of, 7, 13; at State University of New York at Buffalo, 42, 44-54
Innocent-until-proven-guilty philosophy, 130, 147, 161-162
Innovation: analysis of, 1-25; case study method for, 201-209; characteristics of, and success, 184-188; and compliance, 165-166; defined, 3-4; eclectic school of, 190-191, 210-211; with enclaves, 5; environmental conditions for, 6; factors limiting success of, 191-195; failure related to, 3-10, 155-166; great-ideas approach to, 44, 46-47; great-person approach to, 44-46; with holistic change, 5-6; human problems/relations school of, 189; as an idea, 12; initiation-implementation stage of, 7, 13; institutionalization-termination stage of, 7-9, 13, 14-15, 16, 63-151; knowledge about, 4-10, 184-195; literature on, reviewed, 167-199; need recognition stage of, 7, 12; with new colleges, 4-5; and organizations, 11-25; peripheral to colleges, 6; piecemeal, 6; planning and formulating stage of, 7, 12-13; power school of, 189-190; process of, 188-191; rational school of, 188; recipe for, 190-191; resistance to, 38, 168-176; stages in process of, 6-9, 11-15, 29-88; study of, 27-151; theories on, 210-211; types of, 4-6
Innovation failure: defined, 156; steps in, 166
Institutionalization-termination stage: compatibility and profitability in, 15-25; concept of, 7-9, 13, 14-15, 16; conclusions about, 196-199; conflict resolution and boundary covergence in, 14-15, 16; continuing stage of, 89-151; as continuum, 156-157; law making in, 160-161; and literature review, 167-199; negotiation in, 163-164; norms, values, and goals related to, 162-163; outcomes in, 196-197, 198; as political process, 160, 163-164; process in, 196, 197; at State University of New York at Buffalo, 63-88, 105-115; switch or control mechanism in, 196-197; validity of model of, 155

Johns Hopkins University, atomistic organization of, 178-179
Johnson, D. B., 8, 214

Kalman, H., ix
Kalman, R., ix
Keniston, K., 175, 214
Kennedy, D. B., 198, 214
Kerber, A., 198, 214
Kerlinger, F. N., 214
Kerr, C., 30, 215
Ketter, R., viii, 35-39, 41-43, 59-63, 79, 84-88, 89-90, 92-93, 97, 98, 99-100, 102-103, 105, 114, 116, 118, 130, 146, 156, 159, 161, 215
Kivlin, J., 16, 213
Kohlmeier, L. M., 215
Kolko, G., 58
Kuhns, E., 190, 210-211, 215

Ladd, D. R., 42, 215
Law making: and norms, 65-67; as political process, 160-161
Lawrence, P. R., 213
Leeds, R., 198, 215
Lemert, E. M., 215
Levine, A., 3, 6, 7, 9, 170, 215
Levine, K., ix
Levine, M., ix
Lewis, L., vii
Likert, R., 189
Lindquist, J., 190, 210-211, 212, 215
Lippitt, R., 189, 215
Loris, S., viii

MAC 1 (Meyerson Advisory Committee 1), 35-36, 38, 39, 41-43
McGregor, D., 189
Maguire, L., 8, 215
Mann, F., 6, 7, 215
March, J. G., 215
Marlinski, D., viii
Martorana, S. V., 190, 210-211, 215
Maslow, A. H., 81, 215
Mathematical Sciences, College of, 47;

## Index

described, 120, 126-127; evaluation of, 137-138, 145, 147
Matthews, D., 21
Mayhew, L. B., 215
Meiklejohn, A., 24
Merton, R., 31*n*, 215
Metropolitan State University, as new college, 4
Meyerson, M., viii, 31-45, 48, 52-56, 58-65, 67, 69, 73, 78, 79, 85, 92, 113, 135, 156, 161, 182, 215
Middle States Association of Colleges and Schools, 32, 102, 215
Miles, M., 215
Millett, J. D., 174-175, 176-177, 215
Mills, T., 58-59
Minnesota, University of, General College of, 22-23
Mott, N., 6
Murray, D., 84, 86-87

National Academy of Education, viii
Need recognition stage: concept of, 7, 12; at State University of New York at Buffalo, 29-35, 42
Neff, F. W., 6, 7, 215
Negative profitability, concept of, 81, 158
New College of Modern Education, 123, 159; described, 120, 124-125
New York University, 174, 175
Norms: defined, 11; and law making, 65-67
Norms, values, and goals: in institutionalization-termination stage, 162-163; of organizations, 11-12, 13-14, 15, 17, 19, 21, 23; at State University of New York at Buffalo, 64, 79-80, 82, 85, 86, 87-88

Organization of Afro-American Awareness, 69
Organizations: atomistic, 178-179, 180-181, 182; bureaucratic, 179-180, 181; character of, 173-176, 182-184; collegial, 176-177, 180-181, 182; host, 9, 13-14, 157-158, 159, 160, 162, 164-166; and innovation, 11-25; literature on, reviewed, 168-176; norms, values, and goals of, 11-12, 13-14, 15, 17, 19, 21, 23; political,

180-182; stability of, 168-170; of universities, 176-184; variables of, 170-173
Oxford University, cluster idea at, 4

Padgett, W., 215
Palola, E. G., 215
Paris, University of, collegial organization of, 177
Parsons, T., 215
Perkins, J., 182, 216
Pesch, L., 56
Piecemeal innovation: concept of, 6; at State Universtiy of New York at Buffalo, 41, 43
Planck, C., 45, 46, 125
Planning and formulating stage: concept of, 7, 12-13; and observability, 186-187; at State University of New York at Buffalo, 35-43
Political process, institutionalization-termination stage as, 160, 163-164
Political organization, 180-182
Positive profitability, concept of, 81, 158
Pressman, J. L., 216
Profitability: criteria for, 131-132; defined, 17-18, 19; examples of, 22, 23, 24; general, 18, 19, 23; and innovation failure, 158, 159, 160; in institutionalization-termination stage, 15-25; and literature review, 171-173, 187, 188, 191, 193, 195, 197; and research bias, 17; self-interest, 18, 19, 22; at State University of New York at Buffalo, 81, 83, 110, 113, 123, 127, 129, 130, 133-149
Progressive Education, College of, 160; continuing institutionalization at, 99; evaluation of, 133, 139-140, 145, 148; formation of, 125

Rachel Carson College: described, 120-121; evaluation of, 140, 145, 147; merger of, 124
Reed College, innovation at, 170
Reeschi, K. H., 213
Regan, P., 54, 59, 63, 70, 71, 73, 77, 79, 80, 84
Regulation, and innovations, 164-165
Reichert, J., viii, 104, 105-106, 109, 110, 111, 114, 116, 117, 123, 124, 125, 127,

## Index

128, 135, 149, 157, 163, 164, 216
Research, organization for, 178-179
Research for Better Schools, 8
Resocialization: concept of, 15, 19-20; continuing, 89, 110, 114-115, 127, 147, 148-149; cues on, 13, 52-53; and innovation failure, 155, 157, 158, 163
Revolutionary Communist Youth, 112
Rheinehold, R., 3, 216
Riesman, D., 8, 39, 54, 175, 214
Rockefeller, N., 47, 84
Roethlisberger, F. J., 189
Rogers, E., 6, 7, 16-17, 18, 185-186, 187, 188, 198, 199, 216
Rosa Luxemburg courses, 86-87
Rossberg, R., 75-79, 82, 216
Rudolph, F., 177, 180, 216
Rudy, W., 177, 212
Ruyle, J. H., 213

Sapp, A., 45, 46, 48
Sarason, S., 216
Schachner, N., 177n, 216
Schlesinger, L., 216
Schwartz, R., 217
Scott, J. W., 34, 216
Seashore, C., 216
Sechrest, L., 217
Selznick, P., 8, 216
Service, organization for, 179-180
Shea, J. R., 213
Shepard, H., 168, 216
Shoemaker, F. F., 6, 16-17, 185-186, 187, 198, 199, 216
Sikes, W., 189, 216
Smelser, N., 6, 7, 216
Smith, P., 92, 93, 95, 98, 101, 216
Snell, F., 45, 46, 49-54, 70, 73, 77, 79, 84, 85, 87, 103
C. P. Snow College. *See* Urban Studies, College of
Social Science College: academic freedom at, 97; described, 121, 126-127; evaluation of, 140-141, 145, 147, 148
Somit, A., 84
Spencer Foundation, ix
Spicer, E., 38, 43, 216
Spitzberg, I. J., Jr., viii, 116
Stanford University, subunit innovation at, 3, 5, 7, 9
State Universtiy of New York, 30-34
State University of New York at Buffalo (S.U.N.Y.A.B.), vii-viii, 10, 216-217; and accountability, 63; activist, thematic, and residential colleges at, 94-95; autonomy at, 84-85, 91, 93, 162, 165; budget cutting at, 150; chartering committee at, 106-107, 115-118, 129-133, 145-146, 149, 150, 203-204, 206, 208; college council at, 108-109; college committee of, 47, 96, 101, 105-106; colleges of, listed, 46-47; collegiate assembly at, 76, 84, 85-86, 87, 90, 94-96, 110-111; collegiate concept for, 36-38, 40-41, 66-67; compatibility at, 79-88, 92-101, 107, 109-110, 123, 125, 126, 128, 129, 133-149; continuing institutionalization at, 89-151; curriculum committee of, 51; decentralization at, 45, 53, 61, 64, 92; enrollments at, 33, 55-57; executive committee at, 67, 73-74, 77, 78, 83, 101; external review at, 90-91, 101, 102-105; faculty at, 41, 51, 58-59, 63-66, 82, 98, 99, 100, 123, 125, 126, 127, 159-160, 208; faculty senate at, 39, 42, 44, 47, 53-54, 64, 67-68, 73, 76, 78-79, 80, 87, 97, 100, 105, 111, 112-114, 115, 128-129, 149-150, 160-161, 165, 203, 206, 209; funding for, 57-58; goals of, 32-34, 40-41, 60-63, 92, 97, 98, 99-100, 102-103; grading system at, 42, 51, 86-87, 98, 99, 123, 125, 126, 127; history of, 29-32, 203-204; initiation-implementation stage at, 42, 44-54; innovation failure at, 155-166; institutionalization-termination stage at, 63-88, 105-115; mergers at, 124; method for study of, 202-209; need recognition stage at, 29-35, 42; new prospectus at, 89-91; norms, values, and goals at, 64, 79-80, 82, 85, 86, 87-88, 162-163; planning and formulation stage at, 35-43; political process at, 114, 182; profitability at, 81, 83, 110, 113, 123, 127, 129, 130, 133-149; revamping colleges at, 118-129; rioting at, 69-70, 80, 81, 84, 97; steady state at, 54-63; students at, 42, 68, 74-75, 77, 82, 91, 111-112

State University of New York at Stony Brook, 70
Steady state, 54-63, 161
Stern, R., 75-80, 82, 83-84, 85, 86, 87, 89-91, 156, 157, 163, 164, 217
Straus, M., 16, 212
Strivers, R., 213
Stroup, H., 174-175, 179, 217
Supplements, alternatives distinct from, 52, 158
Swarthmore College, innovation at, 170

Teaching, organization for, 176-177
Temkin, S., 8, 215
Termination: concept of, 15, 19-20, 24-25; continuing, 89, 123-124, 148; and innovation failure, 155, 156, 159, 161, 163
Tolstoy College (College F): continuing institutionalization at, 98, 99, 103, 115; described, 119, 125-126; evaluation of, 133, 141-142, 145, 147, 148; initiation-implementation stage of, 46, 48-49, 53; institutionalization-termination stage of, 70-73, 74, 82, 84, 85, 86
Tönnies, F., 31$n$, 217

U.S. Bureau of the Census, 56
U.S. Department of Commerce, 56
U.S. Department of Labor, 12-13, 56
U.S. Senate, 68
Up the Colleges Committee, 68, 75, 77, 83, 217
Urban Studies, College of (C. P. Snow College): described, 121, 125; evaluation of, 138-139, 145, 147; merger of, 124

Values, defined, 11. *See also* Norms, values, and goals
Van Hise, C., 179
Vico College: continuing institutionalization at, 98; described, 121-122, 126; evaluation of, 132, 142-143, 145, 147
Von Moltke, K., 85-86, 92
Vroom, V., 217

Waddington, C. H., 58
Watson, G., 192-193, 194, 195, 217
Watson, J., 215
Webb, E., 217
Weber, M., 61, 179$n$, 217
Weingart, J., 3, 9, 170, 215
Welch, C., viii, 44, 49, 50, 51, 53, 68, 73, 84, 105, 115
Westley, B., 215
Wildavsky, A., 58, 216
Wisconsin, University of: bureaucratic organization of, 179-180; Experimental College at, 24-25
Women's Studies College, 123, 125, 159; described, 122, 126, 127, 128; evaluation of, 143-144, 145, 148-149

Xerox, college degrees from, 6

Yale College, natural sciences barred from, 100
Yankelovich, D., 111-112, 217
Youth Collective Conspiracy, 68-69

Zald, M. N., 8, 217
Zaltman, G., 7$n$, 170, 185, 199, 217
Zweig, F., 56